The Non-Designer's Web Book

an easy guide to creating,
designing, and posting
your own web site

Robin Williams
and John Tollett

Peachpit Press
Berkeley ∗ California

The Non-Designer's Web Book

Robin Williams and John Tollett

©1998 Robin Williams and John Tollett

Cover art and production by John Tollett
Section dividers designed by John Tollett; quotes by Robin Williams,
   inspired by Brian Andreas, a wonderful artist who creates the magical StoryPeople
   (see his most delightful website at www.storypeople.com)
Interior design and production by Robin Williams
Edited by Jenifer Blakemore and Nancy Davis
Production management by Kate Reber

The incredible variety of art in this book—cartoons, life drawings, portraits, the Url and Browser characters, illustrations, examples for techniques, fake logo designs for sample pages, etc.—were all created by John Tollett. He's amazing.

Most of the web sites shown in this book were created by Dave Rohr and John Tollett at West of the Pecos Web Design and were used with permission. The other web sites were also used with permission. From West of the Pecos: Roadrunning, Loopless, Pueblo Harvest, Santa Fe Mac User Group, Home Sweet Home Page, Santa Fe Stages, First National Bank of Santa Fe, Belthor Furniture/Sculpture, Santa Fean Magazine, Sherman Asher Publishing, Dayton Lummis, Cowboys & Indians Magazine.

Peachpit Press

1249 Eighth Street
Berkeley, California 94710
800.283.9444
510.548.4393
510.548.5991 fax

Find us on the World Wide Web at http://www.peachpit.com

Peachpit Press is a division of Addison Wesley Longman

ISBN

0-201-68859-X

10 9 8 7 6 5 4 3

Printed and bound in the United States of America

Hey Mom—
this book's for you!
Now you have to make
our family web site!
yer ever-lovin' daughter,

Robin

To Robin
Repaying your kindness
and generosity
will take several lifetimes
and I look forward
to every minute.

John

Andy Warhol was wrong:
in the future, everyone won't be famous for fifteen minutes.
But everyone will have their own web site.

Jon Winokur
author
(and great third baseman)

many thanks

John: To Dave Rohr for being the quintessential designer and business partner. His design expertise, computer hardware and software knowledge, his ability to analyze and organize complex projects, and his absolute professionalism are unmatched. He is responsible for the creativity, technical expertise, and innovation of the sites designed by West of the Pecos.

To West of the Pecos clients who have let us design their sites with an uncommon amount of freedom.

To Robin Williams for letting me help her with this book and for using so many West of the Pecos sites as examples.

To Peachpit Press for being encouraging, enthusiastic, and incredibly kind and gracious.

To David Brownlow for introducing me, and many others, to the Internet a few years ago, through studio x, a New Mexico ISP.

Robin: To John Tollett, for adding so many riches, so much creativity, so much expertise, and so many wise thoughts to this project. Because of you, this is not just a good book—it's a great book.

To Nancy Davis and Jen Blakemore, editors and friends—once again, what would I do without you?? You're wonderful, invaluable, and dear.

To Kate Reber, for getting yet another book through that production process with so much care and professionalism.

To David Brownlow of studio x and Canton Becker of ResRocket Surfer for teaching me much of what I know about the Internet and the World Wide Web.

To my students and workshop attendees, for teaching me how to teach people about the Internet, the World Wide Web, and making web sites.

table of contents

Part Two: Making Web Pages

Part Three: Design Issues on the Web

Part Four: Color, Graphics, and Type

Part Five: You're Done—Now What?

The Stuff at the End

Introduction

If you are reading this book, we can safely assume you fall into one of two categories:

1. **The Experienced Designer Category,** a person who has lots of design experience and is capable of designing circles around 75 percent of the current web designers on the Internet.

2. **The Unexperienced Designer Category,** a person who has little or no design experience and is capable of designing circles around 75 percent of the current web designers on the Internet.

Its not that there's a scarcity of great design on the web. There are many web sites, large and small, commercial and personal, that serve as great examples of design, navigation, and organization. But since web publishing is so accessible, affordable, and alluring, an extraordinary number of people have become "web designers" practically overnight. In the past, if someone knew how to produce a brochure or an ad, they were called a production artist or a production manager. Seldom were they called upon to actually *design* the brochure that they *produced*. The advent of first desktop publishing and now web publishing has brought with it a whole new concept of publishing, along with its own jargon and technology. Since web design depended upon programming to make it work, the majority of web designers at first came from programming backgrounds. Some designers began to see the creative and commercial potential of web design and started learning HTML, the HyperText Markup Language that's used to create web pages.

That leaves us with all sorts of web designers: programmers learning design; designers learning programming; and people learning both so they can be a part of this exciting new medium. Which brings us back to the original point: poorly designed web pages are everywhere, but as more excellent web sites are created—sites that demonstrate creative interface design, visually compelling graphics, convenient navigation, and functional site organization—more people will become aware of the difference between a well-designed and a poorly designed page.

Don't be scared

Design can be intimidating. Given the directive to "go design," you may find yourself stressing out, sweating, and mumbling, "Where do I start? What's a good solution? What will make a good design? What will make an interesting site?" Aha! These are exactly the questions that the most experienced designers ask themselves before starting a project. It's extremely important to remember that, as a designer, you're not looking for the *one* idea that will work as a solution (a graphic needle in a design haystack). There are many possible solutions to any given project—a dozen different designers will have a dozen different solutions.

Bridging all worlds

In the web design world, we need to combine technical skills with design skills and creative copywriting. We need to learn to do things differently to publish on the screen than we do to publish on paper. So this book covers the gamut of what you need to know technically, with a strong emphasis on the design of the web pages—the creative content is up to you. The intent is to take you from beginning to end of the construction of a web site in a logical way that builds your skills to the point of confidence and empowerment, bridging the very different worlds of technical expertise and creative sensibility.

So you're off, have fun, don't look back, and we'll see you there.

Robin and *John*

part one
Using the
World Wide Web

IT'S THE WORLD WIDE WEB,
HE SAID.

What's it do, I asked.

I DON'T KNOW, HE SAID.
IT'S NOT FINISHED YET.

"Computers in the future may weigh no more than 1.5 tons."

Popular Mechanics, forecasting the relentless march of science, 1949

What is the
World Wide Web?

If you've been poking around the World Wide Web already and feel comfortable with online services, the Internet, web pages, links, plug-ins, etc., **skip this chapter.** Jump to the quiz at the end—if you can easily fill in every blank, then move right on.

If you haven't spent too much time on the web yet, or if you've never actually been there at all, this chapter will fill you in on the things you need to know before you start designing your own pages. This chapter covers information such as how the World Wide Web is different from the Internet, what a modem does for you, how you get connected, what's a browser, a web page, a web address, and more.

You probably already have at least a vague idea that this hoopla called the Internet allows computers to send messages to each other. You really don't need to know much more than that to get your work done, but it is rather satisfying to understand what those hot shots are talking about, and to start talking yourself about modem speeds, search engines, and downloads.

The Internet

Yes, what you've heard is true—computers send messages to each other. The **Internet** is a vast collection of computers all over the world that store information and send it out.

When you connect your computer to the Internet, you are establishing a line that will reach out and jump on the "freeway" (network) that is buzzing overhead, that Internet freeway. Your computer itself, though, is not a stop on the Internet, but is more like an access point on the virtual highway. As a user, you're part of the Internet, but if your computer broke down, it wouldn't affect anyone else. No one on the whole Internet would give a hoot.

Most of us are users at our computers. When you hear talk about the numbers of people on the Internet, it's us. The number of computers actually on the freeway itself, of course, is also rapidly growing. But it is the users who are forcing it to happen.

This is the vast Internet, moving quickly and changing constantly.

This is you and your computer.

This is an Internet Service Provider (ISP) or an online service (page 19), giving you access to the Internet.

Modems

You're probably already connected to the Internet through an *Internet Service Provider* (*ISP*) or to an *online service* (we'll talk about the difference between the two in a minute). You probably have a **modem** inside of your computer or sitting in a little box next to it. Most people at home or in small businesses or schools use modems. (There are other ways to connect, but you don't need to worry about that right now.) The reason you have a modem is that your computer sends messages to other computers through the phone lines, but computers and phone lines use two different technologies.

A computer is *digital,* meaning it can only work with information that is in concrete, finite, countable little chunks. The phone lines are *analog,* meaning they work with information (like sound) that is infinite, flowing, uncountable.

So a modem has to **mo**dulate and **dem**odulate the information between the two systems—the modem on one end turns the digital information into analog information so it can go over the phone lines; the modem on the other end turns the analog information back into digital info so the other computer can understand it.

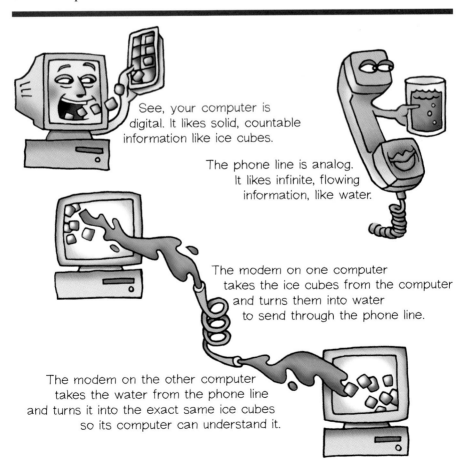

See, your computer is digital. It likes solid, countable information like ice cubes.

The phone line is analog. It likes infinite, flowing information, like water.

The modem on one computer takes the ice cubes from the computer and turns them into water to send through the phone line.

The modem on the other computer takes the water from the phone line and turns it into the exact same ice cubes so its computer can understand it.

Modem speeds

Modems are not all the same. Their biggest difference is their speed. When you hear people say things like "I just bought a twenty-eight eight," or "I can't believe it's only twenty-four hundred," they are talking about how fast the modem can send and receive information, which is called the **baud rate** (pronounced *bod*).

The baud rate refers to how many **bits** (digital pieces of information, or ice cubes) **per second** the modem can send and receive. You can think of the baud rate as the size of the pipe: a higher baud equals a fatter pipe down which more ice cubes/water can travel.

Part of the problem with understanding modem speeds is the way we have abbreviated their speed labels; for instance, "28.8" is faster than "2400." The chart below shows what these numbers mean.

speed	say it	write it	how is it
2400	twenty-four hundred	2400 (2.4)	slo-o-o-o-o-ow
9600	ninety-six hundred	9600 (9.6)	not much better
14,400	fourteen-four	14.4	pretty good, a little slow for the Internet
28,800	twenty-eight eight	28.8	fairly fast; the Internet isn't too bad at this speed
33,600	thirty-three six	33.6	great for home or business
56,000	fifty-six k	56K	don't get spoiled

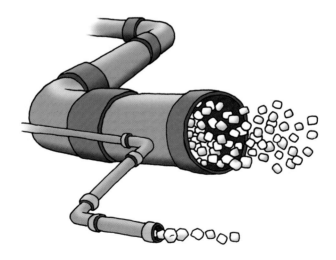

The faster the modem,
the more information it can process at one time.

Online services and ISPs

So through the modem your computer connects to the online world. You may be part of or have surely at least heard of **online services** such as America Online (how many disks do *you* have?), CompuServe, Prodigy, and others. These services are *not* the Internet! You may be a member of one of the services, but that does not mean you are on the Internet!

An online service such as America Online is like a little village. Inside the "village" you have access to organized groups, clubs, stores, services, parties, mailboxes, conferences, etc., and there is a "mayor" who runs the show. There are "police officers" who run around the village helping some people and admonishing others. Everything is already set up for you, maps are drawn, directions are available, guides are present, and it is fairly safe, controlled, and easy to get around in. *Every online service provides a back door that leads to the Internet. When you click that "Internet" button, you are leaving the village.* Good luck.

If you are not a member of an online service, you can get a "direct connection" through an **Internet Service Provider,** affectionately known as an **ISP.** A provider has a computer that is connected to the Internet 24 hours a day, usually with a very fast connection (not a modem) and you can *log in* to their service and connect directly to the Internet.

On page 30 we'll talk about how to decide whether to use an online service or go straight through an ISP.

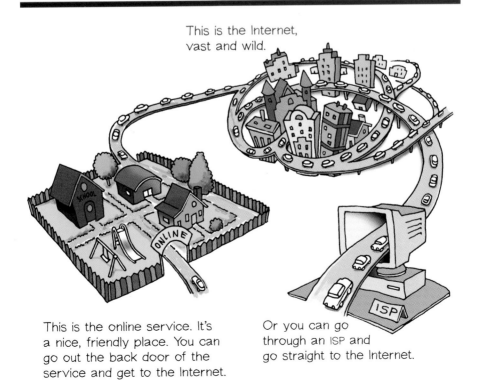

This is the Internet, vast and wild.

This is the online service. It's a nice, friendly place. You can go out the back door of the service and get to the Internet.

Or you can go through an ISP and go straight to the Internet.

What's on the Internet?

If you picture an online service as an independent, controlled village, then the **Internet** itself is a vast, uncontrolled, and basically uncontrollable anarchistic world. No one is the boss. No one has made nice neat compartments for you. No one is policing the bad guys. Once on the Internet, it is up to you to make sense of it, to find your own clubs, form your own groups, figure out how to participate in a conference, search for the things that interest you.

There are many parts to the Internet. There are **newsgroups,** which are comprised of groups of people around the world who have common interests, such as women who are giving birth in August, classic Porsche owners, Robert Burns' fans, etc. There are about 24,000 newsgroups. People in the each group "post" their news on the Internet, kind of like pinning a message on a bulletin board, and everyone in the group can read it and post their own answers, comments, or questions.

There are also **mailing lists,** or **listservs,** which are similar to newsgroups except instead of posting messages on a bulletin board, you get e-mail delivered to your box. Once you join a mailing list, any e-mail message sent by anyone on the list automatically goes to everyone else on the whole list. In an active list, this can mean *lots* of mail.

The World Wide Web

The part of the Internet we all hear about the most these days is the **World Wide Web.** The Internet has been around since the early '60s, but not many people cared much about it because you had to be a nerd to know what was there and how to access it. There were no pictures, no sounds—just ugly yellow text on a black background and weird codes to get what you wanted. Today's World Wide Web, however, has color, sound, graphics, animation, video, interactivity, and ways to jump from place to place.

The World Wide Web actually consists of millions and millions of individual **pages,** very much like the word processing pages you are used to making. That's all it is—a bunch of pages.

These individual pages are **linked** to other pages, which we'll see in a minute. Usually a business or a person creates a unified collection of pages that are all related, as for a business, family, products, service, etc. A collection of related pages is called a **web site.**

Each web site has a **home page.** This page is like a table of contents. Usually the home page is the first page of a site, but more and more sites are including an **entry page** (also called a splash page or front door), which is sort of like the title page in a book, which then leads to the home page.

This is an entry page to a web site. It leads to the home page, or table of contents.

This is the home page. From here you can go to other pages in the site.

These are other pages in the site. Each of these pages may lead to other pages. The other pages do not have to be in the same site—you might go to a page in Japan or Istanbul or next door.

Getting around the web

On the web, you get around from page to page through **links.** This is one of the big features of the World Wide Web—these links are called **hypertext:** text that is "connected" to other pages so when you click on the hypertext, you "jump" to other pages. Imagine if, in a book, you could touch one of the topics in the table of contents and instantly the book would fly open to that page. That's linking. That's hypertext.

On the web, you can recognize hypertext links by their **underline,** and they are usually in a contrasting color. Graphics can also be links. Even if the text does *not* follow the convention of displaying an underline and different color, and even if a graphic does *not* have a colored border around it to indicate it is a link, you can always tell by the **little hand:** when the pointer on the screen is positioned over a link, the pointer turns into a little hand. This is your visual clue that if you click, something will happen (usually you jump to another page). After you click on a link, its color usually changes; this clue indicates that you have already been to that linked page.

As the page appears on your screen, we say it is **loading.** Graphics also load, and you will probably complain about the amount of time it takes to load all the graphics on a fancy page.

 You will see a little hand that looks like one of these (depending on your browser) when your mouse pointer is positioned over a link.

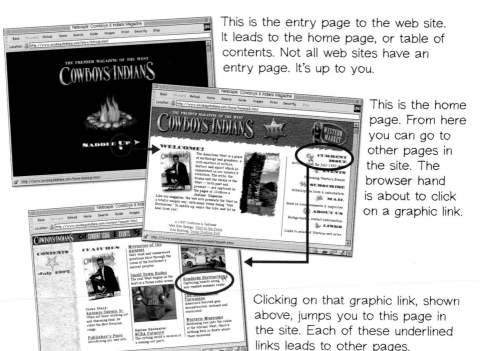

This is the entry page to the web site. It leads to the home page, or table of contents. Not all web sites have an entry page. It's up to you.

This is the home page. From here you can go to other pages in the site. The browser hand is about to click on a graphic link.

Clicking on that graphic link, shown above, jumps you to this page in the site. Each of these underlined links leads to other pages.

Browsers

To see the pages on the World Wide Web, you must have software called a **browser.** As you already know, to type pages to be printed, you need a word processor; to create a spreadsheet, you need spreadsheet software. And to see web pages, you need browser software.

The browser lets you see the graphics, color, links, etc. It reads the information on the web page and displays it on your screen. Browsers are either free or shareware! (Shareware means it is free to acquire, and if you like it and use it, you send in a small fee.)

When you click on a link or otherwise try to find a certain page, the browser finds the web page on the computer where it is stored, translates the coded information for you, and displays the lovely and colorful page on your screen.

As the page loads onto your screen, you will see several visual clues that tell you the browser is working, as noted below.

Netscape makes the most popular and best browser. Versions 1, 2, and 3 are called Navigator. Version 4 is called Communicator.

Netscape Navigator

Netscape Communicator

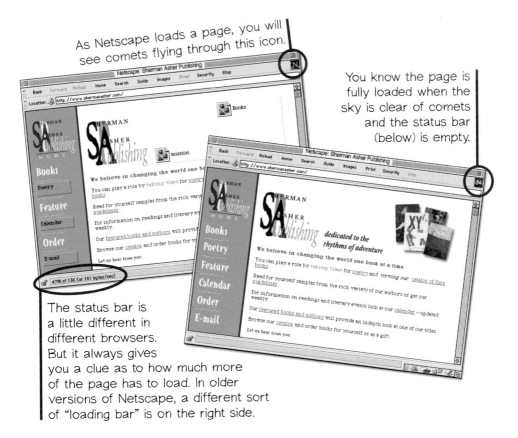

As Netscape loads a page, you will see comets flying through this icon.

You know the page is fully loaded when the sky is clear of comets and the status bar (below) is empty.

The status bar is a little different in different browsers. But it always gives you a clue as to how much more of the page has to load. In older versions of Netscape, a different sort of "loading bar" is on the right side.

Browsers are not equal

Not all browsers are the same. Every browser and each new version of every browser displays web pages slightly differently, which presents major challenges to web site designers. The most popular browser is **Netscape Navigator** (highly preferred), and there is also **Microsoft Internet Explorer.** Online services include browser software, so when you sneak out the back door of America Online or CompuServe, you are actually using a browser supplied to you by the service.

Below you see the same web pages that are displayed on the previous page, but through a different browser. Notice the differences. There are other differences that each user at their own computer can impose, but we'll talk about those later. The point to keep in mind is that everyone does not see exactly the same page in exactly the same way.

Microsoft Internet Explorer is another browser.

Internet Explorer

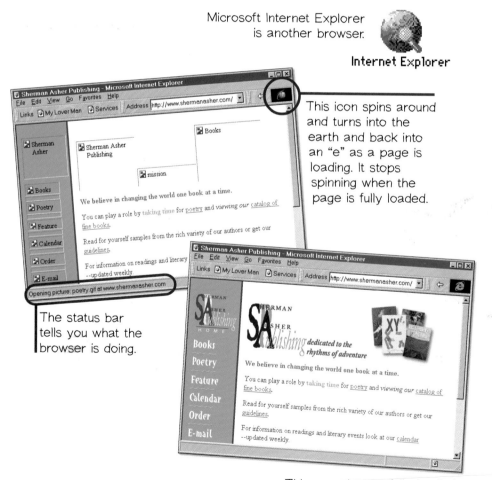

This icon spins around and turns into the earth and back into an "e" as a page is loading. It stops spinning when the page is fully loaded.

The status bar tells you what the browser is doing.

This page is now fully loaded.

Web addresses, or URLs

Every page on the World Wide Web has an **address**, just like we have addresses for our homes and businesses. This address is called the Uniform Resource Locator, or **URL** (you can go ahead and forget the term "uniform resource locator"). The abbreviation "URL" is usually pronounced as its initials: *you—are—ell.*

When you finish your web site, you will **post** it on a **server**, which is a special computer directly connected to the Internet 24 hours a day. Every page on the World Wide Web is stored on a server; there are millions of servers. (Unless you are in a big company, you usually don't own your own server.) Whoever does own the server and is **hosting** your site will work with you to determine what your personal URL will be. Once you know the URL for your site, you can tell everyone and they can visit your fun and enchanting pages. There is a chapter at the end of this book that teaches you how to post your pages—it's easy, really easy!

This **www** stands for World Wide Web, but it's really just a convention; that is, www is not the part of the address that means the file is a web page. Some URLS do not have www in their address.

This is the domain name. It tells you who owns the site. For instance, you have perhaps seen apple.com, toyota.com, nfl.com, etc. You can buy a domain name for yourself. I bought ratz.com.

http://www.ratz.com/robin/hats.html

This stands for **hypertext transfer protocol.** Who cares. The important thing is that **this** part of the URL is what tells you that the file you are looking for is a page on the World Wide Web. Instead of **http://**, in some URLS you might see **news://, ftp://,** or other abbreviations. These refer to other files that are not web pages.

After the domain name, the rest of the address is just a path telling the browser where to find the page you need. For instance, in this address, the browser finds ratz.com, and the slash tells it to look inside the ratz.com folder and find a folder or directory called robin. Then the next slash tells it to look inside that robin folder and find the file called hats.html. (All web pages are called "html files." We'll talk about that later.)

Entering an address

If you know the address, or URL, of a page, you can type it into the **Location box** at the top of the browser window, hit Return or Enter, and the browser will go find that page.

Type the URL in here, then hit Return or Enter to send your browser off to find the page.

Actually, you don't have to type the **http://** part. In fact, on a Macintosh, if the address is in the form of www.**somewhere**.com, all you need to type is **somewhere**. Really. You can type yahoo, apple, or ratz, hit the Return or Enter key, and you will go directly to www.yahoo.com, www.apple.com, or www.ratz.com. In Windows, you can use this shortcut in Netscape, but not in Internet Explorer.

Details of the domain name

The "com" part of the address gives you a clue as to the nature of the web site. "Com" stands for commercial, meaning it is a commercial web site. Below are some of the other abbreviations (called "top-level" names) you will also find in all web addresses in the United States:

.com	**com**mercial oganizations (peachpit.com)

.edu	**edu**cational institutions (cornell.edu)

.gov	**gov**ernment organizations (nasa.gov)

.mil	**mil**itary organizations (army.mil)

.net	**net**work organizations (internic.net)

.org	**org**anizations that don't fit in any of the other categories, usually non-profits (santafecares.org)

Because there are so many web sites, new top-level extensions are being created. You will also see these:

.nom	personal web pages

.firm	company or firm

.arts	art and cultural sites

.rec	recreation and entertainment sites

.store	businesses selling goods

.info	information services

.web	web-related entity

Other countries have **country codes** in their domain names, so if you see something like **jp** in the domain name, you know the site is being "served" to you from Japan. Below is a list of several country codes.

jp	Japan

ca	Canada

de	Germany

ru	Russia

us	United States

au	Australia

fr	France

mx	mexico

ch	Switzerland

uk	United Kingdom

More address details

The **period** you see in URLs is pronounced *dot*. So **ratz.com** is pronounced *ratz dot com.*

The **slash,** /, in an address is always a forward slash, so you don't need to say "forward slash." Just say "slash."

This character, **~**, is a **tilde** (pronounced *till duh*). It's not very common in English words, but shows up in web addresses a lot. Type it by pressing Shift ~ (usually found in the upper left corner of the keyboard).

This character, _ , is the **underscore.** Type it by pressing Shift Hyphen.

In the domain name portion of the address (the first part, from www through .com), whether you type capitals or lowercase is not critical. However, the rest of the address is **case-sensitive,** meaning it is *extremely* important whether you type capital letters or not. If the address has a capital letter, you darn well better type a capital letter or the browser will not find the page!

And just so you know, there is never an empty **space** in a web address. If you see a web address in print somewhere and it has a space in the address, it's a mistake.

What's a plug-in?

Just one more thing: at some point you will undoubtedly run across a message that tells you something is missing, or there is something you need to install before you can see the animation, play the game, or take full advantage of the site. These are usually **plug-ins,** which are little pieces of software that make special things happen. You can live without many plug-ins if you don't mind missing all the fancy stuff. The really important ones are usually included with your browser software.

If you run across such a message and you want to **download** the plug-in (which means to "load" a copy of it from another computer onto your computer), just follow the links on the screen. There are almost always directions that tell you what to do with the plug-in: they belong in the plug-ins folder that you'll find inside the folder that contains your browser. Some plug-ins require that you restart after you install them, so be sure to read the directions on the screen where you click to download.

LiveAudio   FutureSplash   NSPcon32.exe   Plug-ins   Plug-ins   Plugins

These are typical icons for plug-ins.

This is what your Plug-ins folder might look like. It's already in your browser's folder. Put the plug-in in this folder, if your software didn't do it for you. Sometimes you will have to restart your browser, and possibly restart your computer before the plug-in works.
(Read the directions!)

If you see this, the page you are viewing needs a plug-in that you don't have installed. Nothing terrible will happen if it's not installed—you just won't be able to see that movie, hear that sound, play that game, or whatever it is the plug-in allowed.

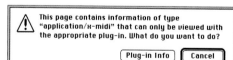

If you click "Cancel" in this message, the browser will load everything except the extra feature that needs a plug-in to work. If you click "Plug-in Info," you are usually taken to a page where you can find out about and download the plug-in.

Which file to download?
(.sit .hqx .bin .zip .sea)

When you find a page that offers files to download, you often have a choice of items. First, of course, you choose the file that is appropriate for your type of system (such as Mac or Windows 95). The extension at the end of the file, such as .hqx or .zip, indicates how the file was *compressed* (made smaller so it would go through the lines faster). The extensions give you an instant clue as to which type of system the file is compressed for:

Mac

.sit	(compressed; fine for AOL files)
.hqx	(binhex; best for Internet)
.sit.hqx	(binhex, same as .hqx)
.bin	(binary; smaller file than hqx, but you need a full-blown compression program to uncompress it)
.sea	("self-extracting archive" that will uncompress itself)

PC

.zip	("zipped" file or collection of files)
.exe	("executable" program; these are often "self-extracting archives" that will uncompress themselves when you double-click or use the Run command)
.sea	("self-extracting archive" that will uncompress itself; it may be a collection of files in the archive)

A file that has been *compressed* must be *uncompressed* to be useful (by the way—lungs *de*compress, files *un*compress). You need a special program to uncompress (also called *unstuff* or *unzip*) files. When you install Netscape on a Mac, it installs a small program called StuffIt Expander that will automatically unstuff most files you download (but not .bin). On a PC, you need to download a program that will unstuff your files—you can get WinZip from www.winzip.com, or PKUNZIP from www.pkware.com.

We clicked this link to download this program. We can continue to work— files will download in the background.

gif-builder-05.hqx
GifBuilder 0.5 is a program to create animated GIF files, which quickly become a popular way to include short movies in Web pages. Its input is an existing animated GIF, a bunch of PICT, GIF, TIFF and/or Photoshop files, or a QuickTime movie, Premiere FilmStrip, PICS file, or the layers of a Photoshop file; and its output is a GIF89a file with multiple images. ...

After that file downloaded, we found these icons on our desktop:

GifBuilder 0.5.sit   gif-builder-05.hqx

GifBuilder 0.5

On a Mac, these two files both down-loaded. Netscape automatically used StuffIt Expander to uncompress them. Once the files are uncompressed, you can throw away the .sit, .hqx, or .bin files.

This is the real uncompressed file—this folder contains the documents for GifBuilder. Keep this file.

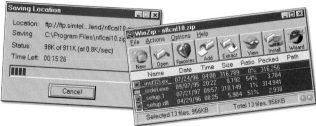

On a PC, open the zipped file in WinZip or PKUNZIP. Extract and install it.

nflcal10.zip

Online Service or ISP?

If you're reading this book, you are probably already connected to the Internet either through an online service or an Internet Service Provider. But just in case you're not, these are some things to think about when trying to decide if you should use an online service or get a direct connection to the Internet through a service provider.

Commercial online service

Connecting through an online service is easy. You just click some buttons, answer some questions about your personal life (like credit card numbers or checking accounts), and you're on.

Getting around an online service is easy. Everything is spelled out for you, and at all times there are live humans available who can help.

Participating in chat groups (people "talking" to each other by typing) is easy. Participating in "live conferences" (a "speaker" with an audience in windows called "rooms") is easy.

Figuring out how to do e-mail, send attachments, download files, etc., is easy.

Using an online service can be more expensive, depending on which service you choose and how much you use.

Internet Service Provider

Connecting through an ISP is not always easy. Unless you are a computer geek, we suggest you hire someone to hook you up. It's worth the fifty bucks (average cost). If you have a Macintosh, make sure you hire a Mac expert. If you have a PC, make sure you hire a PC expert.

At first, nothing is as easy on the Internet as it is on an online service. But once you kind of figure out what's what, then you can get around and chat, download files, find web pages, join mailing lists, and do everything else fairly easily.

A direct connection can be cheaper than using an online service.

What we suggest is that if you are new to the online world, start with an online service. Become familiar with e-mail, downloading, chatting, sending and receiving files, etc. Go out the back door and poke around the Internet. When you find that you are using your online service only to get to the Internet, it's time to get a direct connection. Many people have both.

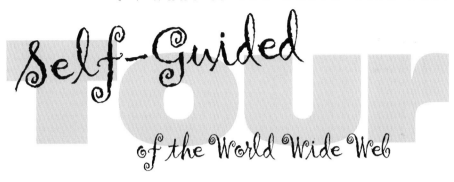

Self-Guided Tour
of the World Wide Web

If you've never been on the World Wide Web, you had better go now. We're assuming you have a connection that works. If you're the least bit intimidated about putting the connection together yourself, hire someone to set it up—a direct Internet connection is sometimes tricky to put together. Once you have a modem, connection software, a connection that works, and a browser, you're ready to go. *Once all that stuff works, the rest is easy.*

Open your connection first, then open your browser. Or if you are using an online service, open your service, then find the button that takes you out the back door to the Internet.

Poke around the web, clicking on links. Notice these things:

☐ What color are most links?

☐ Click a link, then go back to that page. The link you clicked has probably changed color—why is that?

☐ When does the little browser hand appear?

☐ Position the pointer over a link so you get the browser hand. Before you click, look at the status bar at the bottom of the browser window. You will see the address, or URL, of the page you will jump to when you click that link!

☐ Be conscious of the comets in the Netscape icon or the revolving Earth in Explorer. What are they telling you?

☐ Watch for the little bar at the bottom right of the window that gives you a clue as to how long it will take for the page to load.

☐ Did you run across a page that told you something was missing and you wouldn't be able to see the game or animation? You are probably missing a plug-in. Did you follow the links to go get the plug-in? You should try it. (Remember, after the plug-in has downloaded and has been uncompressed, you need to put it into the plug-ins folder, which is somewhere in your browser folder.)

When you are finished surfing, be sure to quit your browser (don't just close the window!), then disconnect your connection.

Oh boy, it's a Quiz!

Okay, let's see how well you picked it up. Taking a few minutes to go through this quiz process will help cement these new concepts into your brain. It doesn't hurt. Just fill in the blanks with one of the words or phrases listed at the right.

The _____ is a network of computers all over the world. To connect to the Internet, most people use a _____. A modem is necessary because computer information is _____, while phone line information is _____; the modem "translates" the two technologies. How fast a modem can interpret data is called its _____ rate, or ___ ___ _____.

There are several parts to the Internet, including _____, _____ _____, and the most popular (and fun) of all, the _____ _____ ___.

The World Wide Web consists of millions of individual _____. A related collection of these pages is called a ___ _____. The first page of a web site is usually the _____ _____, although more and more web sites feature an _____ _____, which leads the reader to the home page. The home page is like a _____ ___ _____.

On each web page you will find _____ that you click to jump to other web pages. You can usually tell if text is linked because it is _____ and in a different _____. Linked text is called _____. Often graphics act as links, also. Even if there are no visual clues such as a _____ or an underline, you can tell if an item is a link because the pointer turns into a _____ when it is positioned over a _____.

To see web pages on the World Wide Web, you must have software known as a _____. To find a particular topic on the web, you need to use a _____ _____. Sometimes you can't see the fancy stuff on web pages because you are missing a _____-__ or two. You can always _____ the plug-in you need.

A web page address is known as a __ __ __. You know the address refers to a web page if you see the letters and symbols _____ in the address. The "www.company.com" part is called the _____. The rest of the address is the _____ of file names, telling the browser where to find the web page.

Internet
modem
digital
analog
baud
bits per second
newsgroups
mailing lists
World Wide Web
pages
web site
home page
entry page
table of contents
links
underlined
color
hypertext
border
little hand
link
browser
search engine
plug-in
download
URL
http://
domain name
path

How to Search the Internet 2

So now you're having a good ol' time surfing all over the web, clicking all kinds of links, dropping into servers all over the world. But you want to find something.

Someone once complained to me that the Internet was useless because when you tried to look something up, you got back 350,000 pages to look through. This is not the Internet's fault—it is *your* responsibility to learn how to intelligently enter your search request so as to limit your results to meaningful ones. Finding what you want on the Internet is an incredibly important skill, especially as the Internet becomes more and more of an indispensable tool. It's true that with so many millions of web pages and other resources out there, if you don't know how to find what you want, all that information is not going to do you much good. Blaming the Internet for not being able to find things is like blaming the car for bumping into things. You need to take responsibility and control.

As a web designer, it is even more important for you to know how search engines and directories work because you want those services to be able to find you. Knowing how they operate goes a long way toward helping you create a site that can be found. In Chapter 16 you will read more specific information about how to "register" your site with the various search tools; this chapter just gets you familiar with how they operate and gives you a few tips on how to find what you want.

Searching the Internet

There are two basic kinds of search tools on the web: **search engines** and **directories.** You don't have to buy these tools or download them—they are just there on the web for your use. They are web pages, just like the rest of the web pages you browse. Addresses for where to find the most popular search tools are on page 42.

You have probably already used a search tool—you type in a word or two, click the button that says "Search," and you get back an extensive list of web addresses that may or may not have anything to do with what you want. An important thing to know is that when you click that button, *no one is running all over the world looking at every web page trying to find what you want.* No: every service has its own database of information. When you click a service's Search button, *you are searching through that service's database.*

Services search in different ways, and each service has different criteria for their databases. Some use humans to sort through web sites, catalog information, and rate the sites. Others use automatic software called *robots* or *spiders* that identify a site's content depending on how many times a word appears on a page or how many other pages are linked to it. A search tool might look at the title of your page, the first paragraph, or other information to determine where your site belongs in its database. That's why you get three different lists of results when you search through three different services.

The following pages explain the difference between a search engine and a directory, with a few tips on how and why to use either one.

Excite Search
Twice the power of the competition.
◉ Search the entire Web   ○ Search Excite Web Reviews   Search Tips
○ Search NewsTracker   ○ Search Usenet newsgroups   Advanced Search
search

mermaids

Searching the web can be this easy: type in a word or two and hit Return or Enter. But to get *useful* results, you need to know what you're doing.

Directories

Directories group web pages into subject categories. The most efficient way to use a directory is to start with a topic and "drill" (click) your way down through various categories until you find what you're looking for. Yahoo is a directory (plus). Go to Yahoo and click on a topic; that topic leads to various categories under that topic, each one leads to more categories and more subcategories. This is a great way to find entire web sites on subjects, such as Shakespeare, auto mechanics, or Persian cats. It is not a good way to find your grandmother's web page that is part of her nephew's site, a current theory of anti-gravity that is one small part of a scientist's research paper, or the brilliant twelve-page dissertation of Robert Burns that is on a Harvard student's thesis page.

Most directories are compiled by humans (as opposed to robots), and they do not usually go looking for things to put in their database. That is, if a web site owner has not registered her site with the directory, it probably will not be found in that directory.

Use a directory when you want to find entire web sites about a particular topic, or when you know you can find your information within a particular web site, such as a college's site.

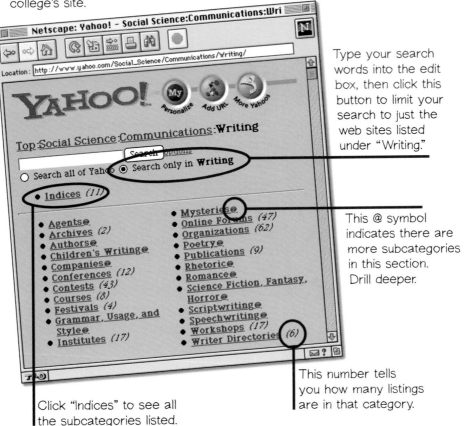

Type your search words into the edit box, then click this button to limit your search to just the web sites listed under "Writing."

This @ symbol indicates there are more subcategories in this section. Drill deeper.

This number tells you how many listings are in that category.

Click "Indices" to see all the subcategories listed.

Yahoo

Yahoo is the most popular directory, so it is important that you learn how to use it and that you register appropriate sites you create with it so web users can find you (more about that in Chapter 16). Once you are comfortable with Yahoo, branch out into some of the other directories.

Here are two important features Yahoo provides: 1) it lets you search within a limited selection of web sites, and 2) it passes on your search to other search engines in case you want to search them. The first feature is important because it lets you narrow your search to those pages that might actually have something for you; the second feature is important because there are lots of things that Yahoo doesn't have in its database, but it sends your search through another engine.

Try this experiment:

- Go to Yahoo's web site (www.yahoo.com).
- Type in "Stanford entrance requirements" with quotation marks around the phrase so Yahoo will find only pages that have the words "Stanford entrance requirements" as one complete phrase.
- Hit Return or Enter.

How many web pages did Yahoo "return" (display for you)? None? Try the search again, this time without the quotation marks. You'll probably come up with several pages that have any combination of those words on them. But this is not the best way to use a directory. You know Stanford must have a web site. Try this:

- Go to Yahoo's web site (www.yahoo.com).
- Click on the link to <u>Education</u> (see **A** on the following page)
- Click <u>Higher Education</u> (not shown on the following page)
- Click <u>College Entrance</u> (see **B**)
- Now type in "Stanford" (but you don't need the quotes; see **C**). Don't hit Enter yet!
- Click in the button that says "Search only in College Entrance" (see **D**)
- Now hit Return or Enter.

How many pages did you get? (See **E** on the following page.) One? If you click that link, you will go straight to the Admissions page on the Stanford site. You could also get to that same link by drilling down a different route (such as Education:College Entrance:Admissions Offices:Stanford). But the point is that searching using *words* is not the best way to use a directory; it's usually more effective to dig through the subjects.

Another nice thing about Yahoo

The other feature of Yahoo that I mentioned on the previous page is that it passes on your search to other search engines. That is, on the page of results from your search in Yahoo, you'll notice links to several other tools. If you click any of these, that other search tool will perform the same search Yahoo did, but it will, of course, look through its own database. The results will be different—not always better, but different.

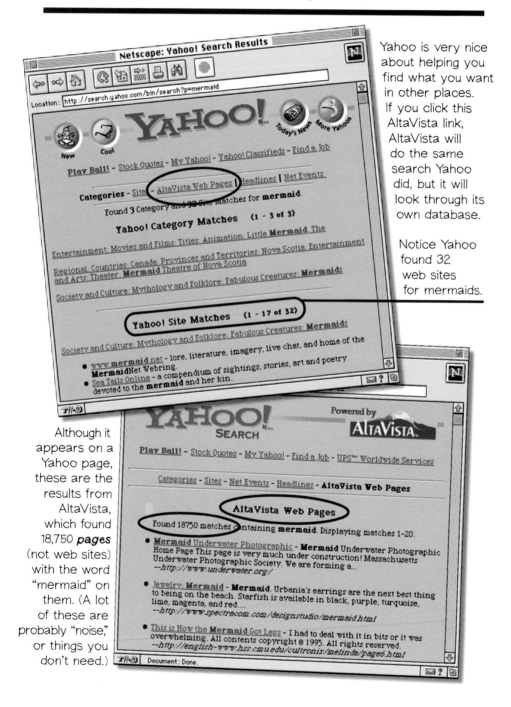

Yahoo is very nice about helping you find what you want in other places. If you click this AltaVista link, AltaVista will do the same search Yahoo did, but it will look through its own database.

Notice Yahoo found 32 web sites for mermaids.

Although it appears on a Yahoo page, these are the results from AltaVista, which found 18,750 *pages* (not web sites) with the word "mermaid" on them. (A lot of these are probably "noise," or things you don't need.)

Search engines

Search engines have automatic software "robots" or "spiders" that search through the web, newsgroups, or other sources, and look for *words* rather than *subjects.* How each robot or spider selects information varies, but it is all gathered and organized into the search engine's database.

A search engine is the place to go when you are looking for particular words, answers to questions, or tidbits of information. For instance, if you are looking for Spam, try the search engine AltaVista. There are not many web sites devoted to Spam, but there are lots of individual pages where interesting tidbits about Spam are mentioned. Try this experiment: search for Spam in Yahoo, then search for Spam in AltaVista. You'll be surprised.

There are other services, such as Excite and Infoseek, that allow you to type in questions such as, "Where was Abraham Lincoln born?"

Some services have both directories and word searches, so you can choose which way you want to find things.

AltaVista is a search engine, searching by words or phrases.

Infoseek is both a search engine and a directory, although its directory is not quite as comprehensive as Yahoo's.

RTFD: Read The Directions!

This is the best tip of all regarding searching the web: **read the directions.** Every search service has tips and tricks and detailed information about how to best find the information you are looking for *in their site.* For instance, some services will give you different results if you look for **Robert Burns** with capital initial letters or **robert burns** with all lowercase. Some need quotation marks to specify words that must be next to each other, some use a + or – symbol to narrow the selection, some use brackets, some use parentheses, some use "Boolean operators" (the words *and, or, and not, near*) and more. It is critical to know how to limit your search or you will go crazy: if you find 63,782 pages with the word "alien" on them, you're no better off than before.

Click the Help button or the Tips button in the service, read the directions for how to search efficiently, and do it.

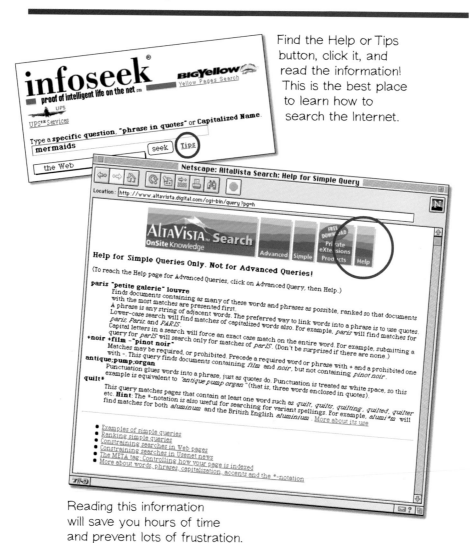

Find the Help or Tips button, click it, and read the information! This is the best place to learn how to search the Internet.

Reading this information will save you hours of time and prevent lots of frustration.

For more information on how to search

Drill down through Yahoo for online information on how to search the web. Try this path: Computers and Internet:Internet:World Wide Web:Searching the Web:How to Search the Web. You can also get there by drilling through the Research section. You will find links to great sites that provide detailed instructions on how to search, plus information about which services are best for various searches. If you really want to learn this skill (which you must if you don't want to waste a lot of time), you will find the best, most complete, and most up-to-date resources right on the Internet itself, rather than in a book.

We will also refer back to this resource when it comes time to add your finished web site to the directories and search engines. If you are anxious *now* for this information, look for "A Webmaster's Guide to Search Engines and Directories," by Danny Sullivan, Calafia Consulting. You'll find this web site in the Yahoo area mentioned above, and shown below. And get the great book, *Getting Hits,* by Don Sellers, from Peachpit Press.

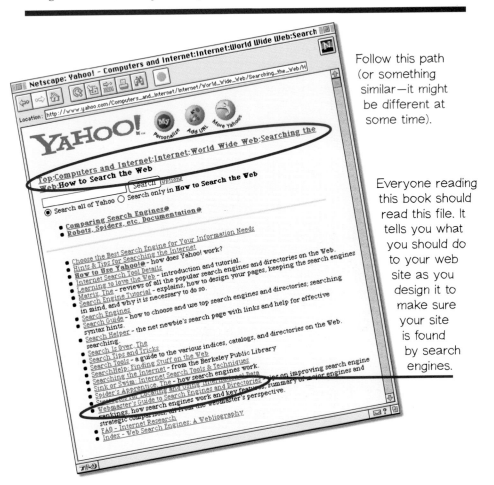

Follow this path (or something similar—it might be different at some time).

Everyone reading this book should read this file. It tells you what you should do to your web site as you design it to make sure your site is found by search engines.

Addresses for searching

These are the addresses for some of the most popular directories and search engines. The description that follows each address does not infer that that is the *only* thing the tool does—it just indicates one of its strengths.

Yahoo **www.yahoo.com** (best used as directory to drill down, not to search for words)

AltaVista **www.altavista.digital.com** (word search; searches web and newsgroups)

Lycos **www.lycos.com** (good for simple searches on standard topics)

WebCrawler **www.webcrawler.com** (not so fast, but good; click "Surf the Web Backwards" to find out who is linked to *your* site)

InfoSeek **www.infoseek.com** (can search web, newsgroups, *and* FAQs, e-mail addresses, current news, company listings; can also ask questions of it, "Where was George Washington born?")

Excite **www.excite.com** (great for when you don't know the exact term you need; is conceptual/finds related topics; can ask questions of it)

HotBot **www.hotbot.com** (can find sites with specific technology, such as sites that use JavaScript or Shockwave)

Open Text Index **search.opentext.com** (great for finding obscure topics)

DejaNews **www.dejanews.com** (best for searching newsgroup postings)

Search.Com **www.search.com** (provides access to a wide variety of search services)

Electric Library **www.elibrary.com** (30 days free access, then a fee; search magazines, maps, more than 2,000 books and 150 newspapers and newswires, radio and tv transcripts, and pictures)

shareware.com **www.shareware.com** (freeware and shareware)

download.com **www.download.com** (commercial software)

WinSite.com **www.winsite.com** (Windows software)

Mining Company **www.miningco.com** (This is an entirely different search tool—it is created by humans whose face you can see and whom you can contact. Specialists in their fields search the web for the best sites, compile them into categories, and maintain the lists. There's no noise here. Check it out.)

Don't limit yourself

On the previous page are the addresses of the most visible and popular search engines and directories. However, there are lots and lots more, and many of them are very specific, which makes their results very good. There are search engines that limit their finds to such specialities as water-related subjects; summer camps and outdoor programs; humorous sites; paganism, magick, and the occult; mathematical material; investing; the ancient world (appropriately called Search Argos); items for sale; travel; music; many different countries (including Estonia) and big cities; women's issues; and dog breeders. You can find a list of all these search tools, and many more, by digging down through Yahoo's directory, starting with Computers and Internet. Then click Internet:World Wide Web:Searching the Web:Search Engines.

And while you're in Yahoo, click Yahooligans! for Kids for lots of sites for children and those who care for them. Then click all those other buttons you've never touched, and see what they do!

Search.com from c|net has an incredible wealth of resources to offer. Go there (www.search.com) and check out the Specialty Searches, the A–Z List. It's incredible.

So go explore! Find a search engine or directory or two and really learn to use it well. It's the only way to use the Internet.

Oh boy, it's a Quiz!

This quiz will give you practice in searching. Remember, this is one of the most important skills you can have, especially if you plan to be a web designer. For many of these questions, you will need to go to the search page, click on the Tips, Options, or Help button, and find the answer.

1. In **Infoseek,** how would you look for **Babe Ruth** to make sure you didn't come up with all the web sites in the world for babies, sexy babes, or ladies named Ruth?

2. In **Infoseek,** how would you look for **mermaids** that don't have anything to do with jewelry?

3. In **AltaVista,** how do you make sure to find information about the **Vietnam war** without finding every site with the word "Vietnam" on it, plus every site with the word "war" on it?

4. If you wanted to find examples of QuickTime Virtual Reality (QTVR), which would be the best search engine to use?

5. In **Yahoo,** find the page that gives you links to all the search engines on the web. From that list, which search engine would probably be best if you were looking for information on how to grow orchids?

6. Also from that list of search tools, which would be the best one to use if you were planning a trip to Hong Kong and wanted to find places to stay and things to do?

7. Find the full text for the Declaration of Independence. What is the address?

8. Knowing that most major companies have web sites, what is the easiest way to try to find them without going through a directory or search engine?

part two
Making Web Pages

MANY PEOPLE DON'T KNOW
THAT COMPUTERS HAVE ANGELS
TOO.

I SAW ONE ONCE HIDING ON A WEB PAGE
AND I ASKED IF HE WOULD LIKE TO
COME OUT AND DANCE
BUT HE SAID, NO THANK YOU HE HAD
WORK TO DO.

THE NEXT TIME I SAW THAT WEB PAGE
HE WAS GONE BUT
MUSIC WAS PLAYING.

"There is no reason anyone would want a computer in their home."

Ken Olson, President, chairman and founder of Digital Equipment Corporation, 1977

Just What are Web Pages *anyway?* 3

Before you begin to *create* web pages, it's a good idea to know *what* they are and how they work. We think it's important to know why you have to do certain things—it helps you remember how to do them.

In this chapter you'll walk through the process of actually creating a couple of practice web pages, using the web authoring software of your choice (see page 50). Remember, you're making practice pages here that you can throw away later just to get the basic concepts down of how to begin the process of making web pages. Don't worry about the planning of a site, the graphics, or the design at this point—that's what the rest of the book is for. Right now, use this chapter to learn your software and the basic underlying principles of creating web pages.

www. stockyards .com

What are web pages?

All of the many millions of web pages around the world are the same thing: pages of text with coded messages telling a browser what to do. Every web page can be opened in a word processor; in fact, many web pages you see were created in word processors, with a programmer or designer typing in the code. This code is called HTML, and don't you worry about it at all—with web authoring software (which we'll talk about in a minute), you don't have to even think about it.

The acronym HTML stands for *hypertext markup language*. Who cares. Some people prefer to laboriously write the HTML themselves, but you can certainly create wonderful web pages without having to write the code yourself. Because each web page is created with the code, whether *you* wrote it or the *software* wrote it for you, each web page is considered to be an "HTML file." (You'll come across this term "HTML file" later, so try to remember it.)

You see, when you create a page with a page layout application such as Adobe PageMaker or QuarkXPress, the program actually records everything you do on the screen—it records it in PostScript code. But you don't see the code on the screen because your page layout software interprets the code into words and pictures for you. When you send your page down to your printer, the *printer* reads the code and creates a lovely printed page for you.

You can create web pages in the same way, letting **web authoring software** write the code while you just put text and graphics on a page. The code is hidden from you. The software interprets the code and displays words and pictures for you while you work on a web page, just like XPress or PageMaker do when you create a page to be printed. The browser software will read the code and display a web page for you. This is great.

One of the best things about web pages, and this is part of what made the World Wide Web phenomenon happen all over the world, is that *any computer can read HTML files.* You can create the web pages (HTML files) on your Macintosh, PC, Commodore, Amiga, Unix, or any other system you love, and anyone else on any other computer can see your pages. No more having to prepare separate files for every conceivable computer platform or operating system.

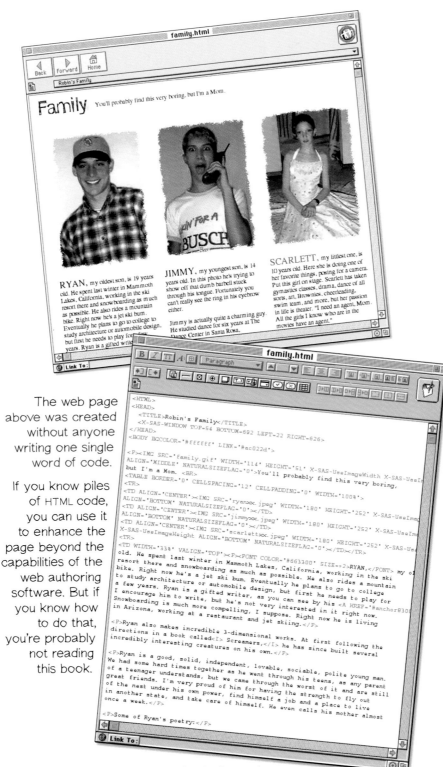

The web page above was created without anyone writing one single word of code.

If you know piles of HTML code, you can use it to enhance the page beyond the capabilities of the web authoring software. But if you know how to do that, you're probably not reading this book.

All the text in blue is the code
that the software wrote, not me.
You can write this code by hand, if you want.

How do you actually make a web page?

To make a web page, you could, as we've discussed, write the code to create the page yourself. Until recently, that was the only way to do it. Now there are a number of **web authoring software packages** that let you create a web page as easily as you make a word processing page. You type the text you want on the page. You select text and make it bolder, bigger, smaller, or italic by clicking buttons. You center the text, or align it to the left or right by clicking buttons. You import a graphic by clicking a button. You tell the text to line up along the right side of the graphic, or at the bottom of it by clicking buttons. You create links to text and graphics by selecting the item and typing in the address of the link. In some programs you can just drag-and-drop to make links.

Because there are so many different software packages and several different platforms (kinds of computers) to use them on, there is no way we can provide step-by-step directions for every program. And besides, if we did this book would be outdated instantly. So what we're going to do in this book is tell you the things that apply to every program—how to make your graphics, how to name your files, how to get your web site posted on the World Wide Web, etc. It will be up to you to learn to use the individual software package you choose. Trust me, though, it's easy. It's very early in the web design game, so the programs are easy because they are early versions.

To make web pages without writing any code, you need to buy a software package. Listed below are the most popular commercial packages and their approximate prices (which may change, of course). Almost all of them are available for both Macintosh and Windows.

Adobe PageMill www.adobe.com	$99	**SoftQuad HoTMetaL PRO** www.softquad.com	$159
Claris Home Page www.claris.com	$99	**NetObjects Fusion** www.netobjects.com	$489
GoLive CyberStudio www.golive.com (Mac only)	$349	**Microsoft FrontPage** www.microsoft.com	$149
Symantec Visual Page www.symantec.com	$99	**Netscape Composer** www.netscape.com (comes with Communicator)	$35

For brand-new beginners who might be feeling a wee bit intimidated, I suggest **Adobe PageMill** or **Claris Home Page.** They're both great, have good manuals, are easy to learn to use, and will do everything you need. They are so good, in fact, that advanced users will be happy also. Adobe PageMill is particularly a good deal at the time of this writing because you get Adobe Photoshop LE (Limited Edition) with it, as well as SiteMill, a site management program that gives you lots of management control over big sites. This bargain may change.

It can be this easy

Okay okay already, let's do it. These directions might not be specific to your particular software, but you'll find equivalent features somewhere in your package.

- First, make and name a folder in which to store this practice web site.
- Open your web authoring software.
- From the File menu, choose "New Page." mermaids

  1. Type a headline on the page.
  2. Hit Return or Enter and type a paragraph of information.
  3. Hit Return or Enter and type another paragraph of information. Hit Return or Enter. (Does this process sound familiar?)
  4. Type a sentence such as "If you have nice things to say, please respond to gwenevere@seamaiden.net."
  5. Type the text that you would want to link to another page, such as "The Life of a Mermaid." Hit Return or Enter.
  6. Save the page into your folder. In the next chapter we'll discuss appropriate file names and titles. For now, just save it.

Your page will look something like the one shown below—boring and pretty ugly, but it's a web page. We'll add more to this.

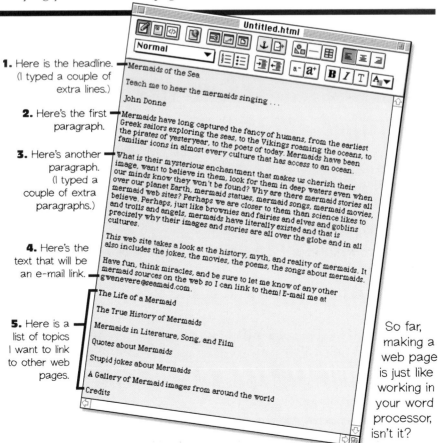

1. Here is the headline. (I typed a couple of extra lines.)

2. Here's the first paragraph.

3. Here's another paragraph. (I typed a couple of extra paragraphs.)

4. Here's the text that will be an e-mail link.

5. Here is a list of topics I want to link to other web pages.

So far, making a web page is just like working in your word processor, isn't it?

Untitled.html

Normal

Mermaids of the Sea

Teach me to hear the mermaids singing . . .

John Donne

Mermaids have long captured the fancy of humans, from the earliest Greek sailors exploring the seas, to the Vikings roaming the oceans, to the pirates of yesteryear, to the poets of today. Mermaids have been familiar icons in almost every culture that has access to an ocean.

What is their mysterious enchantment that makes us cherish their image, want to believe in them, look for them in deep waters even when our minds know they won't be found? Why are there mermaid stories all over our planet Earth, mermaid statues, mermaid songs, mermaid movies, mermaid web sites? Perhaps we are closer to them than science likes to believe. Perhaps, just like brownies and fairies and elves and goblins and trolls and angels, mermaids have literally existed and that is precisely why their images and stories are all over the globe and in all cultures.

This web site takes a look at the history, myth, and reality of mermaids. It also includes the jokes, the movies, the poems, the songs about mermaids.

Have fun, think miracles, and be sure to let me know of any other mermaid sources on the web so I can link to them! E-mail me at gwenevere@seamaid.com.

The Life of a Mermaid

The True History of Mermaids

Mermaids in Literature, Song, and Film

Quotes about Mermaids

Stupid jokes about Mermaids

A Gallery of Mermaid images from around the world

Credits

Format the text

On the page you just created, let's do a little formatting. First of all, you don't like the text so close to the edge, do you? It is disturbing to have text crowd the edge like that.

- Select all the text. (There is probably a "Select All" command in the Edit menu.)
- Find the button or menu command that says something like "Block Quote" or "Indent Right." Click the button or choose the command. (This command actually indents the text from *both* sides.)

Looks better already, doesn't it? Now let's format some of that text. Would you like some text bigger, italic, or bold? You can do that. Do you want to use another typeface? You can't do that. (We'll talk more about fonts later.)

- Select that headline you typed.
- Look either in the toolbar across the top of the page or in the menus for the command that says something like "Largest" or "Heading 1." Choose it. This command makes *the entire paragraph* larger, whether you had selected the entire paragraph or not.
- Find a word in the paragraph that you want bold. Select the word. Find a button with a "B" on it in the ruler, or find the "Bold" command in the menu. Click the button or choose the command. This command makes *just the selected characters* bold.
- Find a word that you want italic. I'll bet you know how to make it italic, yes?
- Let's make the first word or two in the second paragraph larger and bolder:

    Select the text. Make it bold.

    While that text is still selected, find the button or command that says something like +1 or has an up arrow. This command makes *just the selected text* larger (remember, the "Largest" command you used earlier made *the entire paragraph* largest).

Paragraph vs. Break

When you hit Return or Enter at the end of a line, that "Paragraph" command makes a space between the lines. **If you don't want a space between the lines,** use the "Break" code. A combination of one of the following keystrokes will give you a Break instead of a Paragraph: On a Mac, try Shift-Return, Option-Return, or Command-Return. On a PC, try Shift-Enter, Alt-Enter, or Control-Enter. On the opposite page, we used a Break to prevent the quote from having space between the lines.

The example on the following page shows the formatting changes. It's still pretty ugly, but it's getting better.

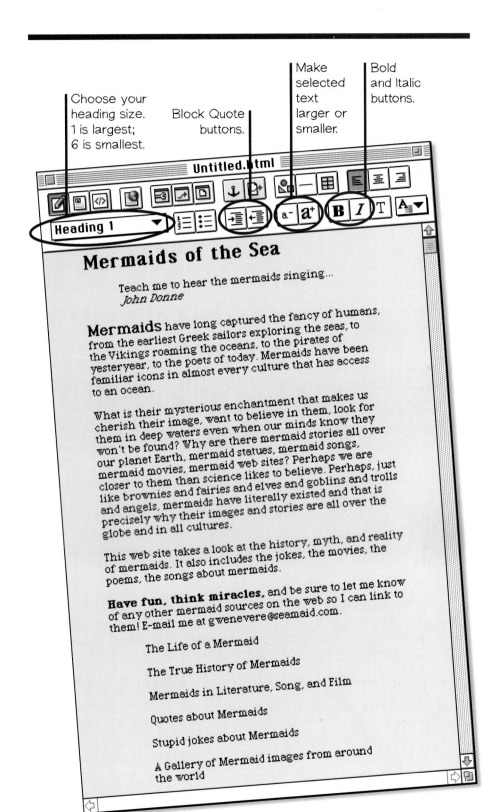

Choose your heading size. 1 is largest; 6 is smallest.

Block Quote buttons.

Make selected text larger or smaller.

Bold and Italic buttons.

This example is from Claris Home Page.

Change the colors

One thing you must always do is get rid of the **default gray background** of the web page. That color is a very dull gray with no redeeming value—changing to a more pleasant color is a sign that you know what you're doing. The steps to change the background are different in different software programs, so you'll need to read your manual to find out how to do it.

Do you want a patterned background? Any correctly formatted web graphic can be used as a background pattern. We're going to talk in great detail about the formats for web graphics (GIFs and JPEGs), but for now, if you happen to have one, you can drop it in as a background. (If you don't have that kind of graphic at the moment, don't worry—just watch the example and know you can do it later.)

Most patterned backgrounds make the text very difficult to read. Be very careful with patterns. This is the rule about type on a patterned background: if it looks hard to read, it is. Nothing magical happens to it when the page gets to the Internet. If the text is hard to read to now, it will be hard to read then, so don't do it.

Do you want to change the color of the text? Simply select the text, then find the menu command or toolbar button that changes the color.

In Claris Home Page, for instance, click the Document button to get the dialog box shown to the right.

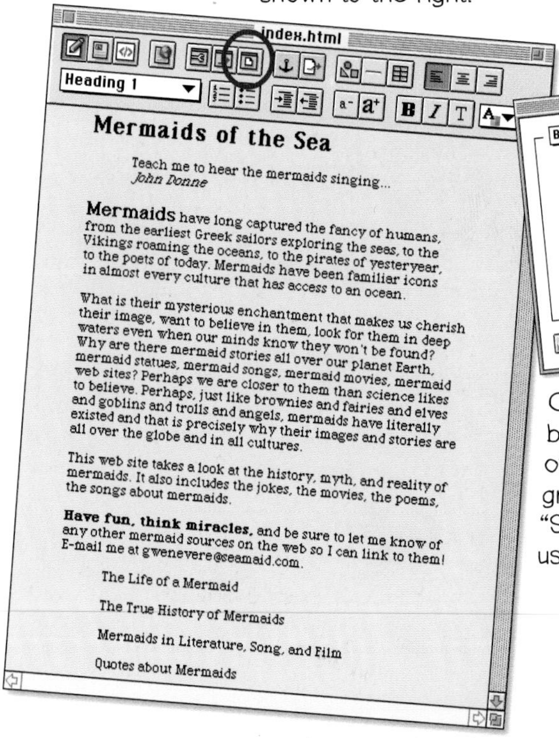

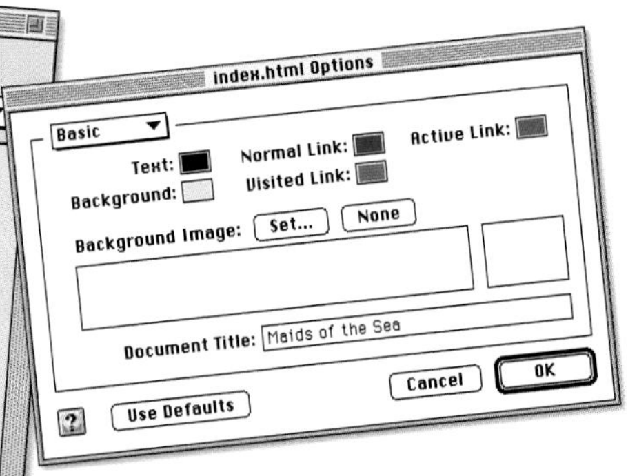

Click the buttons in the dialog box above to change the colors of default text, the page background, the links, etc. Click "Set..." to go get a graphic to use as a background.

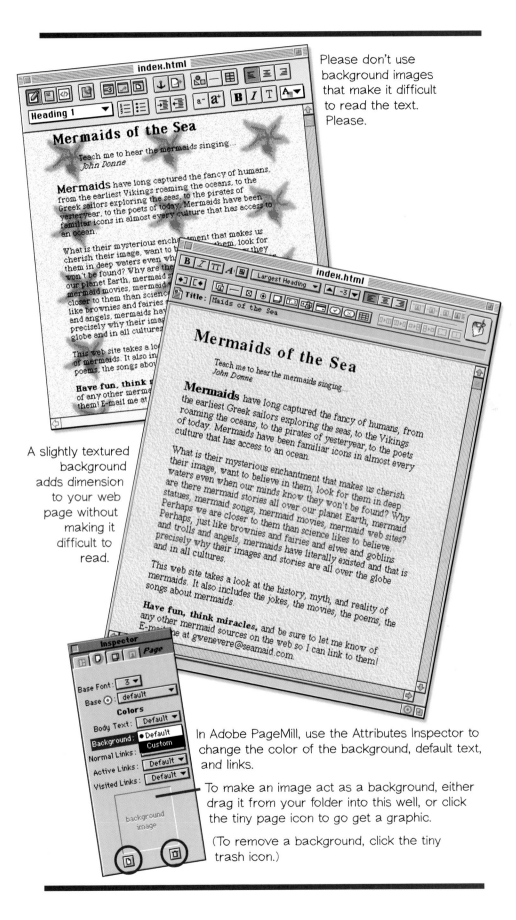

Please don't use background images that make it difficult to read the text. Please.

A slightly textured background adds dimension to your web page without making it difficult to read.

In Adobe PageMill, use the Attributes Inspector to change the color of the background, default text, and links.

To make an image act as a background, either drag it from your folder into this well, or click the tiny page icon to go get a graphic.

(To remove a background, click the tiny trash icon.)

Create links

There are several different kinds of links you can make:

- **Internal links** that link to other pages in *the same* web site. Also called "local" or sometimes "page" links. Internal links all have the same domain name (navy.mil, adobe.com, etc.).
- **External links** that link to pages *outside* of a particular web site. Also called "remote" links. You can link to any other web page in the world, and you don't have to ask permission. External links have a different domain name from the web site you find them in.
- **E-mail links** that don't take the user to another page, but instead open up e-mail forms.
- **Anchors** that generally don't jump the user to another page, but to somewhere else on the same page. These are very useful for long pages.

To make an **internal,** or local, link you first have to have another page to link to. So make another quick page and save it. (We'll talk about the rules for naming files in the next chapter.)

The exact steps for making internal links in each program is a little bit different, but the basic process is:

- Select the text or the graphic on the first page that you want to link to the newly created page.
- Find the "link editor" for your program.
- Then, depending on your software, either type in the name of the file you want that text or graphic to link to; or choose a file name from a menu; or simply drag-and-drop a link icon onto the text or graphic (shown on the opposite page). The steps are neither difficult nor complicated, but you should *read your manual* to find out exactly what they are.

To make an **external,** or remote, link you must first know the exact URL (web address) of the page you want to link to. Then:

- Select the text or the graphic that you want to link to another page.
- Find the link editor for your program.
- Type in the exact URL, including the http:// and any slashes at the end of the address. Click OK or hit Return or Enter.

As you read your manual, you will probably discover shortcuts. For instance, in PageMill you can select the text or graphic on your new web page, then drag bookmarks from the Netscape Bookmarks window onto the selected item. Or drag a file from a folder onto the selected text or graphic and PageMill will create a link to that file with no typing at all.

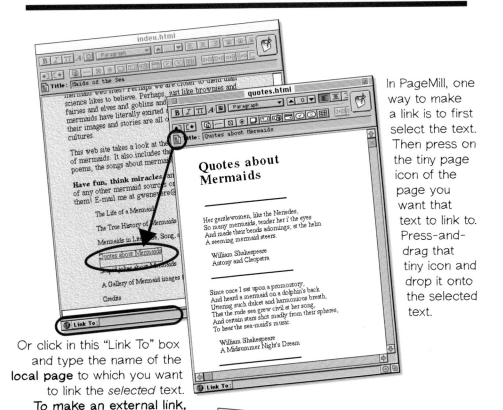

In PageMill, one way to make a link is to first select the text. Then press on the tiny page icon of the page you want that text to link to. Press-and-drag that tiny icon and drop it onto the selected text.

Or click in this "Link To" box and type the name of the **local page** to which you want to link the *selected* text. **To make an external link,** type an http:// address here.

In Claris Home Page, one way to make a link is to select the text, then click on the "Insert Link to File" button in the toolbar to select the page to link to.

Or, as in PageMill, you can drag the "Insert Link to File" button from one page onto the selected text in another page.

You could also select the text, then Command-Press (Mac) or right-click (Windows) on the text. You will get a menu of files to link to, or you can enter a URL, or go *look* for a file (called "browse" in Claris Home Page).

Make an e-mail link

An e-mail link does not jump you to another page, but (in most browsers) brings up an e-mail form pre-addressed to that person, and with a return address from the user's computer already entered in the form. The link is very easy to make.

- On that first page you created earlier, select the e-mail address you typed.
- In the link editor for your software, type in this code, including the colon: **mailto:**
- Immediately after that code, with no space between, type the entire e-mail address that you want linked. It should look like this:

  mailto:samantha@seamaids.com
- If your software requires you to hit Return or Enter or to click OK after you make a link, do so. If your e-mail address on the page is now underlined, you did it right. If it isn't underlined, read your manual.

There are a couple of guidelines to follow when making e-mail links.

- Please don't make an e-mail link that people cannot tell is for e-mail.

  For instance, if the text For More Information is underlined, people expect to click on it and go to another page with more information. If that's what they expect, then don't make it an e-mail link! Be clear. Type something like, "For more information, please send e-mail to info@seaweed.net."

  If there is a list of officers on a web page and each of their names is a link, such as Ryan Williams, visitors assume the link will take them to a page with more information about that person. So don't surprise the visitor by making the link pop up an e-mail form instead of a page of information.

- Don't create an e-mail link without spelling out the address. That is, don't do something like "E-mail me!"

  Some people have browsers that cannot do e-mail forms. If there is no address spelled out, a visitor cannot write to you.

  Also, someone might want to write you later, like from their home or office computer. Or they might want to put your address in their address book. Or they might want to print the page. Obviously, if the e-mail address is not typed on the page, the visitor cannot write it down or print it for later use.

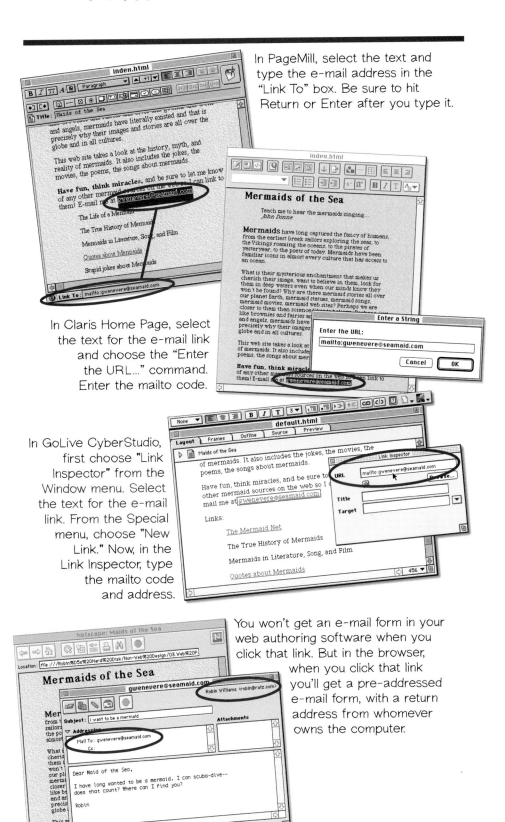

In PageMill, select the text and type the e-mail address in the "Link To" box. Be sure to hit Return or Enter after you type it.

In Claris Home Page, select the text for the e-mail link and choose the "Enter the URL..." command. Enter the mailto code.

In GoLive CyberStudio, first choose "Link Inspector" from the Window menu. Select the text for the e-mail link. From the Special menu, choose "New Link." Now, in the Link Inspector, type the mailto code and address.

You won't get an e-mail form in your web authoring software when you click that link. But in the browser, when you click that link you'll get a pre-addressed e-mail form, with a return address from whomever owns the computer.

Add a graphic

Later in this book we spend quite a bit of time on how to make graphics that will work properly on the web. For now, see if you can find a GIF or a JPEG file in the samples that came with your web authoring software (they will be labeled something like "image.gif" or "image.jpg"). If you do, you can add it to the web page. If not, just read the following simple directions and know that when you get your graphics it will be this easy.

- One **very important rule** about graphics is that *the graphic file* **must** *be in your web site folder before you put it on the page!*

  We'll talk about why this is so important later; for right now, just get in the habit of putting the graphics into your web site folder before you place them on your page.

- Find the toolbar button or the menu command that says something like "Place Image," "Insert Image," or anything similar. Click the button or choose the menu command.

- *From your web site folder* select the graphic that you want on the page. Click OK.

Easy, huh? Save your page.

Take a look at the code you didn't have to write: find the menu command for "Source code," "Edit code" or something similar. Aren't you glad you didn't have to write that?

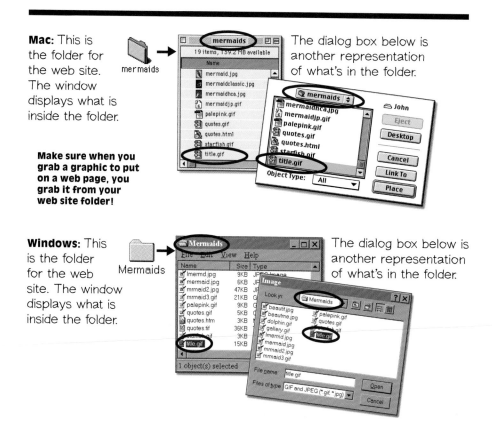

Mac: This is the folder for the web site. The window displays what is inside the folder.

Make sure when you grab a graphic to put on a web page, you grab it from your web site folder!

The dialog box below is another representation of what's in the folder.

Windows: This is the folder for the web site. The window displays what is inside the folder.

The dialog box below is another representation of what's in the folder.

In PageMill, click this button **to add a graphic.** Or drag the graphic from your folder and drop it on the page.

To see the code, from the Edit menu, choose "HTML Source." To go back to the display page, choose the same command again.

(This is the same page, opened in Claris Home Page.) Click these two buttons to switch back and forth from a preview of the web page to the code.

This circled code tells the browser that the image source (IMG SRC) is called **title.gif**.

Make a table

There is one more feature of web pages that you can skip for a while, but eventually you really need to have control over, and that is **tables.** Tables allow you to put things in columns. Without tables, you can only have one long list of text and graphics. The examples on the following page show the same web page with and without tables.

If you've ever made a table in a word processor, you can make a table on a web page—it's exactly the same concept. Even if you've never made a table before, you can make one on a web page. Read the directions in your particular software for the details of making and formatting tables.

Basically, it's a matter of clicking the table button or choosing the table command from the menu. Enter how many rows and columns you want and click OK.

- If you don't want the **border** to show around your table, change the border amount to 0 (zero).

- If you want a thicker or thinner border, including the interior lines between the cells, select the table and change the **cell padding** value.

- If you want to move the text further away from or closer to the edge, select the table and change the **cell spacing** value.

- If you want to make the text align at the top, bottom, left, right, or along the baselines of the text, first select the individual cell. Then find the button or command in your software and make your choice.

You can resize the entire table, resize the individual rows and columns, group several cells into one cell, add or delete rows or columns, etc. Most applications let you color the background of individual cells. Once you've got a table on the page, you can insert text into it, format text, insert graphics, make links from the text and graphics inside the table, and do everything else you've learned to do on the web page. The cells will expand as you type text or insert graphics.

Absolute vs. relative table widths

Your software lets you determine whether the width of the table will be *absolute* or *relative.* If you choose a certain, **absolute pixel width,** such as 400, then your table will remain that exact size no matter how a visitor changes the size of their browser window. If you choose a **relative percent,** then the table will resize according to the size of the browser window. You almost always want to set absolute values for the width of your tables and the individual cells. See the dialog box on the facing page.

Tables can be a little frustrating because they don't always behave very well. Start with a simple table and get to know the techniques for managing it well. Work your way up to more complex tables.

This page, created in GoLive CyberStudio, is just text on the page with illustrations next to the text. You don't have as many options in a layout without tables.

This page has been arranged with a table. You can see the borders of the table. Tables are made of rows (across) and columns (down). Each individual spot within the table is called a cell. You can group several small cells together to make larger cells, as in the purple sidebar.

This is the same web page, but the table border has been "turned off." Without the borders showing, the information appears to be in neat columns.

Your software will have a table dialog box where you can enter the specifications for your table. This example is from GoLive CyberStudio.

To set an absolute pixel width, enter a value.

To remove the borders, change the "Border" number to 0 (zero).

What are frames?

Frames are very different from tables, although at first glance they might seem similar because frames can make it appear as if there are columns on the web page. Frames are tricky and have to be done thoughtfully and correctly—you will need to study your manual. Many people dislike frames on a web page because they can cause confusion, and if not created well they look junky. All we want to do right now is teach you to recognize a frame when you see one.

A frame is a stationary part of a web page that stays put while you scroll through another part (that other part is also a frame). You can tell if there is a frame on a page by scrolling: anything you see that does not scroll along is another frame.

You can spot most frames by their border, which might or might not include a scroll bar. It is possible to make borderless frames, though. Whether it has a border or not, if part of the page stays still while you scroll another part, the page is in frames.

Each frame is actually a separate web page. When you see a page with three or four frames, that is actually three or four web pages all squished into one "frameset." That's why it might be confusing when you hit the Back button—sometimes you just go back through another page *within that frame,* not all the way back to what you thought was the last real page you saw.

A thoughtfully created frameset can be very nice. It's often used to keep navigation buttons along the left or right side of a page, or a banner across the top. With a frame to hold buttons, the visitor can browse the entire web site and always have those buttons or that banner accessible.

As you wander around the web, keep your eyes open for frames. Notice whether they clutter the page and confuse the navigation, or provide a good anchor point for browsing the site. Put into words what you like or dislike when you find a frameset, and use your discoveries as guidelines if you ever decide to create frames on your own site.

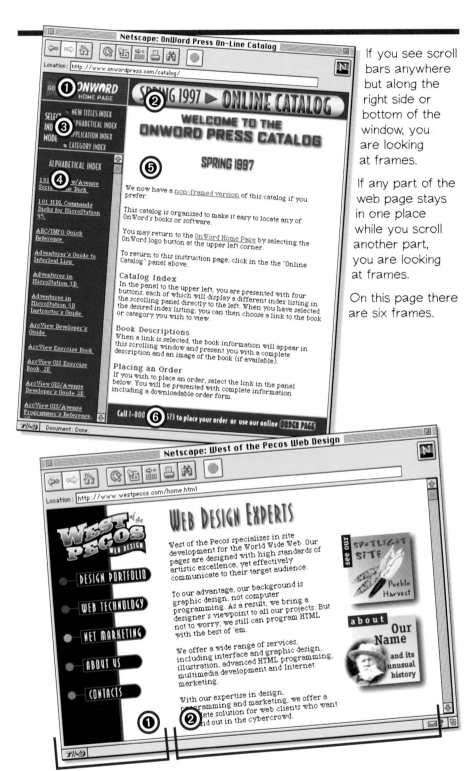

If you see scroll bars anywhere but along the right side or bottom of the window, you are looking at frames.

If any part of the web page stays in one place while you scroll another part, you are looking at frames.

On this page there are six frames.

This page also has frames, but you can't tell instantly because the frames are "borderless." There are two frames.

If you scroll the scroll bar on the right-hand side of the window, you'll notice that the information bar on the left does not move.

If you click one of the buttons on the left, only the information in the right-hand frame changes. Try it and see.

Add code, if you like

There may be times when the software just doesn't quite do what you want it to. Part of this may be the limitations of web design, and part of it may be the limitations of the software itself. All of the web authoring software packages have a way for you to add code yourself, if you know how and so choose. In some packages you can add it right to the source code. In others you'll find a command called something like "Raw HTML," "Extra HTML," or "Script." On pages 245–247 you'll find directions for adding some easy HTML code to enhance your pages.

If you don't want to deal with it, don't. But if you know HTML and want to add code, the option is there. And if you want to learn more about HTML, get Liz Castro's book, *HTML for the World Wide Web: Visual QuickStart Guide,* from Peachpit Press.

Build more pages

Basically, to finish the rest of your site you simply make more pages, adding your graphics and making links, just as you did in these last few pages of the book. The next chapter provides a few important details that are specific to creating web pages, as well as some other things to think about before you begin your real site. And the rest of the book talks about design principles, how to make your graphics, tips and tricks, and more.

Then what?

When you're finished with the web site, you will test it, upload it to a "server," test it again on the World Wide Web, and then tell the world your site exists. Details for that are in Chapters 14, 15, and 16. But you have a lot to do before then.

Self-Guided Tour
of the World Wide Web

Now that you know how web pages are put together, go back to the World Wide Web and notice these things:

☐ Find a page where the text bumps up against the left edge. Is it appealing? What would you do to make the page more appealing and the text easier to read?

☐ Find a page with the standard gray background (besides Yahoo). What is your impression when you come across a gray page like that?

☐ Find a page that has an icon for a missing graphic. Why might the graphic be missing?

☐ Look for this address: www.uxorious.com. Did you get a message? Why did you get that message?

☐ Find a table with the borders showing.

☐ Find a page where it is obvious the designer used tables, even though the borders are not showing. How can you tell?

☐ Find a page or two where the designer probably should have used tables. How would tables have made it a better page?

☐ Find several e-mail links. Do you find any e-mail links that you don't know are for e-mail until you click them or check their address in the status bar?

☐ Find several pages with anchors (links that jump you to somewhere else on the same page, instead of to another page).

☐ Find at least two external links and two internal links. How can you tell whether they are external (remote) or internal (local)?

☐ Find a page with several frames. Spend some time there and poke around. Notice how frames are not like tables! What do you think?

Oh boy, it's a **QUIZ!**

This is a quiz on the most important aspects of creating your pages. If you can't answer these correctly, please reread the material, consult your manual, or ask your friend, and make sure you know the answers before you move on.

1. Every web page is basically the same thing:
a) a page of text with formatting specifications in HTML code
b) a database
c) a spreadsheet
d) http code

2. What do you need to do before you create your first page?
a) Adjust your monitor settings.
b) Design the headlines.
c) Make and name a new folder in which to store your web pages.
d) Create all of your graphics.

3. Each of the following is an **e-mail link.** Which one is most appropriate? Why and why not?
a) Robert Burns
b) Send me e-mail!
c) Please e-mail us at countryinn@bucolic.com.
d) Order Tickets

4. If you want to make the headline text larger, which of the following would you choose?
a) Select the text and apply "Heading 1."
b) Select the text and apply bold, plus apply a larger type size.
c) Either of the above would work. The difference is:_____.

(hint: experiment and discover the important difference!)

5. What is the best way to make columns on a web page?
a) Draw guidelines across the page.
b) Create tables.
c) Type the text in short lines, hitting the Spacebar between columns.
d) Use graphics to contain the text on either side.

6. The difference between a Paragraph and a Break is:
a) A Paragraph contains a complete thought; a Break doesn't.
b) You must have more than one line in a Paragraph; a Break can have only one line.
c) A Paragraph cannot change color.
d) A Paragraph has space following it; a Break has no space following it.

7. Which of the following are you **not** going to do?
a) Leave the default gray page color.
b) Make a background that is hard to read text on.
c) Type in all caps.
d) I promise I won't do **any** of the above.

8. How can you tell where a **link** is going before you click on it?
a) You can't.
b) Ask your mother.
c) Position the pointer over the link and read the status bar at the bottom of the browser window.
d) Type "link = ?" in the location box, then hit Return or Enter.

Things to Know Before You Begin Your Web Site

In the last chapter we showed you the basics of making an actual web page, which is very similar to making a document in a word processor or a flyer in a page layout program. In this chapter we want to fill in a few other details about making web pages that you don't need to worry about when you are making any other kind of printed piece, such as exactly how you must name and title your pages and how important it is to keep your files organized.

We'll also discuss what you need to think about before you begin your site, such as making a map to follow, establishing a relationship with a service provider to host your site, getting your very own web address, buying your own domain name, collecting materials, and more.

Organizing your files

From the very beginning of the creation of your web site, you need to be conscious of organizing your files. You're going to be making a lot of them and it can get very confusing.

Organizing by folders

Most smaller sites can be contained in one folder. If you think your site is going to be large, with more than about thirty or forty files (including all graphics, sound files, web pages, etc.), you may want to make subfolders. For instance, you might want to store all of your graphics in one folder. Or perhaps your site is large enough to break down into separate sections, and each section would have its own file.

Whatever you decide, you need to implement your system from the very beginning; that is, you should make all the folders you will need for the entire site before you begin. If you decide later to add a *completely new section,* you can certainly add a new folder and store files in it. But this is what you can't do: you can't decide you want to make a new section *out of existing pages and graphics,* and then move those pages and graphics into a new folder. All of the links will be broken (see pages 74–75). If you plan to make lots of large web sites, you need to invest in "site management" software that makes moving files, rearranging pages, and updating links very easy (see page 252). Some web authoring software has this built in.

Organizing by name

The facing page has details of how you should *technically* name your files so they can be used on the web. But here are a couple of ideas for naming your files so you can find them again.

One option is to give each different kind of file a prefix that indicates what it is. For instance, if it's a navigation graphic, give it a prefix of "nav." If it's a main headline, give it a prefix of "hd." If it's an HTML file, give it a prefix of "a" or "x." When you view these files in your folder, all those of a similar kind will be grouped together. Later when you can't remember what you called a file, you can list files by name and find it within its category.

Another option is to make sure all files that belong on one page start with the same letter. For instance, if you create a page for a workshop you are doing, this page might have a title graphic, a headline graphic, a background graphic, and of course the HTML file. So give them names like worktitle.gif, workhead.gif, workbkg.gif, and workshop.html. This way they are grouped together in your folder and you can easily find all the pieces to the page. This is especially handy when the workshop is over and it's time to take down the page.

These file-naming ideas aren't necessary for the files to work, of course—they're just to help you find things.

Naming your files

It is very important how you name your files. You will be creating HTML files (those are the web pages) and probably graphic files. Because these files are read by all sorts of computers, we have to take the file names down to the least common denominator and make sure there is nothing funny in them that some computer can't understand. The rules are simple:

- **Use all lowercase letters.**
  Technically you can use capital letters, but we find it's easier to keep things straight and organized (plus it looks cleaner) if the names are limited to all lowercase.

- **Use only letters or numbers—no funny characters.**
  That is, don't use apostrophes, colons, semicolons, bullets, slashes, or any other characters except letters or numbers.

- **You can use** the tilde (~), underscore (_), hyphen (-), or period (.).

- **Never use a space** in any file name.

- **All web pages must end in .htm or .html**.
  The .htm is most common on PCs, and .html is most common on Macintoshes. (Whether it's .htm or .html, the pages are considered "HTML files.")

- **Put an extension at the end of your graphic file names** so you know what they are (don't worry if you don't know what these "file formats" refer to yet; we'll explain them in Chapter 10). For instance:
  If the graphic is a Photoshop 4 file, name it **graphic.ps4**.
  If it's a TIFF file, name it **graphic.tif**.
  If it's a GIF file, name it **graphic.gif**.
  If it's a JPEG file, name it **graphic.jpg** (.jpeg is also okay)

  You get the idea. This will save you headaches later, we guarantee.

- **Keep the file name short** for several reasons, not the least of which is that it reduces typos when people have to type the address.

So which of the file names below are correct and won't cause problems? How can the incorrect ones be corrected?

mydogs.jpg	correct (.jpg or .jpeg are both acceptable)
HOMEPAGE.HTM	Is technically okay, but preference is lowercase
car/wash.html	wrong: can't use a slash in a file name
snakes:myFriends.gif	wrong: can't use a colon in a file name
You-Bet-It-Hurts-Tattoos.jpg	technically okay, but is too long; remove caps
Grandma's house.html	wrong: cannot use apostrophe or space. Capital letter is okay, but not encouraged.

Saving and titling pages

You must save and title every web page. Saving and titling web pages is different from saving word processing or spreadsheet files, so don't assume you know everything and skip this—it is very important. Read this whole page before you start to save, because different programs do these two steps in different orders.

You are going to be doing two different things: 1) **saving and naming** the page as an HTML file, and 2) **titling** the web page. Don't get confused.

1. When you Save As, you are **saving** the code as an HTML file, which is a web page. Every web page has a **name** that ends in .htm or .html. This is how the browser knows it is a web page.

The very first page of your web site *must* be named index.html or index.htm, or sometimes default.html. How do you know which one? You must call the service who will be "hosting" your site. We'll talk more about hosting a site in a minute (see pages 76–77), so for now pretend you called them up and asked, "What do you need me to name the first page of my web site, index or default? Do you need the extension of .htm or .html?" Let's pretend they said "index.htm" if you're on a PC, and "index.html" if you're on a Macintosh.

So now go ahead and **save** that beautiful web page you've worked so hard on, with these two important reminders:
Save it with the **name** index.htm or index.html, all lowercase.
Save it into the folder you created for the practice web site!

2. Okay. Now you also have to **title** this web page. The title has nothing to do with the HTML file name you saved it as!

The title is what will appear in the title bar of the window when someone else views your page on the World Wide Web.

When someone makes a bookmark (Netscape) or favorite (Internet Explorer) of your page, this title is what will appear as that bookmark or favorite.

Many search engines look first at your title and decide from that where to add you to their database so others can find you. So make that title relevant to the page!

The title is not limited to the naming conventions of files; that is, you can have capital letters, numbers, odd characters, longer names, etc.

Different software has different methods for entering the title. Look for the appropriate place in your software to enter the title, or check the manual.

Title your practice web pages before you move on.

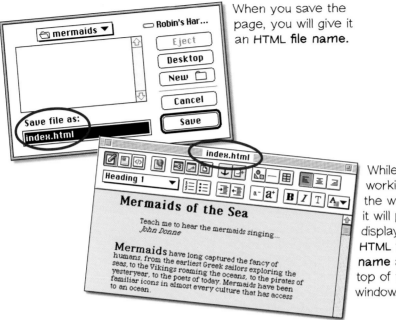

When you save the page, you will give it an HTML **file name**.

While you are working on the web page, it will probably display the HTML **file name** at the top of the window.

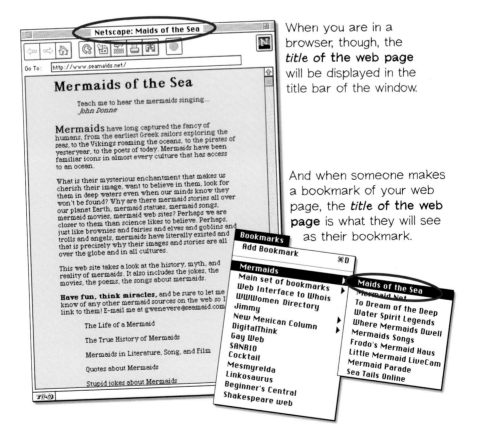

When you are in a browser, though, the *title* **of the web page** will be displayed in the title bar of the window.

And when someone makes a bookmark of your web page, the *title* **of the web page** is what they will see as their bookmark.

What does a browser do?

Your connection software (called something like TCP/IP or FreePPP) is what actually goes out and connects to the other computers in the world, gets the web pages, and feeds them to your browser. The browser interprets the HTML and displays the pages of text, graphics, sounds, animation, movie clips, etc., on your screen.

Now, all those movies and animations and graphic images are not on the HTML page itself. You can see a page of code, opposite—it's just a bunch of text. The code tells the browser that there is an animation file, or a graphic image, or a movie, *separate* from the HTML file, and the code simply tells the browser where to *find* that separate item. The item is most often nearby, like in the very same folder as the web page itself, or in another nested folder. The browser finds the separate item and displays it.

The code is very specific. Let's say the code tells the browser to display the image file called "DogFood.gif," which is stored in the folder called "dogs." If you changed your mind after you made the page and renamed that image file "dogfood.gif" with lowercase letters, or perhaps you renamed it "catfood.gif," or perhaps you put the graphic into a different folder, *the browser cannot find the image.* The browser looks for "DogFood.gif" in the folder "dogs" and nothing else. If you renamed the folder "dog" instead of the original "dogs," the browser cannot find the folder. The browser can only do what the code tells it to do—it does not stop and wonder if perhaps you changed the name of the file or moved it.

This means, then (and **this is important**), that after you put an image on a web page, you had better not change the name of the image, nor change its location. And when you send your web site to the server, you must also send every graphic image, every animation, every movie file, etc., and they all must be in the original folders they were in when you placed them on the page, or the browser won't be able to display them.

Have you ever run across web pages where a graphic is missing? That's because the browser can't find it. Most often the browser can't find it because the graphic file wasn't sent to the server in the first place, someone put the graphic in a different folder, or perhaps someone changed its name. Don't let this happen to you.

 This icon means the image could not be found.

 This icon means the image is available, but is not loaded. Perhaps you turned off the "Auto Load Images" command.

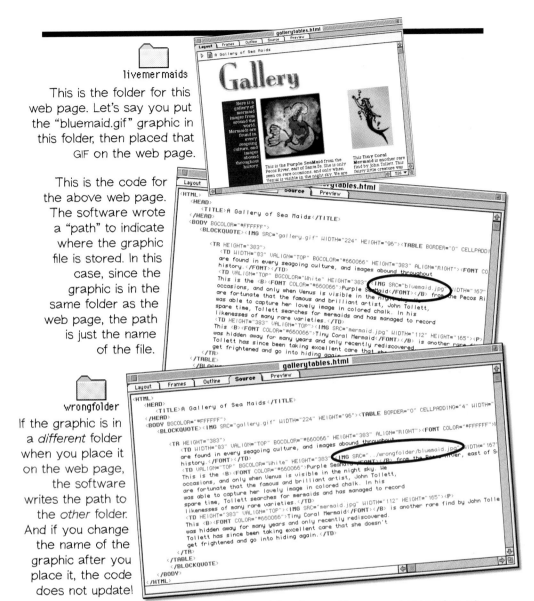

livemermaids

This is the folder for this web page. Let's say you put the "bluemaid.gif" graphic in this folder, then placed that GIF on the web page.

This is the code for the above web page. The software wrote a "path" to indicate where the graphic file is stored. In this case, since the graphic is in the same folder as the web page, the path is just the name of the file.

wrongfolder

If the graphic is in a *different* folder when you place it on the web page, the software writes the path to the *other* folder. And if you change the name of the graphic after you place it, the code does not update!

If you really want to change the name or location of the graphic file, all you have to do is change the code to match the new name and/or path.

To do this, first delete the existing graphic from the web page. Then do what you need to do—put the graphic in the folder where it belongs, rename it, or whatever—and insert the graphic again on the web page. The software will write the new path.

Or use site management software (page 252) to move, rename, and relink files automatically.

Or change the name of the graphic or put it into the correct web site folder, then go into the code and fix it by hand: change the name of the file, or eliminate all of the path except the graphic file name, which tells the browser the graphic is in the web site folder. Change the code from: `<IMG SRC="../wrongfolder/bluemaid.jpg"` to this: `<IMG SRC="bluemaid.jpg"` (just select and delete)

What is a server?

A **server** is a juiced-up computer that is connected to the Internet 24 hours a day. It has special software on it that allows web pages to be "served" to the Internet whenever anyone types in the web address.

If you leave your finished web site on your computer, no one but you will ever see it. A web site cannot be served to the Internet from your home or office (well, you can sort of serve it, but that's another story).

So when you finish your web site, you will find someone with a server who will store, or host, the site for you (for a price, of course). You will send your site, or *upload* it, to the server. We'll explain the exact details about how to upload your site in Chapter 15—it's quite easy. For now all you need to know is that you will be sending your finished web pages to a server, and from there they will be accessible on the Internet.

It is the **domain name** (as explained on page 26) that contains the address of the server. Sometimes you will see a web address that has numbers where you expect a domain name to be—that number is the **DNS,** or *domain name server* for that domain name. See page 80 for details on how to get your own domain name.

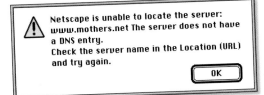

Have you seen this message? "The server does not have a DNS entry." It means your connection software cannot find a server that is hosting the web site you want; *you probably have the wrong domain name.*

Sometimes this message also appears *when your connection has been dropped.* If you **know** the address is correct: quit, disconnect, and start over. Just because all the lights on your modem are still on does not mean you are still connected.

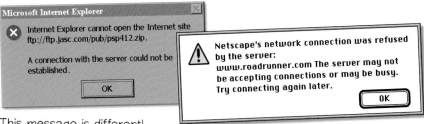

This message is different!
This one means your modem is working, the address is correct, and the server has been found, but the server is too busy serving other people, or it may be down. Try again later.

How to find a server

You need to find someone with a server who will host (store) your site. Here are places to look:

- Commercial online services such as America Online or CompuServe usually store web sites *free* for members. Thousands of people take advantage of this perk. Check the World Wide Web or Internet section of the service—you should find a FAQ (list of frequently asked questions) that explains the process.

- If you use a local Internet Service Provider (ISP), ask them. They most likely host web sites as well as provide connectivity. If they don't host web sites, other service providers in town probably do. Ask your own service provider whom they recommend.

- Is your ISP is a national provider, such as AT&T or NetCom? They usually host web sites as well as provide connectivity. Check their web site or the printed information they sent you.

- Do you know anyone else in town who has a web site that's up and running? Ask them who hosts their site.

- Find other local sites on the web, people from your town who have posted web pages. E-mail them to ask where they post their sites. Sometimes you can find that information at the bottom of their home page or on a credits page. Ask how they like their host.

- Call a local web designer and ask whom they recommend. A good web design firm usually knows all the servers in town, as well as the popular remote servers, because they have a variety of clients who store their pages on various servers.

- Is there an Internet cafe in town? They often host web sites. Check the listings at www.cyber-cafe.com to see if there is one near you.

Cost of hosting a site

The cost of hosting web sites varies quite a bit. Be sure to ask around. Web site storage is usually provided by the megabyte—one place might charge $25 a month for 5 megabytes and $10 for each additional megabyte. Another place might be $50 a month for the same amount of space. Another place might give you the first 3 megabytes free with your e-mail account. As we mentioned, most commercial online services provide members several megabytes free. This business is just starting, so providers are feeling their way around and experimenting with various rates. Prices are quite competitive so it really pays to shop around.

Often your per-megabyte per-month fee is not the only cost involved. Be sure to talk with your provider and see what other expenses might pop up. There might be a setup fee, or a fee for other technical details. If you want your own *domain name* (see page 80) there are definitely several extra costs involved.

Ask these questions of your host

When searching for a place to host your site, ask the following questions. One important factor to consider while they are answering these questions is how nice they are to you. Even if they are cheap, if they treat you like you're stupid, go somewhere else. If they are patient and kind and respectful, it might be worth any extra fees it takes to be able to work with someone nice.

What are ALL the details and costs involved with storing my web site?

We talked about the storage costs on page 77. Ask how much space you get, if you can get more later, whether their fee includes e-mail accounts and how many. Also, ask the host if a report of the "traffic" statistics (how many visitors) on your site is covered by the fee.

If I want my own domain name, what are the extra costs involved?

They may lump a variety of costs into one fee for the domain name, such as an initial setup fee, an extra monthly fee, or other costs.

Will I have "ftp privileges" so I can I update the site myself from home? Are there any extra charges for this?

Updating the site from your home, business, or laptop is called "remote updating" because you are doing it from a remote location. To do this, the provider needs to set things up for you on their server and give you a password so you can get into your own folder on that server. These are your "ftp privileges." Ideally, you want to work with a host that does not charge you for updating the site yourself.

What's your line speed? (meaning, how fast does their server provide data to the person on the other end?)

Smaller service providers might use modems instead of fast, dedicated lines. If they use 14.4 modems—go find somebody else. Even if they are the only provider in town, look for a national provider. A speed of 28.8 is minimum for a modem, 33.6 and 56K are better, and if there are faster modems by the time you read this, that's even better, of course. A 56K *line* is even better than a modem.

Any good service provider will have at least a line called a T1 or even a T3; a big provider might have multiple T1s or T3s, or some new techology that's even faster. This is really the host you want to use.

Do you host sites that are extremely popular?

If they brag that five of their sites get 50,000 hits a day (requests from the server), that means their server might be so busy it won't be able to send out the data from your pages very fast.

As we mentioned earlier, though, working with nice people can override some of the less important details or not-too-significant cost differences.

Domain names and your web address

When you post your web site, your service provider will give you your very own web address. It will start with **http://**, then the **domain name** of the server you are buying space on, then a **slash** (which tells the connection software to go down one more level, to another folder), then the folder name that directs the browser where to find your home page on that server. The path may include more folders, HTML file names, and slashes. For instance, a web page that Peachpit Press made for Robin and that is stored on Peachpit's web site has this address:

http://www.peachpit.com/peachpit/meetus/authors/robin.williams.html

This address tells the browser (the software browser, not you):

http://www.	The destination is a page on the World Wide Web.
peachpit.com/	This is the domain name, telling the browser which server in the world stores this site.
peachpit/	Once the browser gets to the server, it looks in the folder called "peachpit." The slash tells the browser to look inside this folder. It does, and finds there are lots of other folders inside this "peachpit" folder!
meetus/	The browser finds the folder inside of "peachpit" called "meetus" and looks inside of it. Inside the "meetus" folder are other folders for staff, authors, company, etc.
authors/	The browser finds the folder inside of "meetus" called "authors." Inside this authors folder are lots of web pages, one for each Peachpit author.
robin.williams.html	The browser looks for the html file, the web page, called "robin.williams.html." Since this is the last item in the path and it is indeed an HTML file, the browser displays it on the screen.

Your web address will look somewhat similar, although the browser probably won't have to dig so deep as it does to find Robin's page on Peachpit's vast site. For instance, if you store your site on a server whose domain name is cactus.com, your web address might look something like this:

http://www.cactus.com/yoursite/

When someone types in that address, the connection goes to that domain name, looks down one level for the folder called "yoursite," and displays the index.html file (your home page).

Your own domain name

Are you wondering how you get your own domain name? You don't have to be the NFL or AT&T or the White House to do it. We own several domain names ourselves.

There is a company called InterNIC. InterNIC is the God of Domain Names. They keep a master list of all the domain names in the world and parcel out new ones. It costs only $100 to register your domain name with Internic for two years, the name is renewable every two years, and the fee is payable directly to InterNIC. They will bill you.

You can get in touch with the *webmaster* at the place where you will be storing your site (the webmaster takes care of all the web sites on the server). Ask her to check to see if the domain name you want is already taken. If it isn't, the webmaster or service provider will probably charge you a small fee, such as $25 or $50 to register your requested domain name with InterNIC, then InterNIC will send you a bill for $100 in the mail. Or the provider might arrange everything and you pay the provider for the entire fee, including InterNIC's fee.

You can, if you feel so inclined, register with InterNIC yourself. You will need pertinent information from your host before you can register a site. InterNIC's site is at http://rs.internic.net.

You can do a quick check on the web to see if someone else has already posted a site with the domain name you want, but even if you don't find anything, that doesn't mean someone else hasn't registered the name yet. To see if your desired domain name is already taken, go to InterNICs "Whois" database at http://rs.internic.net/cgi-bin/whois. Type in the domain name you're interested in and hit Return or Enter—it will tell you who owns the name. If the domain you want is already taken, you'll have to get creative with a variation. Also see page 26 about the new top-level names (.firm, .art, .nom, etc.) that are coming soon.

Virtual servers

You might hear the term *virtual server* bandied about. A virtual server comes hand in hand with a domain name. "Virtual," of course, means "pretend." If you are a large company, you might buy your own computer to act as a server and hire a staff to run it. But if you don't need or want to operate your own server, you will store your site on someone else's server. Once you get your own domain name, though, it *looks* like you have your own server. You really don't, of course—what the webmaster set up for you is a *virtual server* in name only so your domain name can pretend it is sitting on its own server. Often there is an extra cost involved to create a virtual server for you.

Planning ahead

Later in the book we talk more about specific concepts to think about when designing the pages, the graphics, and the navigation of a web site. But even at this point you should start thinking about a few things as you conceptualize the site and gather your images and the other files you'll use to create the pages.

Your web audience

Two important questions you should ask about a site are 1) Who is the target audience, and 2) What do I want this site to accomplish? Obviously, if the site is a personal site for you or someone you know, these questions are easy to answer and as long as you're having fun, who cares if the site is slightly unfocused. But if the site is for your business or someone else's, you need to think carefully about the answers. The answers most clients give to these two questions are "everyone" and "everything." After all, this is the World Wide Web so why not make the entire world my audience and have the web site be the answer to all my business and marketing problems? The answer is "focus."

The more you focus your site on its goals and the more precisely defined your target audience is, the more efficiently and effectively you can present the information. Without a focus for design and content, some features or information that would be valuable may be left out. Or, more likely, lots of unneccesary junk may be included. Clients sometimes say "I hear links are good. Should I have a links page?" Maybe or maybe not, depending on what you're trying to accomplish. "I've got a bunch of really adorable photos of me on a nude beach in Hawaii. Should I put them on my home page?" Maybe, maybe not. Sorta depends on who your target audience is. "I've got a dozen written pages of information about my company. Do I need to put it all on the web site?" Same answer. "Should my web site be four pages or ten pages or what?" You can guess the answer.

Although these questions seem obvious, they become very important when designing a site for a client or company you're not familiar with. You'll find that asking these questions will bring up issues you hadn't thought of and will draw out of the client valuable remarks and information that would have been left unsaid—unsaid, that is, until the client sees the final project and *then* decides it doesn't fit their audience.

Making an outline

Making a written outline of the site serves several purposes. It gives you a quick visual reference of the project without doing any actual construction of pages, and it allows you to quickly and easily organize the structure of the site. A problem for many designers is that they have to work on several projects at one time. An outline offers an easy way to refamiliarize yourself with the site after several days on other projects. Even though computers are great organizational tools, sometimes the multiple pages and many graphic images needed for a particular project become a confusing mess in our minds as we try to remember which files go where. A quick glance at the outline can remind you of the site's organization and content.

In Chapter 7 we'll talk more about detailed outlines, lists, and visually organizing the site. For now, write up an outline—put into words—how you or your client envision the site. You will add to this outline and elaborate as you go along, and it will serve as a valuable reference all during the site's construction. Web sites and all their attendant files have a way of growing beyond everyone's expectations.

Collecting and storing material

In most cases, you will need to gather content materials before you start. Based upon the outline you created and all of your discussions with the client, make a checklist of the copy and visuals you want to include in the site. Typically, you'll get photos that need to be scanned, digital photo files (photos that have already been scanned), graphic files, and text files. Plus, you'll almost always need graphics that the client can't supply— you'll have to create or find these, such as navigation buttons or special type treatments for headlines.

Keep a manila file folder for original files, copies, print-outs, and other hard copy material. Also keep one main folder on your hard disk for each web site in which you store everything, organized into separate, well-labeled subfolders. Set aside a Zip disk or other storage media for each large web site or collections of small ones, and make back-ups onto it as you go along. Staying organized at this early stage will prevent a lot of time-consuming confusion and stress later on ("I know I saved that logo somewhere on the hard drive yesterday and now it's gone").

Saving source files

Inside your **main project folder** on your computer (not the actual folder for the web site itself), create a subfolder named "Source Files." Inside this folder create subfolders for the different types of source files you will keep: Text Source Files, Graphics Source Files, Photo Source Files. This is particularly important for the images—later in the project if you decide to make changes to a photo or graphic, you can make the changes on the original file, ensuring much better quality than you'd get by altering a GIF or a JPEG.

In the graphics chapters, we spend a lot of time talking about saving your graphics at the low resolution of 72 ppi. But you will want to save those original source files at a higher resolution so they will be more flexible later in certain situations. For instance, if you've saved a photo source file as 3" x 3" at 72 ppi and later decide you want it to be 4" x 4", you'll find that enlarging the image makes the photo seriously "pixelated." At 72 ppi, it doesn't look bad at all on the screen (it doesn't look so good in print), but when the image is enlarged, even on the screen it looks awful.

A 72 ppi image (above) can look great on the screen. But if you enlarge it (right), it will look just as bad on the screen as it does here in print.

If you had the original source file at either a higher resolution (even just 100 ppi, preferably 144 ppi) or a larger dimension (5" x 5"), then you could make another copy of that original image, reduce the copy to the 4" x 4" size you want, and change the resolution to 72 ppi without a noticeable loss of quality.

In Chapter 13 we show you a Photoshop technique for creating navigation buttons on multiple layers in one file. Saving the layered version as a source file enables you to easily make changes and additions later. If you don't save that original source file, you will have to recreate those navigation buttons all over again.

The original source files can take up a lot of room on your hard disk. You may be tempted to just convert the files to whatever size and format you need and not bother to save the high-resolution originals. You can live dangerously if you want to, but it's amazing how often those original source files are useful.

Checklist: before you begin

If you haven't already, dive in and make a small, disposable site, two or three pages long, just to get the feel for how things work in this new world. Make it something silly so you won't care if things don't work. You will learn so much from your first site! And you'll be so glad you learned them on a site you are going to throw away.

If you're too anxious to spend time on a pretend site, then *forward, in all directions!*

But before you begin:

- Buy a **web authoring software** package and **read the directions** on how to use it.
- Spend some time thinking about your site, jotting notes on paper. Create a **visual map** of the pages and how they will relate.
- Establish a relationship with a **provider** who will **host** your web site when you're finished.
- If you want your own **domain name,** register it now.
- Start organizing.

  Make a **manila folder** in which to store all the hard copy materials, including your outline.

  Make a **main folder** on your hard disk in which to store every single file relating to the web site. Create separate folders in here in which to store text files, source files, etc.

  Make a **web site folder** (which can be outside of your main folder if that's easier for you) that will contain *the web site and nothing but the web site* and its critical files.

- Finish reading this book.

Self-Guided Tour
of the World Wide Web

Now that you know a few more details about naming files, domain names, and the file structure that the web address indicates, go back to the World Wide Web and notice these things:

☐ Find a page with an inappropriate **title,** such as "index.htm" or "hexidec.html." What do you know how to do that the person who created that web page doesn't?

☐ Find a page that has an icon indicating a missing graphic. Why might the graphic be missing?

☐ Look carefully at a few web addresses. Can you visualize the file structure now? That is, can you tell which folders are inside of which folders, and which file is the actual name of the web page you see?

☐ When you come across business sites, take note of their domain names. Do you find a business that does not own its own domain name? What kind of impression does that give you?

Oh boy, it's a Quiz!

This quiz will help you clarify the things you need to think about before you begin your web site. As you read through the rest of the book, keep these items in mind.

1. Which of the following is not a **"legal" file name,** and why not:
   a) designers.htm
   b) tall_tales.html
   c) honey bunny.gif
   d) gargoyles.jpg

2. In what **order** should the following tasks be completed:
   a) Make a folder in which to store all of your web site files.
   b) Put your graphics in your web site folder.
   c) Name and title the first page of your web site.
   d) Type your text on the web page and add your graphics.

3. What does it mean to save and **name** your web page:
   a) You must save it with an HTML file name.
   b) Every web page is an HTML file, so you must save them as such.
   c) Browsers can only recognize HTML files as web pages, so you must name each page with an HTM or HTML file name.
   d) All of the above.

4. Why must you **title** your web page:
   a) The title is what appears in the title bar in the browser.
   b) The title is what appears in a visitor's bookmark or favorite list.
   c) The title is used by many search engines to add the site to their databases.
   d) All of the above.

5. What **restrictions** are on **title** names, as opposed to file names?
   a) No capital letters.
   b) No spaces.
   c) No apostrophes.
   d) None of the above.

6. If you make **graphics,** what reason could there be for saving the original, high-resolution files that won't be used in the web site?
   a) You might need them for print media.
   b) You might need to go back and make changes or corrections.
   c) You might need to make more of the same, such as buttons.
   d) All of the above.

7. Why should you establish a relation-ship with a **host** provider before you make your first web page?
   a) They need to tell you how to name your first page.
   b) You might need to take out a loan.
   c) They need to reserve space on their server.
   d) It takes several weeks to set up a system for you.

8. If you must **rename or move a file,** how can you fix the code?
   a) By hand.
   b) Delete the old file from the page and replace with the new file.
   c) Use site management software.
   d) All of the above.

part three
Design Issues on the Web

E-MAIL IS BAD, HE SAID,
I LIKE TO TALK TO PEOPLE
FACE TO FACE.

I said, communication
is not in your eye or your hand
or your voice.

I said, communication is in your heart.

Of course, that doesn't make it any easier.

"But, what is it good for?"

Engineer at the Advanced Computing Systems Division
of IBM, 1968, commenting on the microchip.

Print
vs. Web *and how it affects design*

Even though designing a web page has similarities to designing a printed page, your awareness of the *differences* between the two media will help make you a more effective web designer.

Some of the differences are technical, such as using the proper formats for graphics, naming files properly, or being careful to keep the file sizes small. Who cares if the full-page, full-color photo on the cover of a brochure is a 100 megabyte TIFF file? You can still turn the page in a half-second or less. Try that attitude on a web page and even your mother is not going to sit through the incredibly long download.

There are also differences in the way we conceptualize the project and start planning solutions. Web design presents challenges that don't exist in print media. As a traditional designer, when you designed a printed brochure you probably didn't spend a lot of time looking for creative ways to get the reader to turn past the first page, since everyone knows how to navigate through a book or a pamphlet. Now, however, making the navigation of a web site easy and intuitive is one of the designer's most important tasks. We'll go into more detail about interfaces and navigation in Chapter 7, but in this chapter we'll look at the different issues presented by print and web publishing, and how the differences should affect your web design decisions.

Cost of publishing

Most people who have some design experience got it in the print media world designing brochures, magazines, print advertising, outdoor boards, annual reports, and anything else that needed to be printed. If you came from the print media world, you got used to being able to do just about anything you could imagine . . . if you had enough money in the budget. The cost of publishing in traditional print media is extremely high. If you're designing a color ad to appear one time in a national magazine, or if you design a classy four-page color brochure, the price (not including your design time) will be . . . well, let's just hope that you're the designer and not the client who gets to pay the bill.

By comparison, web publishing costs are surprising low. Companies and individuals who previously couldn't afford even low-budget publishing now have beautiful, full-color web sites that contain much more information than they could have hoped to fit into a twelve-page brochure.

The San Juan Agricultural Cooperative uses its web site (shown on the opposite page) not only to tell you what products they have to sell, but they've also included several pages of recipes, historical photos of the Pueblo, stories by Pueblo elders, a sound recording of a Turtle Dance song, and many other interesting pages. Let's see now . . . do I want a fifty-page full-color web site or a four-page, two-color brochure?

Since publishing is so affordable on the web, there are thousands of great web sites that aren't commercial and don't care if you visit at all. Let me think . . . I'm trying real hard to remember . . . hmm, hmm, hmmm . . . nope, I can't remember one single time that someone designed and printed a full-color brochure just for the fun of it. Or because they simply wanted to share their thoughts with the world. And certainly not just so they could show their relatives their teenage son's pierced tongue. No, this stuff could only happen on the World Wide Web.

The web advantage: The relatively low cost of web publishing gives you the freedom to design your pages in the most effective manner. Web site hosts allow up to a certain amount of storage on their servers for a fixed monthly fee. This is like a commercial printshop saying "We'll print your recipe book this month for $30. Use as many colors and pages as you like. Change the recipes every day if you want, and we'll reprint it for you everyday, for free."

Keep this concept in mind as you plan your site. Instead of trying to squeeze a dozen recipes onto one long, scrolling page, why not let each recipe have its own page. You may even decide to have step-by-step photos of the recipe being prepared. Or perhaps a history of Aunt Emma's locally famous family recipe would be nice along with some old family album pictures.

Plan your site so it takes advantage of the ample space available. In a world where broadcast time is bought by the second and print space is purchased in inches, web sites offer a rare opportunity to present all the richness of the information in a variety of ways.

Full color is free!

Color!

Most color printing on paper uses a four-color process known as CMYK. CMYK stands for cyan, magenta, yellow, and black, the four colors of ink that a printing press uses. All other colors are simulated by overlapping the four process colors in varying percentages. Designers have long been painfully aware that there are many colors that the CMYK process cannot reproduce. But computer monitors use the RGB color model. RGB stands for red, green and blue. The RGB model is able to represent a much larger percentage of the visible spectrum. That means you can use colors that are more brilliant and vibrant than any you've ever used on paper. It also means, if you're not careful, you can use colors and color combinations that are uglier than any you've ever used before. (We explain about color on the web in Chapter 9.)

Color can create moods, add emphasis, attract attention, organize information, and entertain the viewer. It can be subtle, obnoxious, muted, bright, minimal, overdone, harmonious, distracting, beautiful, or ugly. It can scream or whisper, repel or seduce. Color can improve readability or detract from it.

The web advantage: Not only can you use color at no extra charge on the web, you can use colors that don't even exist on printed pages. You can have full-color photographs and colored backgrounds and colored type. Or you can have entirely white pages with just a tiny touch of color, the cost of which is difficult to justify in print. You can be creative in colorfully excessive or muted ways with no limitation of cost.

The beauty of the sepia tone photograph is made more dramatic by the small splashes of color in the food products.

Revisions, updates, and archives

Regarding that expensive full-color brochure: if you make the information in it generic enough, maybe you can avoid reprinting it for a year. If a mistake was printed in it, your phone number changed, or you fired the boss whose photo is on the cover, it is a serious and expensive undertaking to change and reprint the material. And when you reprint, what do you do with all the old material you labored so hard over—those interesting articles and great tips, the short stories, the insightful business reports that people still find useful.

The web advantage: You can keep a web site as fresh as your morning coffee. If your address changes or the price of smoked green chile goes up, you can modify the web page and upload it to the web within minutes. This is a nice little feature when you realize that you've misspelled the president's name just ten minutes before the new web site is unveiled to the board of directors.

And where else could you store all the back issues, out-of-date articles, or archives of older information so they are still accessible to your clients, students, colleagues, or friends around the world? With minimal trouble you can make the wealth of your collective data available.

With this ease of changing your site, there's no excuse for having mistakes and typos on your pages. Also, when you upload your site and test it online, it's very common to discover that a link isn't working or an image file is missing. Making these kinds of corrections usually doesn't require altering the page or graphics, and you can do it quickly and easily.

Corrections and changes aren't the only updates that you'll need to make to your site. You also have an obligation to keep the site current and rich with new content. If visitors to your site can't tell immediately that something is different, they won't dig around looking for whatever new information might be there. Many sites have a "What's New" page that links to the newest information on the site. Other sites make some noticeable design and copy changes to the first page so the visitor will know the site has changed. Another technique is to put a revision date stamp on the first page, such as "Last revised on March 17, 2001."

Updating, revising, and archiving new and old files on your web site, whether it's for personal or business use, will help attract repeat visitors. And in this new medium, visitors *expect* these features.

Distribution

Another problem to overcome in print is the distribution of the printed material. Whole businesses exist that specialize in telling companies how to target their desired audience and get the materials to them, wherever that audience happens to be.

For a site on the Internet, distribution is no longer a problem. It's not even a challenge. Your family reunion web site is just as accessible as IBM's, Apple's, or Microsoft's web site. The challenge is to make your web address known to the greatest number of people possible—your audience has to find you and your web site. Registering web sites with web directories and search engines are the most common avenues of making a site easy to find (Chapter 16). But as the web grows, "cross-marketing" the web site address through traditional media becomes more important (see below and page 274). Clients who register their site with fifty search engines and then sit back waiting for the masses to appear are usually still sitting there a couple of months later, realizing what an ocean of information their little ship is in.

There is encouraging news, however: in printed direct marketing, if five to ten percent of the people you reach are interested in your message, your piece is considered (by marketing people) to be successful. On the web, a much higher percentage of people who visit your site are really interested in what you have to say since they had to actively seek you out.

The web advantage: Cross-marketing the site by using traditional media greatly increases the chances of making your web address known to your target audience. Print your web address on your letterhead and in your brochures. Include it in print ads, radio, and TV commercials. Trade links with other sites that have some connection to yours or that have an overlapping customer base. You may decide it's worth it to advertise your site on some other site, with your ad being a direct link back to your web site. (If your web site is personal, you may not care to publicize the web address at all.)

Once visitors find you, you must give them a reason to come back or to tell other people about you. If your site is ugly, boring, or even just average, don't count on repeat visitors. Even after you've made a web site that is beautiful and interesting, you'll need to commit to updating it frequently to keep visitors coming back.

Depending on the kind of site you have, you could have a new tip each week, a quote a day, a question to ponder, a new layout, a button to click for a surprise, a prize drawing to register for, new and different information, more links that your readers would find exciting. Let your sense of fun and creativity take over.

Customer response

One of the battles always being fought in print media is trying to get the potential customer to respond. Traditional advertising/marketing wisdom dictates one main technique—make it easy to respond. Until now, other techniques were amazingly low-tech: give the customer a pre-addressed, business-reply envelope that doesn't need a stamp; position a coupon on the outside corner of a page so it's easier to cut out than a coupon in the middle of the page; perforate coupons whenever possible so you don't have to ask the customer to find a pair of scissors. After all this, your customer may or may not fill out the form and mail it back to you.

The web, on the other hand, takes ease-of-response to a new level. You can provide your audience with an e-mail form. You can incorporate popup multiple-choice menus and checkbox buttons instead of asking the site visitor to type in answers. One click on a "Submit" button and the information is delivered to you.

The web advantage: By giving the visitor a chance to respond immediately, you've smashed through the biggest barrier between you and your potential customer. This is a chance to collect the information needed to add a customer to your mailing list, or to solicit comments and suggestions. If reader response is not required for your site, it's still smart to offer some form of interaction. The friendlier your site appears, the better your chances are for repeat visits.

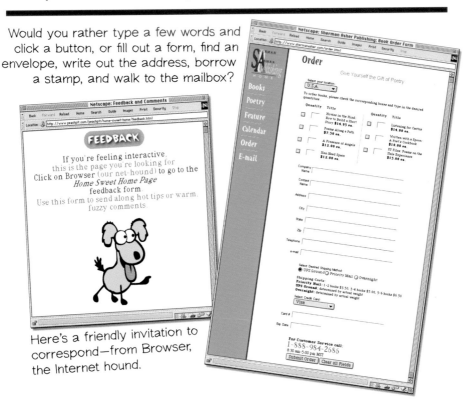

Would you rather type a few words and click a button, or fill out a form, find an envelope, write out the address, borrow a stamp, and walk to the mailbox?

Here's a friendly invitation to correspond—from Browser, the Internet hound.

A world of information

Another great feature unique to web sites is that you can let someone else publish a lot of the information that you would like to include in your site. Let's say, for instance, you have a business that sells mermaid maps (you know, those maps that show when and where the mermaids are schooling). On your web site, you not only want to sell maps, but you have an old college pal who has an Underwater Mermaid Academy. Instead of recreating all the information about tides, schooling, and stuff like that on your own web site, you can link directly to the Underwater Mermaid Academy web site. It's as if you've added all the value of her site to yours for free. And you didn't even have to ask for permission. If she liked you in college half as much as you thought she did, she'll put a link in her site back to your site.

In print media, you certainly wouldn't have the space for all that information, it would cost a fortune to have it printed, and you might not be able to get permission to reproduce it anyway.

The web advantage: Look for web sites whose information would be an enhancement to your own site or a benefit to your reader. Decide if you want to give certain sites prominent recognition by featuring them in a special article on your site or by showcasing them in a graphic element. Perhaps they will just appear on a separate page full of recommended links to other information.

But you don't want to give people a reason to leave your site too quickly and easily! Be careful about where you place these external links. In Chapter 7 we discuss the common problem of obsessive linking and suggest ways to offer extra information to visitors while keeping them interested in and returning to your site.

File size

To do quality work in print, you need to create files that are high resolution. Let's translate that into practical terms: you need to create files that are so large they not only slow down your computer as you work on them, they're a digital pain to move around from your computer to the service bureau to the printer. If you've ever had to retouch (and do frequent saves) on a fifty-megabyte photo to be used in a color brochure, you'll fall in love with this aspect of web design: you need to create files that are low resolution and as small as possible. This not only makes working on the files on your computer very fast, it makes moving them around very easy. The collective file size of a web site that is rich with color images, QuickTime movies, sound files, animation, and dozens of pages of text can be a fraction of what the file size would be if the same information and images were being prepared for print media.

Traditional print media usually requires the resolution of images to be around 266 to 300 ppi (pixels per inch, often referred to as dpi, dots per inch). All web images are 72 ppi and compressed. A 4 x 5-inch color photograph saved as a 300 dpi file could easily be 5MB. The same file saved at 72 ppi and compressed might be as small as 10K. We'll explain more about file sizes in Chapter 10.

The web advantage: Even a small 72 ppi file can seem too large when you're sitting in front of your monitor and waiting for a web page to load. As you design web pages, your primary goal is to have a reasonable balance between visual interest and page download time. If a page has so many images that it takes longer than 30 seconds to appear on the screen, divide it into two or more separate pages. If the client wants a full-screen image of his new baby boy, convince him to use a small, thumbnail-sized photo that, when clicked on, links to a larger version on a separate page. Even navigation buttons that are less than 5K each can start to add up and slow things down if you have too many of them. Remember, even though file sizes on the web are small, careful planning is required to prevent slow-loading pages.

Sound and animation

Did you notice we said "movies" and "sound" just a page ago? The World Wide Web is also an interactive multimedia experience. Many sites don't have the budget for all the multimedia bells and whistles, but some of the bells and whistles are within reach of many sites.

Movie files can be very large but they can be a nice feature, especially if you warn the site visitors how large the file is so they can decide if they want to wait for it to download to their computer. Sound clips are relatively easy to make. Both sound files and movies require special software to convert them to a correct format for the web.

Simple animation is easy to accomplish and can add a lot of visual interest. More and more sites are starting to increase the interactivity and the multimedia experience of their sites by including things such as:

- QuickTime Virtual Reality (QTVR): images you can "walk" through using your mouse
- 3D images: images created in three dimensions that can be rotated and viewed from any angle
- Shockwave: combines animation, sound, and interactivity
- Java: programming that creates applications that can run from within the web site
- JavaScript: scripts, or small programming sequences, that can make certain actions take place
- ActiveX: programming that creates and allows interactivity within the web site
- Database interaction: the browser creates web pages "on the fly," calling upon changing information in a database and combining that information with designated graphics to create a page that reflects the latest possible information

The web advantage: As cool as some of these features may be, they're not necessary for creating great web sites. Before you start feeling overwhelmed, remember that most good web sites are simply designed using attractive images and interesting information. Just keep in mind that the interactive potential is there, and interactivity is one of the very visible ways that web publishing is different from print. When you are ready, you can take advantage of this feature of the web and perhaps add simple animation (it's not difficult; see pages 210-212) or a response form (see page 248). But don't feel obligated or intimidated—interactivity and multimedia are simply options, and many great web sites ignore them.

Amount and accessibility of information

Whatever you're looking for, you'll probably find it on the Internet and it won't be the outdated, twenty-year-old version that's collecting dust on the shelves of the public library. Even if you *could* collect all the printed information available on Adobe software, for instance, that information would soon be outdated, reprinted, and you'd have to collect it all over again. Many web sites are updated daily, especially sites about technical information. And it's just sitting there, available 24 hours a day, accommodating your own strange schedule.

Add to all this the fact that you can search sites anywhere in the world from your office or from your home. I keep having flashbacks of spending hours in the library and not finding what I was looking for. Let's face it—this is getting pretty close to research-nirvana.

The web advantage: No matter which side you're on—looking for or providing information—the variety, convenience, and accessibility of information is the most powerful aspect of the World Wide Web. As a designer, you want to create a site that is not only visually and graphically compelling, but that also offers interesting and valuable content. If your site is updated frequently, the audience will revisit often.

Other web sites may require different updating schedules to satisfy different audiences. Keep these factors in mind as you plan. The better and more current your content is, the better your audience will be.

The Biking Across Kansas site is a great example of accessibility of information through the web that could not be duplicated in print. This site, covering the annual two-week bicycle tour across Kansas, is updated several times a year up until the time of the event. While the ride is in progress, the site is updated daily and includes digital photos from the day's ride and commentary from organizers. The site also allows family and friends to contact participants on the road via e-mail.

Location of designer

As a print designer, you don't have to live in a big city, but it sure makes life much easier if you're close to those big-city clients. And it helps to be close to supply stores and to the service bureau that's going to output your files. And when the job goes to the printing press, it's best for you to be there to approve the job as it's being printed.

The web advantage: The web represents the same unlimited potential to people in rural communities as it does to people in big cities. Remember when designers ran across town to show a client a layout for an ad, a brochure, or a flyer? As a web designer you can upload the files to the "server" (the computer where the web pages are stored so the world can see them) right from your home or office, go online to test the files, make any necessary corrections, and re-upload the files—all without leaving your desk. The clients can view the changes from their own offices, make suggestions, approve or disapprove, all without anyone having to physically meet in the same space. The client may be on the other side of town or on the other side of the world—it doesn't matter. A client in California may hire a designer in Mississippi to design a web site that will be hosted on a server in Florida. The server storing the web site doesn't care if the designer is uploading from Los Cerrillos, New Mexico, or New York City, New York.

Recently West of the Pecos had a potential client who wanted to see some logo and web page designs that had been requested just that morning. The deadline was critical for an emergency presentation to the head honcho that afternoon. John did illustrations and graphics in Santa Fe while his partner, Dave Rohr, who was out of town, did site structure and organization in Kansas. That afternoon the client's account executive called on a cell phone from his car in Portland, Oregon, on a conference call with the art director in Albuquerque, New Mexico, and West of the Pecos Web Design in Santa Fe. While they were discussing deadlines, the account executive found a Kinko's copy shop, got on the Internet, viewed the logos and layouts at a private URL (still on his cell phone) while the art director viewed them from Albuquerque, and the account exec approved the designs for presentation.

Designers in remote locations who have long fought the battle of being geographically challenged now have just as much to offer as anyone, including better parking. Whether you want to get information or distribute information, the World Wide Web makes your location irrelevant.

The print advantage

Before we make it sound like print media is right up there with petroglyphs and parchment scrolls, let's reassure ourselves that print is still an irreplaceable medium. Once the cost and distribution problems are overcome, print is, without a doubt, a viable and important part of life. The two mediums are different, and each has its advantages and disadvantages. One is not better than the other; they are just different.

Print is more portable. It's easier to carry around a book or two than it is to lug around a computer and a monitor. A laptop computer is portable, but when you go to the family reunion at Hog Scald Hollow, Arkansas, you won't find a place to plug it in. And if you've ever been to Hog Scald Hollow, you know that when that laptop battery does go down, the nearest electrical outlet is about fifteen hollows away.

Print is cheaper to read. You don't need a computer or even a TV-box. You don't need to pay an ISP. You don't need to buy any software.

Print is more familiar. It has a history. We feel comfortable with it. The texture of the paper, the weight and size of the book, and the typographic design all add to the aesthetic experience of reading. Print allows us to see beautiful, high-resolution graphics that put the best monitors to shame. Printed pieces can have embossing or metal foil stamping. If you want to make a strong visual impact with large images, print can make it happen.

You can read print in the bathtub. You can read it when the electricity goes off. You can read it in broad daylight. You can read it in the car. You can read it with children in your lap. You can start fires with it. You can put it on billboards or matchboxes. You can send it through airport security without having to turn it on. You can put it in your pocket while you hike to a secluded reading spot. You can read it on the beach. You can write notes in the margins and phone numbers on the back.

Print tools are better developed. We've been creating books from printing presses for over 500 years, and by hand for a couple thousand years before that. The process of getting the written word into published form is well established. Even though the tools have changed in the past few years, we still follow basically the same process.

Print is reliably WYSIWYG. If you're a designer working in print, the desktop publishing tools you use are more predictable and more WYSIWYG (pronounced "whizzi-wig," or What You See Is What You Get) than web authoring tools. For the most part, a page layout program shows you a page exactly as it will print. If it looks okay on the screen, it's going to look okay as final output. You don't have to test PageMaker or XPress files in other programs to see if they look all right. But web page authoring has to deal with the fact that people view the web pages with different computers using a number of different browsers, each of which interprets and displays the web pages a little differently. So, not only do you have to test your web pages on various computers and using various browsers to know how people will see your web pages, but when something is acting goofy you have to figure out what's wrong with the file and fix it. Even though web publishing tools often claim to be WYSIWYG, you may be surprised at what can pass for WYSIWYG these days. Some of these products should be labeled WYSIWYWYG (What You See Is What You Wish You Got).

Print is faster. When you look at a beautifully designed brochure or coffee table book, isn't it nice how quickly those images download on the page? And have you noticed how rare it is to crash or run out of memory while reading a book?

As vast as the web is, there are still two billion nine hundred seventy-six thousand published works available in print that are not on the web. That's a rough estimate, but you get the point.

Oh, the advantages of print!

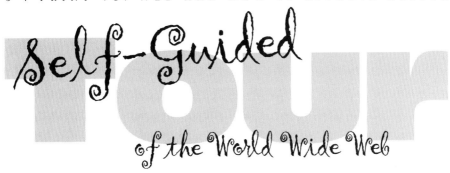

Self-Guided Tour
of the World Wide Web

Take a tour of the World Wide Web, this time looking at the features web sites offer that can't be implemented with print media. Remember, we're not saying that web sites are better than print, just that they are different, and we need to design differently.

Listen carefully to your own reactions. You are a typical visitor. If you feel put off or delighted by something, that is probably the same reaction many other visitors would also have. Keep those things in mind when you design your web pages.

- ☐ Find a large, industrial-strength site (toyota, apple, adobe, att). There is often a button for the "index." Take a look at the index. Do you think this company would have made that many pages in full-color print? Would you ever own or want to own all those printed pages?

- ☐ Do you find sites that put too much information on one page? Do you find pages that could easily be broken down into several topics, each with their own page?

- ☐ Do you find pages that are *too* broken up, pages where you would rather not have to click another time and wait for another page to load to get to the information? Do you find pages where there is only one short paragraph and wonder why the designer made you jump? Or pages with one large photo and no caption or buttons or other reason to be there? Making lots of pages is cheap, yes, but make sure each page is important enough to make it worth someone's while to get there.

- ☐ Find a site, like www.weather.com, that is updated every few minutes. How useful would a weather site be if it could only be updated every three months?

- ☐ When you come across a form that the designer wants you to print, fill out, then mail or fax in, do you respond as quickly as you might if the form had a Submit button?

Oh boy, it's a QUIZ!

For each problem, choose whether Print or Web media would be the best solution, and circle your choice. Most problems would benefit from using a combination of the two media (as well as other media, of course), but circle a choice for the predominant vehicle. Write a short statement justifying that choice.

1. Your corporation has an annual report that must get to every one of its stockholders.

Print Web Why?

2. You're a graphic artist and you want to relocate from a small town to a big city. You can print up four-color brochures to send to all the ad agencies and studios, or you can put part of your portfolio in the mail, or you can send every agency and studio your web address.

Print Web Why?

3. You're a small software company and every few months you have updates to your software. You need to notify existing customers and find a way to get them the updates.

Print Web Why?

4. You have valuable information that your clients pay a lot of money for. But the information changes regularly—sometimes as often as weekly.

Print Web Why?

5. You're a teacher/businessperson and you have a great collection of small booklets that are extremely useful for your students/clients. You know the rest of the world would like the information, but publishers complain the booklets are too small and don't want to deal with them. Because your readers' responses have been very strong, you are willing to publish the booklets yourself.

Print Web Why?

6. Your sweetheart has decided it is time for the world to recognize the phenomenal breadth of your artistic talent. She wants to compile a high-quality collection of your life's work.

Print Web Why?

Basic Design Principles for Non-Designers

Anyone can learn the mechanics of making a web page. And anyone can make an ugly web page. Lots of people do. But the only reason so many people make bad web pages is that they don't understand the very basic design principles. If you have read *The Non-Designer's Design Book,* by Robin, you can skip this chapter, except perhaps to see how those same principles apply to web pages. If you haven't read that [bestselling and award-winning] book (we strongly suggest you do), then this section may well be the most important chapter in the book for you. The following chapters talk about things like "interface" and "navigation," which require a little more thought and planning. The concepts in *this* chapter are very simple things that will easily and quickly change dorky web pages into more professional-looking pages. They won't make you a brilliant designer, and they won't land you $20,000 web design contracts, but they will keep you from embarrassing yourself in front of millions of people.

The four basic principles this chapter highlights are **alignment, proximity, repetition,** and **contrast.** These principles are the underlying factors in every printed piece you see anywhere, on screen or elsewhere. If you just remember these four principles, your web (or printed) pages will look clean, neat, and professional. They will communicate more clearly, people will enjoy them more, and you will be proud.

We took the examples in this chapter straight from the World Wide Web. We don't want to hurt anyone's feelings, and we certainly don't want to get snotty about "sites that suck," so most of the bad examples are ones we recreated based on someone's idea, but we won't tell you who did it. When you look at some of these examples and think, "Nobody would have done that," know that somebody did. And they often did it on "award-winning" and "professional" pages. In many cases, a client had to *pay* a designer to do these things.

Our point here in this chapter, rather than to make fun of anyone's bad design work, is really to remind us all to work together to increase design consciousness on a global level. It will be better for all of us.

Alignment

Alignment simply means that items on the page are lined up with each other. Lack of alignment is the single most prevalent problem on web pages. It's a big problem on printed pages, as well, but it seems to be even more ubiquitous and disastrous on web pages.

You know you can align items on the left side, the right side, or centered. This is the rule to follow:

> **CHOOSE ONE.** *Choose one alignment and use it on the entire page.*

Seriously. This means if you choose to align the basic text on the left, then don't center the headline. If you center some of the text, then center all of the text. **Don't mix alignments.**

This one principle will radically change the appearance of your pages. We've put several examples on the following pages. The layouts are directly from existing web pages, but we changed the words to protect the innocent.

We know from teaching thousands of non-designers that you might at first find it difficult to line everything up. A centered alignment is safe—it's balanced, symmetrical, calm, formal. And we know that it makes a person with no background in design feel like they are doing cool things by making some text flush left, some flush right, and some centered. But it looks terrible. It's messy. It gives an unprofessional appearance.

And while you're lining up text and graphics, get that text away from the left edge. It is annoying and distracting to have your eyes bump into the left edge of the browser page every time they swing back to get the next line. When you indent text (also called "block quote"), it also indents from the right edge, helping to prevent the text from ending up in those long, dorky, difficult-to-read lines.

Horizontal alignment is just as important as vertical alignment. It's very common to see buttons as in the example above, where the type does not align horizontally. This "up/down/up/down" shift makes the whole strip look messy. So in addition to thinking about vertical alignment, watch the horizontal alignment of your buttons and links.

Type sits on an invisible line called the "baseline." By aligning all the text on the same baseline, the strip of links is neater and more organized. In most web authoring software there is a button for baseline alignment, usually in the table specifications.

This form has a great start—there are some strong alignments in place. But there are also several places where the type seems to have been thrown on the page at random.

There's a strong alignment down the side of the form. So strengthen it by aligning the other elements to this line.

In general, nothing should be placed on the page arbitrarily. Everything should have a reason for being where it is. Don't just throw it and see where it sticks. You should be able to state in words why an element is placed where it is.

With the one simple move of aligning all the elements along one edge, the page is instantly cleaner and more organized. When things are clean and organized, they communicate better.

Alignment doesn't mean that everything is aligned along the *same edge.* It just means that everything has the *same alignment*—either all flush left, all flush right, or all centered.

In the example above, draw lines along all the flush left edges. Don't forget the sidebar. When a strong edge repeats, it gains even more strength.

We discourage beginning designers from centering everything. A centered alignment has its place, but it has to be done consciously—not because you can't think of anything else. One problem with a centered alignment is that it is weak—there's an invisible line down the middle, but the edges have no definition. And because it is so symmetrical and balanced, it's very calm and formal. Is that what you want?

In the right-hand example, you can practically see the invisible line down the side of the elements. Isn't that invisible line stronger than the one going down the center of the example on the left side? The strength of that flush left edge adds strength to the visual impression of the page.

Now, that centered alignment in the left example actually looks rather nice by itself, doesn't it? But it was on a page where everything else was flush left, which made this centered information look weak, which weakened the whole page.

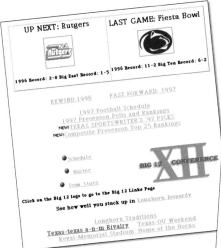

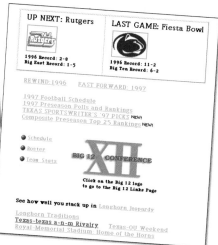

On pages where there is lots of information to present, it is critical that the layout follow some strict alignment guidelines. This is not just to make it look prettier—it is for clearer communication. If a visitor's eye has to wander all over the page trying to follow the flow of information, they're going to miss something or get tired and go away. Glance over the two examples above. Which one can you skim faster and still have a better grasp of what's available? Look at the information in the table cells at the top of the pages—which page presents the information more clearly?

On the left-hand page, it looks like the person took a handful of data and threw it at the page—there are no reasons for any of the items being placed where they are. Don't do that. It doesn't take any more time to line things up than to not line them up.

Margaux	Romanee-Conti	Ramonet
Petrus	Mouton	Latour
Vogue	Henry Jayer	Dujac
D'Yquem	Caymus Special Selection	Opus
Montelena	Heitz Martha's	Talbot
Kistler	J.J. Prum	Biondi-Santi
Taylor's	Graham's	Gaya

Margaux	Romanee-Conti	Ramonet
Petrus	Mouton	Latour
Vogue	Henry Jayer	Dujac
D'Yquem	Heitz Martha's	Opus
Gaya	J.J. Prum	Talbot
Kistler	Graham's	Biondi-Santi
Taylor's	Caymus Special Selection	Montelena

Turn the dang borders off. In this example, the strong edges of the aligned text *can* create the visual separations necessary for the columns, but not if the text is centered and the baselines don't align.

Again, the result of cleaning up the alignment is not just that it looks better, but it communicates better. The table is easier to read.

Pages with strong flush left or flush right alignments usually look more sophisticated than pages where there is a mixture of alignments. The alignment creates a unifying force.

This is a very typical example of a web page—centered heading, flush left body copy. The flush left elements are bumped up against the left edge.

First of all, choose one alignment—either center everything or flush everything to the left.

Second, move elements away from the extreme left edge of the web page. Raphael looks like he's about to fall off the page.

Third, don't set default type in all caps. It's hard to read and it looks dumb.

Fourth, don't italicize words that are in all caps.

Fifth, get rid of the "Netscape Now" thing. It's totally superfluous and only serves as junk on the page.

Sixth, see page 118 for a note about the contrast on this page.

Proximity

The principle of **proximity** refers to the relationships that items develop when they are close together, in close proximity. When two items are close, they appear to have a relationship, to belong together. When items are physically far from each other, they don't have a relationship. Often on web pages (as well as on printed pages), many items are orphaned unnecessarily, and many other items have inappropriate relationships.

It often happens on web pages that a headline or a subhead is far from the text it belongs with. Sometimes a caption is far from the picture it describes; sometimes a subhead is closer to the text above it than to the text below it. Be conscious of the space between elements. Group items together that belong together.

Open your eyes to the relationships on the screen: squint your eyes and see what elements on the page seem to have connections because of the spatial arrangements. Are they appropriate connections? If not, fix them.

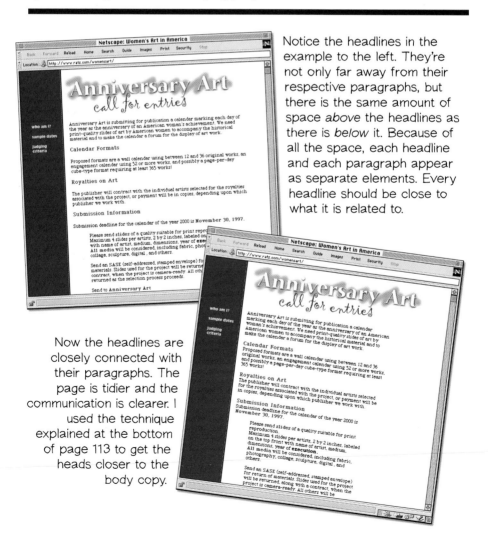

Notice the headlines in the example to the left. They're not only far away from their respective paragraphs, but there is the same amount of space *above* the headlines as there is *below* it. Because of all the space, each headline and each paragraph appear as separate elements. Every headline should be close to what it is related to.

Now the headlines are closely connected with their paragraphs. The page is tidier and the communication is clearer. I used the technique explained at the bottom of page 113 to get the heads closer to the body copy.

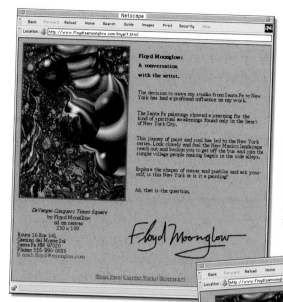

Count how many times your eye has to jump from one element to another on this page. About twelve times? When elements are separated by space, they become visually disconnected from each other. That's one of the reasons you should NEVER hit two Returns between paragraphs—it creates too much separation between items that belong together, as you can see on this page.

When items that belong together are grouped closer together, the information is much more organized and easier to read. The visual spaces create a hierarchy of information.

The individual groups of information are still separated by space, but the space is organized and has a purpose—it's not random space that is breaking elements apart that should be together.

So what is it that maintains the unified structure of the piece, if elements are separated by space? Alignment. Those invisible lines connect the various parts of the page.

Notice how and why the different pieces of information have been grouped. Notice how the elements are aligned. Notice how the spacing arrangements provide visual clues as to the meaning and importance of different pieces of information. If this page was set in another language, you would still know what each piece of text referred to *because of the spacing.*

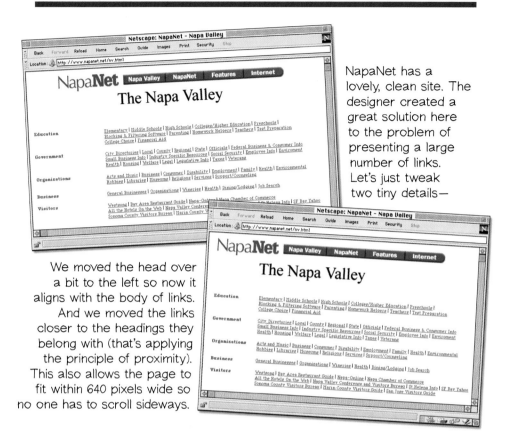

NapaNet has a lovely, clean site. The designer created a great solution here to the problem of presenting a large number of links. Let's just tweak two tiny details—

We moved the head over a bit to the left so now it aligns with the body of links. And we moved the links closer to the headings they belong with (that's applying the principle of proximity). This also allows the page to fit within 640 pixels wide so no one has to scroll sideways.

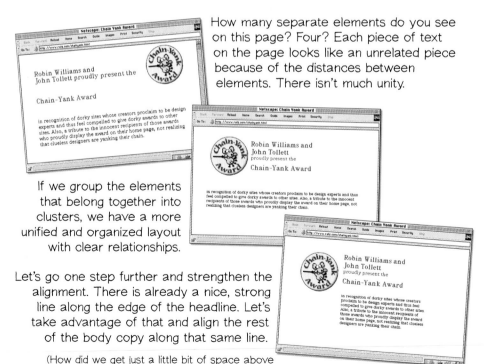

How many separate elements do you see on this page? Four? Each piece of text on the page looks like an unrelated piece because of the distances between elements. There isn't much unity.

If we group the elements that belong together into clusters, we have a more unified and organized layout with clear relationships.

Let's go one step further and strengthen the alignment. There is already a nice, strong line along the edge of the headline. Let's take advantage of that and align the rest of the body copy along that same line.

(How did we get just a little bit of space above "Chain-Yank Award" instead of a whole line space? We typed a period after "Award," selected the period, colored it to match the background, and enlarged its type size. The larger size forced more space above the whole line of text.)

Paragraph vs. Break

Often you can prevent a big gap between items that belong together by using a Break instead of a Paragraph.

- The **Paragraph** code in HTML, `<P>`, automatically creates an extra space between the elements (between the lines of text, or between a graphic and the text, etc.).
  In your web authoring software, **create a Paragraph by hitting Return or Enter.**

- The **Break** code in HTML, `<BR>`, makes the line break at that point where you enter it, but a Break does *not* create an extra space.
  In your web authoring software, **create a Break by hitting Shift Return or Shift Enter.**

  Different software packages might use different keystroke combinations to make Breaks. The combination is always another key added to Return or Enter: it might be Shift Return, Alt Return, Option Return, Command Return, or Control Return. You can either read the manual or experiment in your software.

As you learned earlier, certain formatting is *paragraph specific,* meaning the formatting applies to the entire paragraph, even if you select only one character. All of the Headings, plus the default text (called Paragraph or Normal), are paragraph specific. Indents, block quotes, and alignments (flush left, right, or centered) are also paragraph specific.

Now, the lines or objects separated by a Break are considered by the browser software to be *one paragraph,* even though the lines break at various points. The disadvantage of using a break, then, is that when you apply something like a Heading format, that Heading applies *to the entire paragraph,* even if you inserted several breaks within it.

For instance, you might want a headline above a paragraph of text, but you want to use a Break instead of a Paragraph so the headline stays close to its body copy. But then if you apply a Heading format to the headline, the entire paragraph of body copy also takes on the Heading format.

The solution to keeping a headline close to its body copy: Use a Break, but don't apply a Heading format. Instead, select the headline and apply *individual* formatting to it (as explained on page 52): make the size a little larger, and make it bold and/or a different color (shown below, right).

How's this Headline?

Here is the body copy. I want the headline above to be closer to the body copy. There is much too much space between them now, and it's destroying their relationship.

How's this Headline?

I used Shift Return after the headline this time, instead of Return. Then I made the headline type larger (+2), bold, and changed its color. Now the headline and body copy have a nice, close relationship.

Repetition

The concept of **repetition** is that throughout a project you repeat certain elements that tie all the disparate parts together. Each page in the web site should look like it belongs to the same web site, the same company, the same concept. Repetition makes this happen.

On a web site, your navigation buttons are a repetitive element. Colors, style, illustrations, format, layout, typography, and so on can all be part of the repetition that unifies the entire site.

Besides unifying a web site, a repetitive (consistent) navigation system helps visitors get the most out of your site because they don't have to learn their way around again on every new page.

Notice the repetitive elements within each individual page, in addition to those that tie all of the pages together.

So exactly what is it that makes these three pages look like they belong together? They're very simply designed:

• A left-edge background graphic makes the black and red stripe

• Repetitive headlines pick up the black with a bit of red

• The black type has red accents

• The layout format is repeated on each page

• The subheads and visited links are the same pale color

• The rules (lines) are repeated

(The page below needs some stronger alignment. What would you suggest?)

These three pages are all part of the Kodak Image Magic section of Kodak's site. Each individual page is nicely done, but there is no continuity among them. It looks like three different designers were in three different rooms designing three different pages without ever talking to each other.

In this site, it's easy to see the repetitive elements—background, typeface, link images, and colors. Notice the nice, clean alignments. Notice that the home page is an excellent example of a page that looks great centered—why? Imagine that same page in Times, all caps. Can you visualize the difference?

Hey, do these three pages look like they belong together? Why?

- The home page graphics have been adapted to apply to the rest of the pages. (The separate graphic elements that comprise the rooftop are all the same, so once the graphics download on the first page, the rest of the pages come in very quickly.)

- Certain elements recur on every page in the same place—what are they?

- Although the window area is the same on each page, the image inside of it is different ("unity with variety").

- The plaster splotch behind the headline is the same on every page, but the small image next to it changes. It's a repetitive element, but with a surprise.

- Besides the repetition, also notice the links above the wall—there is a clue that tells you what page you are currently viewing.

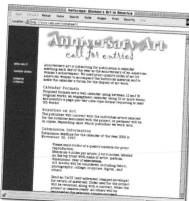

Repetition can be as simple as repeating a color throughout the page. In this example, the color was picked up from the sidebar and logo and repeated in the heads and important words on the page.

So exactly what is it that makes this very simple layout look so sophisticated and elegant? Think about it for a minute or two.

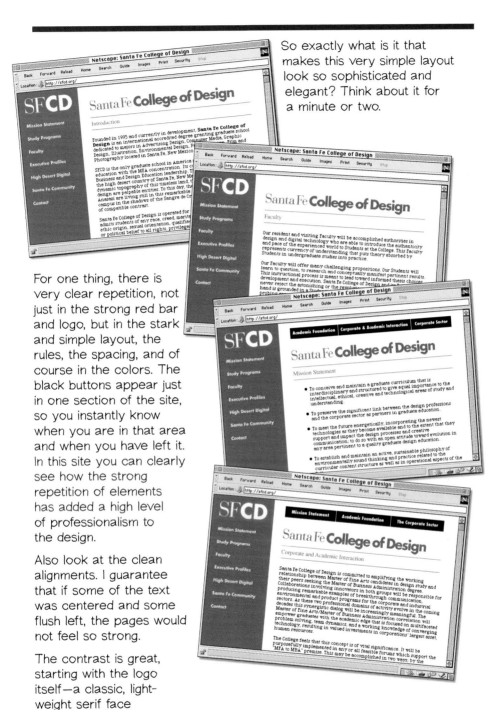

For one thing, there is very clear repetition, not just in the strong red bar and logo, but in the stark and simple layout, the rules, the spacing, and of course in the colors. The black buttons appear just in one section of the site, so you instantly know when you are in that area and when you have left it. In this site you can clearly see how the strong repetition of elements has added a high level of professionalism to the design.

Also look at the clean alignments. I guarantee that if some of the text was centered and some flush left, the pages would not feel so strong.

The contrast is great, starting with the logo itself—a classic, light-weight serif face contrasted with a heavy sans serif. The red and black on the white back-ground is also strong contrast. The size of SFCD in relation to the rest of the text is strong.

It takes a very self-assured designer to recognize and act on the power of simplicity. Don't get fooled or intimidated by all the hoopla and fancy moving objects on the web. Many great and powerful things are created quietly and with grace.

Contrast

Contrast is what draws your eye into the page, it pulls you in. Contrasting elements guide your eyes around the page, create a hierarchy of information, and enable you to skim through the vast array of information and pick out what you need.

The contrast might be type that is bolder, bigger, or a very different style. It might be different colors, graphic signposts, or a spatial arrangement. To be effective, contrast must be strong—don't be a wimp. **If two elements, such as type, rules, graphics, color, texture, etc., are not the same, make them very different—don't make them almost the same!**

There are times when you don't want contrast on a page, most often when you just want to present continuous text, as in a novel or some articles. In that case, don't interrupt the reading process by throwing contrast into it, *including links.* Links are a form of contrast by virtue of their color, their underline, and their interruptive status. If you want people to sit and read through an entire piece, then let the page be very bland and uninterrupted, let the readers' eyes just start at the beginning and continue to the end. Let the words simply communicate.

Create a focal point

On any designed piece, whether it is on screen, paper, or a package, there must be a **focal point.** Something must be the dominating force, and the other elements follow a hierarchy from that point down. This focus is created through **contrast.**

When all of the type is the same size, as in this heading, there is no hierarchy of importance. We have trouble picking out the essential elements because every element is given the same priority. If everything has the *same* priority, then *nothing* has priority. But SOMETHING should be the most important. Contrast helps define what is important.

When you glance at the first example, what do you choose as the most important element of all those words? It's difficult, isn't it—they all have the same value because they all have the same size. Your brain has to spend a moment to come up with a logical answer.

By contrasting the size of the adjectives and the name of the actual event, the event becomes more important.

In the example to the left, what is the focal point? Eh, you say, there are three focal points? But which one appears to be the most important of those three? The sound buttons? Are the buttons *supposed* to be the most important element?

This page is a little confused about its focal point. Something needs to be the boss. Just a couple of simple changes will make a big difference.

To provide **contrast** and create a **focal point:**

- Take the logo out of its confining box and make it LARGE, make it the focal point by virtue of its being the biggest and first thing you see. It's such a great image— show it off!

- Reduce the size of the sound buttons and put them in an appropriate, subordinate position.

- Get rid of the default gray background. Black text on a gray background does not have enough contrast.

And by the way:

- Remove the boxes around the graphics. Strong alignments create their own "containers" for holding elements. Boxes just add clutter.
- There's a great **alignment** started—follow it!
- Paragraphs need space between them OR indents—not both!
- **Proximity!** The name of each person should be close to their own quote.
- **Repetition!** Pull that great purple color into the rules and important text.

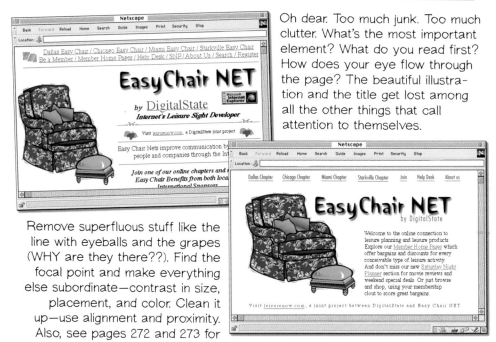

Oh dear. Too much junk. Too much clutter. What's the most important element? What do you read first? How does your eye flow through the page? The beautiful illustration and the title get lost among all the other things that call attention to themselves.

Remove superfluous stuff like the line with eyeballs and the grapes (WHY are they there??). Find the focal point and make everything else subordinate—contrast in size, placement, and color. Clean it up—use alignment and proximity. Also, see pages 272 and 273 for important reasons why you should NOT set your list of text links as the first item your page, and why—instead—you should write a descriptive paragraph as the first text on the page.

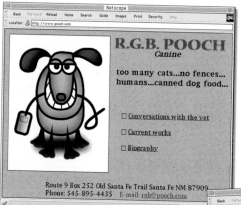

If everything is given the same value, then nothing is important, nothing is the focal point. Establish a hierarchy of information through contrast (combined with proximity). Pay attention to how your eye flows through this page. Where does it go first? Next? Are you sure you've read everything on the page? Does someone else follow the same path you did?

Reorganize the elements into logical groups defined by space (proximity), give the important elements the visual prominence they deserve (contrast), and unify the various elements by aligning them. Do you find that your eye now has a clearer path to follow? Does someone else follow the same path? Also, reduce the "painting" so it fits within the framework of a browser window that's 640 x 460. Then the important information will make a nice visual presentation.

Spell it right!

Yeah, we know, spelling isn't part of design. Neither is grammar. But both bad spelling and bad grammar can destroy the professional effect of your web site just as easily as can bad design. Many web authoring software programs now have spell checkers. Whether your software does or doesn't, have someone else look carefully at your work. Especially check the pieces of type you have set as graphic elements because they are much more difficult and time-consuming to correct later.

From producing so many books, we know too well how easily those dang typos and accidentally misspelled words sneak in. And they hide until the job is printed—somehow they sneak around on the page, avoiding everyone's eyes, until 20,000 copies of the page are printed. There are probably several typos hiding away in this book right at this very moment. Fortunately, it is much easier to correct spelling and grammar on the web than in print. So fix it. All it takes is one really dumb error or some really poor grammar to blow your whole cover as a professional business. The examples below were really and truly taken right off the web. We recreated or disguised them so you can't tell who made them.

Netscape: Great Web Sites

Location: file:///greatwebsites

GREAT WEB SITES For *Tommorrow*

Microsoft Internet Explorer, the second most popular browser, is availabae for free download directly from the Microsoft site. If you are building a web site, you should test its

Recipeints of Url's Pick of the Week

■ Midi files are nice *if* you have a control panel for volume and *if* you cite the song title and artist. If you don't, it will count against you. I like midis but I resent being forced to listen one with no way or controling the volume.

On the other hand, if you state your beliefs in a rational manner and back them up with well-thought out reasons *why* you believe the way you do, you will have eanred my respect (whether I agree with your belief system or not) and most probably an award of one kind of another. Rule of thumb: don't proselytize or preach to me and I won't reciprocate.

Smart Nutriants

WHY PICK US?

We are the web experts which will make your web site better than any other site you can have. with you and us working together, we are making your bussiness sucessful.

100% PROFESSIONAL

Our guaranty is browsers will lust for your pages. Because remember, we are the professionals which you can do no better than - - its just the way we are - - and want to be. You will see.

How do you like the use of proximity in this piece?

Combine the principles

Even though simply applying any one of these principles will radically improve the design of your web pages, you will generally find yourself applying more than one principle, and probably all four. Even if you have never had any graphic training, we guarantee you will see a marked difference in your pages by simply using these four basic principles.

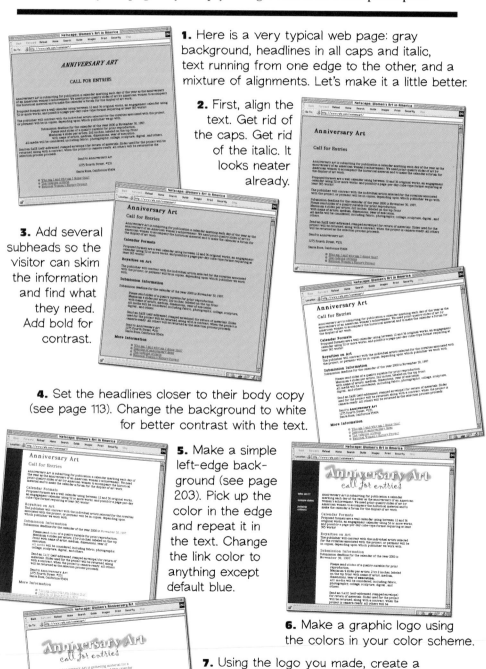

1. Here is a very typical web page: gray background, headlines in all caps and italic, text running from one edge to the other, and a mixture of alignments. Let's make it a little better.

2. First, align the text. Get rid of the caps. Get rid of the italic. It looks neater already.

3. Add several subheads so the visitor can skim the information and find what they need. Add bold for contrast.

4. Set the headlines closer to their body copy (see page 113). Change the background to white for better contrast with the text.

5. Make a simple left-edge background (see page 203). Pick up the color in the edge and repeat it in the text. Change the link color to anything except default blue.

6. Make a graphic logo using the colors in your color scheme.

7. Using the logo you made, create a simple entry page. Can you see where alignment, proximity, repetition, and contrast were used in this one page?

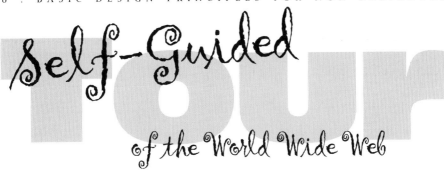

Self-Guided Tour
of the World Wide Web

Watch for the following sorts of design concepts on the web. You might want to save a bookmark or favorite of several of the worst pages you find so you can use them in the quiz on the next page.

☐ Go to ten different pages, chosen at random. How many of the pages utilize strong alignments in the layout? How many have an arbitrary mix of alignments? Which pages have more organized, clean presentations, and why do they appear that way?

☐ On every web page you look at from now on, notice how elements have been aligned. Spend a minute to put into words what the page looks like, how it affects you. When viewing a messy page, think about how it might look if things were aligned.

☐ On the next ten web pages you see, consciously note how the principle of proximity affects your instant impression of the page and what it is trying to communicate, both positively and negatively.

☐ Choose three web pages that are oblivious to the principle of proximity. Put into words how the lack of proximity disrupts the design layout, and how it disrupts the communication process. Think of solutions and put them into words.

☐ Go to several large, corporate web sites. Try some museums or art sites. Poke around in the pages and put into words what the designers have done, using repetitive elements, that unify all the pages of their sites.

If the designers didn't do a very good job, put that into words also: Why doesn't the site appear unified? What could be done to make it unified? Do you see why it is important to use repetition?

☐ Go to five other web pages. You might want to close your eyes until the page is fully loaded, then notice where your eye lands first, and where it goes from there—it is probably following the contrasting elements. Do these elements lead you in a logical path through the information? Do they establish a hierarchy of information that makes sense for the page?

☐ Find two pages where the contrasting elements disrupt the natural flow of the page. What can be done to improve those pages?

Oh boy, it's a Quiz!

Do some simple redesigning of two of your own web pages. Open them in your web authoring software. Print the pages as they are right now, then print them again after you do some easy rearranging.

1. **Check the alignment.** Remember, this doesn't mean everything is aligned on *one* edge—you might have three columns, but they should all be left-aligned (not two left-aligned and one centered, for instance), or maybe they're all centered under a centered head. Just don't mix alignments.

   Does everything on the page have some visual connection with something else on the page? Can you draw a straight line from the edge of each item, such as a block of text, to the edge of another?

2. **Group similar elements into closer proximity.** Make sure headlines are closer to their related body copy than to the text or graphics above them.

   If a headline is two lines, make sure the lines are close to each other.

   Make sure captions are close to their photos.

   Make sure subheads have more space above than below them.

   Make sure there is enough space between elements that are *not* similar.

   Make sure the spatial arrangements provide a visitor with instant visual clues as to the hierarchy of information.

3. **Create repetitive elements.** Especially if this page is part of a larger site (which it probably is), create repetitive elements that will let a reader know instantly that this page is part of the complete site. The repetition might be as simple as a color scheme, a consistent background pattern, an arrangement of elements, graphic headlines, a navigation bar, etc.

   Even if your entire web "site" is only one page, that page could probably use some repetitive elements to unify the various pieces. Find something you're using already, such as bullets, and make them interesting (but not big) bullets—those can be your repeating element.

4. **Create contrast in appropriate places.** Avoid a flat, gray page. Use a background that contrasts with the text and graphics.

   If there isn't one already, establish a hierarchy of information so the reader can easily skim to the section they need. Use contrast of size and weight (boldness) to create the hierarchy.

   Pick up a color from your color scheme and use it in headlines and important words.

Designing the Interface & Navigation

As you evaluate the content and nature of the site you plan to build, you should begin thinking about *(drum roll . . .)* the **Interface Design.** This sounds like something lonely, grouchy programmers do in windowless rooms, but it's really one of the fun, creative parts of web design. It's the interface design that's going to make your web site visually interesting (or ugly) and enjoyable (or irritating) to move around in.

"Interface" refers to how the pages look, and also how the pages work and interact with the viewer. Some aspects of the interface design are pre-determined by the nature of how web pages work: underlined words are always hypertext links that will send you to another page; the cursor changes to a hand when positioned over a hot link; the menus help you accomplish certain things.

Different browsers present different interfaces of the same web pages. A browser's interface design is one feature that makes people prefer one browser over another because the interface design is what determines how easy is it to make a bookmark or a favorite; how easy is it to access that bookmark; how much control you have over the size of the type; how easy is it to read and understand the buttons, etc.

You can't do anything about the interface of the browser, except keep the limitations in mind and adjust for them. And always look at your finished web pages in different browsers to see how they were interpreted. If you need to rearrange elements to make them work with the interface of different browsers, then you need to rearrange.

The particular aspect of interface design that we're most concerned with as web designers is the **navigation design,** or the way people get around your site and understand where to go. The interface and the navigation are generally inseparable elements: if people say "The interface is great," it probably means your site is easy to navigate; if people say "It's so easy to navigate," they probably feel comfortable with the interface.

Start with a simple plan

Good web site design begins with a good web site plan. But it doesn't have to be a complicated plan. It can be a simple plan. As a matter of fact, simple is better.

The first step in this plan is to make a list of the information to be included in the site. This list can be rough, as long as it gives you a general idea of what the content will include. Then make an outline based on this list, organize the information. This will serve as the basic structure of the site. You may later make changes in the outline, such as combining several topics into one, or splitting large topics into smaller, separate ones, but you need a basic framework from which to work and design.

Generally speaking, each main item in your outline will be a different page in your web site layout. Instead of an outline, you may prefer to make a rough sketch of a flow chart incorporating the same information. You can sketch a rough diagram of the site, using simple boxes to represent main sections, adding any notes in the margins that will help you visualize the site. You'll be surprised how effectively these crude sketches will keep your vision of the site organized and focused—whether you're working on a personal site or especially if you're working on multiple sites for a variety of clients.

General Topics in Belthor site
Contact Info
Background/bio information
Current works
Older works
The Studio—
Price List
Commissions
Photos of the studio
Comments about the studio process
The studio philosophy
Information about finishes and glazes
Series/Collections
Reviews/Shows/Schedule
Awards
Links
What's New page
Details and close-ups
Sound files/Shannon
Video clips
Index of site contents

The first step in designing the Belthor site (featuring museum-quality furniture) was to make a written list of general topics that we wanted to include in the site.

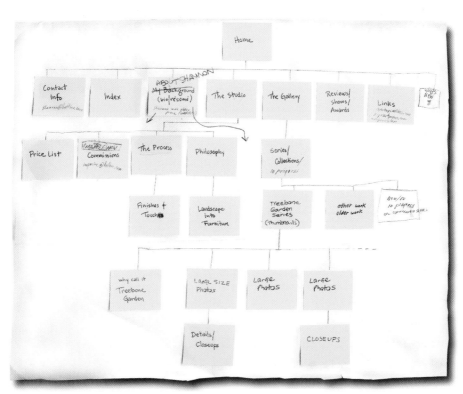

Working from the list of desired features and subject matter, we made a diagram of the site. Using a yellow sticky note to represent each web page, it was easy to move things around and visually play with organizing the structure of the site. This rough diagram was presented to the client and we worked on it together to further refine the organization. Then we made a to-do list for the project.

To-Do List for Belthor Site:

Shannon
Write copy for main sections
Prepare price list
Collect existing photos
Photograph new pieces
Get CD of new images from brother
Supply copy of logo
Review video tape for selecting
  short clips
Prepare list of 10-15 key words
  to submit to search engines
Write 25 word description
  of the site
Prepare list of desired site links

John
Design structure and organization
Experiment with horizontal
  navigation bar vs. vertical
  navigation bar
Design layout for main page
  and a typical secondary page
Process all available images
  (optimize, retouch, convert
  to proper file format)
Spellcheck all text files
Register site name (URL)
Set schedule for showing structure
  diagram and design ideas

Horizontal format

An extremely important aspect of the interface design, and one that is too often neglected, is the page orientation. Pages can have a "traditional" vertical orientation (the 8.5 x 11–inch format we are accustomed to) or a horizontal orientation. In most cases, a horizontal format makes more sense because monitors are wider than they are tall. Also, some of the display area is occupied by the browser toolbar, which means the "live" area of a web page is even more horizontal than the monitor itself.

One-Size Surfing

Lots of designers ignore another small detail . . . that most people have 13-inch monitors which measure 640 pixels across by 480 pixels down. About 20 pixels are needed to display the menu bar, so you only have a 640 x 460 space left in which to display a web page. If you design a site that looks great on a 17- or 20-inch monitor, you'll be asking most people to scroll more than you realize. It takes a while to get used to designing for a smaller, wider page. But if you create your site so the full impact of the page is visible on a 13-inch monitor, you'll know that the highest percentage of viewers possible will be seeing your pages the way you intended.

Even though we have larger monitors, we are strong proponents of **One-Size Surfing.** We hate having to resize our screen for every web page. So now we set it at 640 x 460, a common denominator, and look at the design of the pages from that one standard. We encourage you to do the same.

Now, this doesn't mean that *every* single page must fit within that 640 x 460 space. We do recommend that your *entry page,* if you use one, fit entirely within. Your home page should also be a complete unit within that space, with perhaps the boring details tucked away where a visitor could scroll to if necessary. All other pages should have a neat, compact, consistent appearance within 640 x 460, but obviously many of these pages will have more information to scroll to. Take a look at Adobe's site (www.adobe.com) and notice how everything fits neatly in the home page window, and the other pages have a consistent, repetitive format with the important information still in that horizontal layout. **The initial visual impression should be contained within 640 x 460.**

Many web design books show incredibly beautiful, tall, and narrow web pages that, printed on the page of the book, are stunning. But few web visitors will ever see those tall, skinny pages—they will see only the portion that fits on their smaller monitors. Seldom does an individual section of a page look great when isolated in chunks.

Start thinking in a horizontal format. Notice web sites where a designer has thoughtfully designed within the common screen size, and sites where they haven't. Set your browser window to 640 x 460 (one-size surfing) and see what happens to the variety of "award-winning" pages.

This page was designed last year on a 17-inch screen without considering what the result would be for people with smaller monitors. Fortunately, this was a personal site and didn't risk alienating business customers. Unfortunately, it didn't score points with friends and relatives who had smaller monitors. We're going to re-do it when we have time. (yeah, right)

Scrolling up or down a page to see the content is common and expected. Okay, no big deal—do it everyday. But now they want us to scroll sideways? Pleeeeze . . .

Design at least the first page so it fits neatly within a 640 × 460 pixel rectangle. Details that are not so important (such as credits, dates, etc.) might be tucked away in a lower position, but anything critical for the visitor should be set within this space.

Even though Loopless had a lot to say on the home page, the page still fits into the 640 x 460 format.

There is something so comforting about being able to view a complete and well-designed page in one window.

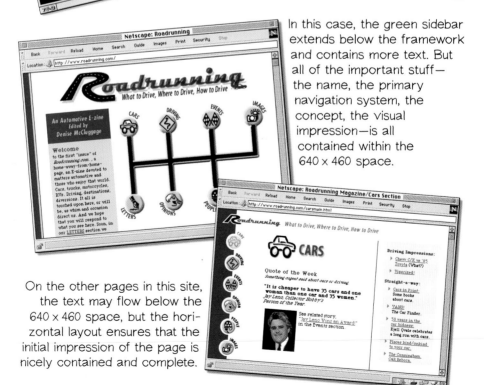

In this case, the green sidebar extends below the framework and contains more text. But all of the important stuff—the name, the primary navigation system, the concept, the visual impression—is all contained within the 640 x 460 space.

On the other pages in this site, the text may flow below the 640 x 460 space, but the horizontal layout ensures that the initial impression of the page is nicely contained and complete.

At West of the Pecos Web Design, we often develop web pages in Adobe Illustrator before we start writing code. We made a screen capture of a browser window sized at 640 x 460 pixels, then placed it in an Illustrator file. This gave us a template to design on top of. Working within this template we can experiment with the overall design and the sizing of elements without having to think about HTML code.

The type we create here for headlines and subheads can later be saved as GIF files to use on the final web pages.

We use the Illustrator measuring tool in the tool palette (the ruler icon) to measure graphics for final resizing in Photoshop, and to determine the sizes of tables (or individual cells of tables) that we anticipate creating.

You can create a template in Photoshop, Macromedia FreeHand, CorelDraw, or any program you feel comfortable working in. The point is to have a 640 x 460 space to work within, and also to be more free about design without having to worry about making it work on a web page. As you design on a template, though, always keep those final web page limitations in mind!

To make a screen shot, arrange the item on the screen the way you want to save it. Then:

Mac: press Command Shift 3. If you are on System 7.6 or higher, press Command Shift 4; with the cursor that appears, drag around the area you want to capture.

This makes a file called Picture One on your hard disk. Open it in your paint program and remove any excess stuff.

Windows: press PrintScrn. To capture only the open window, press Alt PrintScrn. Open your paint program and paste. Remove excess stuff.

To measure a web page, go to www.shareware.com and look for screen rulers, such as Screen Ruler for Mac or Reglo for Windows.

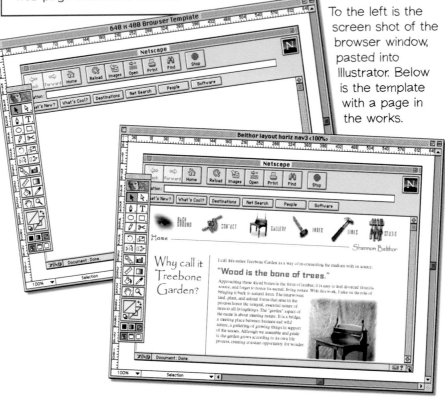

To the left is the screen shot of the browser window, pasted into Illustrator. Below is the template with a page in the works.

Navigation design

If you can easily find your way around a site and find your way back to the home page at any time from any page, the **navigation is well designed.** On the other hand, if the web site you've visited is vague in its presentation and organization of content and you get lost in the site, the **navigation is poorly designed.**

The focus of good navigation design is organization, not graphics. Although creative graphics can add to the aesthetic value of the navigation, your primary goal is to make it easy for visitors to find their way to and from any part of the site you design.

As you explore the web, notice the different styles and techniques used for navigating pages—some sites use simple text links, while others use graphical icons. These icons can be simple buttons with words on them or they can be custom illustrations. While the navigation system is a design opportunity for you to have fun with and an opportunity to use your skills to make the site visually interesting, your primary consideration is to ensure that navigating the site is easy and enjoyable. Whatever style you choose, "clear" and "simple" should be your goals.

Sometimes designers abandon the best solution—the most obvious one— simply because it is obvious and they want to be clever and original. Remember, in your quest to be creative and original, the most obvious solution is sometimes the best. Don't trade clear communication for unclear cleverness. While you're thinking how clever you are, most of us are thinking, "Huh?"

Occasionally we find a site whose designer proudly presents us with a "new" type of navigation with directions on how to use it. We don't want to stifle anyone's creativity, but clear and simple are still the best ways to make friends and win customers—if you have to explain how to use your navigation system, it's wrong.

The Home Sweet Home Page web site is focused on beginners so the initial design decision was to have a fun, friendly, and casual look. This, along with the title of the site, brought us to the obvious solution: a casual cartoon of a home and neighborhood with different sections of the home representing the sections of the site.

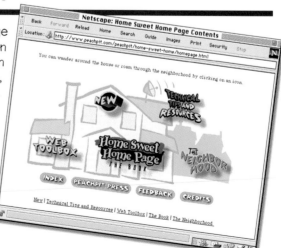

Navigation styles

There are many styles of navigation: navigation buttons, navigation bars (usually a group of icons), plain text links, fancy animated graphics, and more. You can use illustrations, photographs, or graphic images to show a visitor around. You might use an image map as in Home Sweet Home Page, shown on the previous page—one graphic with different "hot spots" (invisible buttons) that link to other pages.

The primary navigation system to the main sections of your web site should be kept together in a compact package, either at the top of the page, the bottom, or off to the side. If you have a long, scrolling page, it's useful to place a navigation system at both the top *and* bottom of the page. A common variation to this approach is to place the fancy graphic version of the navigation system at the top of the page, and a simple, all-text version of the links at the bottom of the page.

You may have noticed that some sites have beautiful graphical navigation buttons, and right next to or below them is an all-text version of the same buttons. That's because some people browse with their graphics turned off and this technique allows them to still see and use the links. Some people might be using very old browsers that can't display image maps, or very old modems that make downloading the graphics painfully slow, so they turn off the graphics. It's thoughtful to accommodate these situations in your navigation system by having text links that match the graphic links, and by always providing an "alternate label" (shown below), which we'll discuss in more detail on page 184.

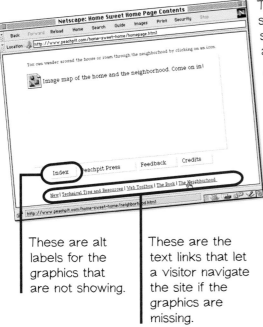

These are alt labels for the graphics that are not showing.

These are the text links that let a visitor navigate the site if the graphics are missing.

To accommodate those who surf without graphics, make sure every graphic link is also accessible as a text link.

And make sure every graphic has an "alt label." This is the text that appears if the graphic doesn't. In most browsers, this label appears as the page is loading. Your web authoring software has a place for you to type in the alt label for each graphic.

In many browsers, the alt label appears when the cursor is positioned over the graphic. This means you can put special messages in the alt label that do more than simply name the graphic. Describe the product, add a love note, elaborate on the image—be creative with it!

Navigate with frames

Another technique that can aid in navigating a site is the thoughtful use of *frames*. Frames allow you to divide the browser window into two or more separate areas (frames) that can act independently, yet still interact with each other. This can be very useful in some situations. For instance, if you want the navigation area to remain visible at all times, you can put the navigation items (buttons, words, or icons) in a separate frame. As a visitor clicks the links, the navigation frame stays put and the new information loads into a separate part of the page (another frame). See pages 64 and 65 for more examples and explanations of frames.

Be careful with frames. In the wrong hands, frames can be a disaster. They can be ugly. They can make the site navigation impenetrable. Don't use frames until you have studied sites where they have been used appropriately and studied sites where they have been used stupidly. Have a good reason to use frames.

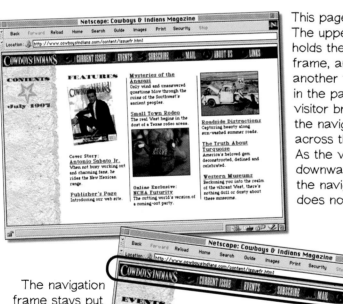

This page uses frames. The upper section that holds the buttons is one frame, and the rest is another frame. As shown in the page below, as a visitor browses the site, the navigation frame across the top stays put. As the visitor scrolls downward on that page, the navigation frame does not move.

The navigation frame stays put when you jump to another page and while you scroll down the rest of a page.

Repetition

Repetition and consistency of the navigation elements from page to page is important. If a visitor sees the same navigation system on every page, it adds a comfort level of familiarity and orientation. If visitors have to search for the buttons on every page, or if the links have different words, techniques, or icons they get annoyed. Don't you?

Where are you?

A good navigation system gives the visitor a clue as to what page they are currently on. This can be as simple as unlinking the text link on that page so it's neither underlined nor in the link color. (That might sound obvious, but we have seen many pages with active links that take the visitor to the exact same page they are already on. Don't do that.)

If you use graphic icons in your navigation bar, create a visual clue in the graphic. A common technique is to fade the icon for that page into a shadow (and unlink it). Some people do just the opposite—the icon for the page you are on might be the only one that is not a shadow. You might have a triangle pointing to the icon representing the visible page, or a small symbol next to it, or a checkmark. It doesn't need to be obtrusive, but it does need to be clear. Things don't have to be big to be clear.

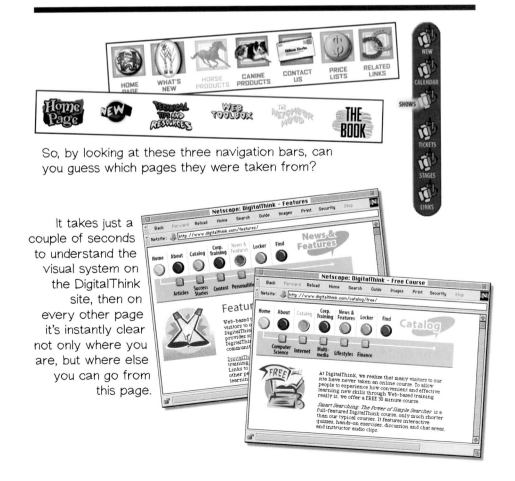

So, by looking at these three navigation bars, can you guess which pages they were taken from?

It takes just a couple of seconds to understand the visual system on the DigitalThink site, then on every other page it's instantly clear not only where you are, but where else you can go from this page.

More than one way to navigate

You can have different kinds of navigation styles on the same page. The content of the site and how you want to present the information will help determine how you approach the navigation design, as well as the overall design of the site.

When designing the Santa Fe Stages site (shown below), the client wanted all the current productions to be prominently displayed on the first page so anyone visiting the site would have access to every production without digging any deeper into the site. And, naturally, they wanted a way to navigate to all main sections. So, you can get to the page of productions by clicking the "SHOWS" button in the main navigation bar on the right side of the home page; you can also click on any title listed on the left side of the home page, and it will take you to that title's exact position on the long, scrolling productions page. It's not always necessary to provide multiple ways to navigate to the same information, but in this case, the client's request led to this solution.

Repeating a navigation bar such as the stage lights on subsequent pages doesn't add to the download time of those pages. Once the graphic files are loaded the first time, they are then stored in your browser's memory (referred to as the "cache"). Each time you go to a page with the same navigation bar, the browser displays its cached version instead of downloading the graphic all over again.

Creating the look of this site revolved around using simple backgrounds that suggested theater curtains and brick walls plastered with theater posters. The theater identification is reinforced by using stage lights in the navigation bar. When you go to a page, the stage light representing that page "turns on," confirming your location in the site.

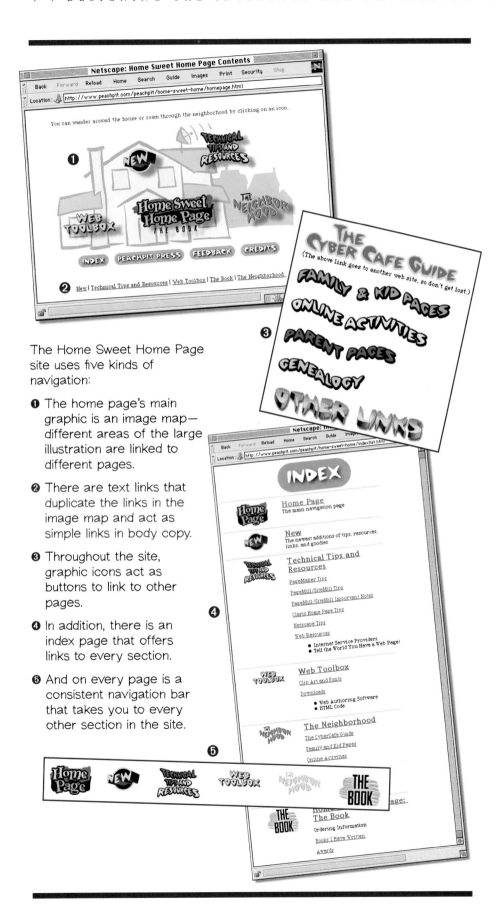

The Home Sweet Home Page site uses five kinds of navigation:

❶ The home page's main graphic is an image map— different areas of the large illustration are linked to different pages.

❷ There are text links that duplicate the links in the image map and act as simple links in body copy.

❸ Throughout the site, graphic icons act as buttons to link to other pages.

❹ In addition, there is an index page that offers links to every section.

❺ And on every page is a consistent navigation bar that takes you to every other section in the site.

The site decides the navigation style

Once you've gathered as much information as possible about what goes in the web site, and you've created a rough sketch of a flow chart of the site, use your overall impression of the material to decide what kind of personality the site should have: casual and friendly, technical and serious, businesslike or goofy—anything is possible.

Next, find a visual theme that represents the overall content and that can be carried throughout the site. The Roadrunning site (an online magazine about cars and driving) uses a gear shift for navigation. The *Cowboys & Indians* magazine web site uses western brands against leather backgrounds (as shown on page 134). Belthor's site uses furniture and woodworking tools to set the tone for an artisan's site.

Not all sites use complex graphics for navigation links. Navigation elements can be as simple as key words or phrases in plain text grouped together somewhere on the page. This is a good solution when you don't have the necessary visual space for more graphics and icons, or you may just want a look of simplicity or sophistication. If so, why bog down the page with lots of navigation icons? Robin's ratz.com site is easy to navigate and its elegant simplicity is more attractive than many heavily designed and illustrated sites.

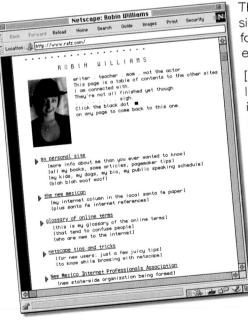

The ratz.com site combines simplicity and elegance, allowing for clear navigation and extremely fast download times.

[John said that—isn't he kind? I can't say it's elegant, but it is simple and downloads in 8 seconds on a 14.4 modem. Because this is only a list of links and their descriptions, I didn't try to keep it in a horizontal format. No one stays on this page very long— it's for leaping off to other sites. *Robin*]

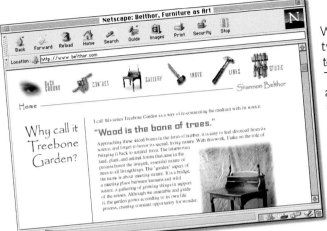

Woodworking and art are the two messages we wanted to send in the Belthor site. The home button is designed as a page divider—it allows more room above for other icons and can be used alone on some pages. The name of the site appears on the right side of the divider so every page of the site is identified as the Shannon Belthor site.

The Loopless Sound site is partially commercial and partially personal. The subject is motion picture sound recording, but the mood is, "Let's make a movie and have fun." The main navigation graphics center around an old-fashioned clapboard that was already part of the existing logo.

A gear shift sets the mood for this site about cars and driving. Special programming called JavaScript makes different icons appear on the gear shift knobs when the mouse is positioned over each one of the gear knobs. Subsequent pages do not have room for the gear shift diagram but the knobs are repeated on every page (as shown on page 130).

Index or site map

Of course you have links to the major sections of your web site. But if your site is large and/or complex, you may want to add a feature that will help readers find the specific information on that page they stumbled across last week and now can't remember under which section it appears. Why not use a technique that's been around for hundreds of years, that people are familiar with using, and the implementation of which is even better on the web than in print. We're referring to the underrated, dependable **index.** It can be an alphabetical listing of key words that link to appropriate pages in the site, or, as in the Home Sweet Home Page site, an outline of the site that is similar to a table of contents. This provides the reader with the familiar task of glancing through an outline to see the specific content. They can click on a title or subhead to take them directly to a particular place on that page—much easier than flipping through pages looking for a page number!

Another way to help readers understand your site and how it's organized is to offer a **site map.** This is nothing more than a graphic representation of the site, a diagram that shows the site organization and the structure of the page links. Clicking on one of the pages in this diagram will take you to the actual page. This approach usually doesn't have as much detailed information as an index/outline technique would, since the size of the graphic could become very large if not kept fairly simple.

Keep your eyes open for the ways other designers have created and implemented indices or site maps. In this new world, people are developing very creative ways of presenting information. As web sites get more complex, an index or site map is going to become more and more valuable and intrinsic to the navigation of a good site.

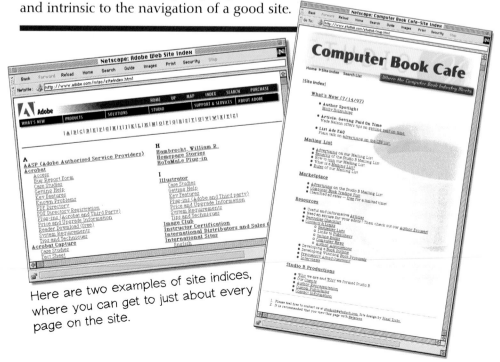

Here are two examples of site indices, where you can get to just about every page on the site.

Selective linking

Generally speaking, most sites contain two types of links: *internal,* or local, links (those that connect to another part of your own site) and *external,* or remote, links (those that connect to someone else's site). Even though it's possible to create a site without external links, you'll benefit from having them. External links can enhance the content of your own site without you having to do the work. Unfortunately, it's easy to get carried away with the thrill of linking anywhere and everywhere, only to realize later that you've created a page (or a site) that offers so many external links that it damages the readability of your own content. Also, too many links in body copy make the reader feel anxious, afraid they're missing something if they don't follow the link. So use some judgment and restraint when you start linking about.

Keep in mind that reading text on a monitor is more tedious than reading text on a page—and the distraction of colored, underlined hypertext links doesn't help any. As a visitor is reading along, out of the corner of their eye they see a bright blue, underlined word that seems to be screaming "CLICK HERE! READ THIS! NOW!" What have you done? First, you distracted the reader's attention; then you invited them to leave your site completely, *hoping* they find their way back after they follow the link you supplied. What's a web designer to do? Well, for one thing, if the link is external at least have it open up in a new window so *your* site stays on the screen (see page 247 for easy directions on how to make that happen).

Don't make irritating links

It's possible to create links that irritate your readers:

Check your links often to make sure they're still working. External links are often broken because the other site addresses change or shut down.

Make a link worth jumping to. Please don't link to pages that are a waste of time, such as a whole page with one line of credit to someone, a page that tells me the page is coming soon, or a larger image of a photo with no new information. Make it worthwhile.

Avoid giving the reader a link just for the sake of supplying a link. It's very annoying to leave what you're reading to follow a link and have it go to some barely relevant page. For example: imagine that you're reading a web page résumé for Url Ratz (an Internet consultant) and it mentions that he used to work for IBM. The word "IBM" is underlined and in color, so you figure it's going to take you to a page that details Url's work experience at IBM. When you click the link, you are taken straight to the IBM corporate site. Great, thanks for yankin' my chain, you rat.

Learn from others

You may remember, back in the digitally dark ages, that designers used to keep dozens of design annuals on their shelves—award-winning stuff that you could thumb through when you had an important project to work on. If you walked unexpectedly into an art director's office and he suddenly slammed a book shut, you could pretty much bet he had just found an idea somewhere in those pages that was going to show up in his next ad or brochure. This kind of behavior made many of us think there must be something wrong with using these resources for ideas. But studying the work of others is a great way to break out of whatever conceptual or design rut you may be in. Studying the work of other designers broadens your view of how to approach design problems. If it does nothing more than start you thinking in a different direction, it may be all that's needed to lead you to the creative solution you're looking for. Throughout history artists, designers, architects, fashion designers, and now web designers have looked to each other for inspiration.

Not only is it okay to learn from other designers, it's easier than it used to be. No longer do you have to buy design annuals to see other designers' work—you can find it on the web! Find web sites that are in the same field you are. Look at them critically. What is good about them? What is bad about them? Is the page attractive? Does it look interesting? Or does it look like a word processing document in color? Put the good and bad features into words. Don't just say, "I don't like it." Be very specific about what you like and don't like. Use the self-guided tour on the following page as a reference to help you put important concepts into words.

Remember, if you can put the problem or the solution into words, you have power over it.

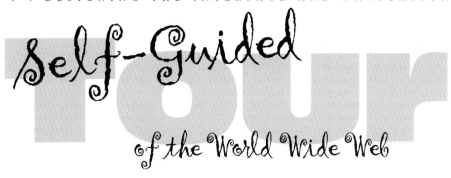

Self-Guided Tour of the World Wide Web

This time through the World Wide Web, focus on the interface and the navigation of each site. Ask these questions:

- ☐ Do you instantly understand what the web site is about, or what it's for?
- ☐ Do you know what to do when you get there?
- ☐ Are the links clear about where they will take you?
- ☐ Can you easily find your way back to the home page or to other sections?
- ☐ At least on the home page, does the entire page fit inside your window so you don't miss anything, so you don't have to scroll, so you see the entire design of the site in one screen?
- ☐ Is the text easy to read? Are the graphics easy to understand?
- ☐ Does the page make you nervous by having too many links on it?
  - ☐ Or too many graphics?
  - ☐ Or too many moving parts that don't stop?
- ☐ On a large site, is there an index that lets you see the structure of the entire site and find the page you want without having to search through every link? Start a collection of the various sorts of site maps you find.
- ☐ Turn the graphics off. Can you still get around?
- ☐ Do the graphics complement the content and navigation by establishing an appropriate personality for the site? Or is the site personality-challenged?
- ☐ Does something about the site catch your attention and tempt you to explore further? Or after one glance do you think, "I wish I were doing something more interesting, like watching a 200-megabyte file download."
- ☐ Does the page look junky? If so, is it because of thoughtless design or because the site is getting filthy rich from all the advertising placed on it? (Under the right circumstances—like offering you piles of money—you may be able to design around junk.)

Very Important Question
- ☐ Can you find a site that breaks the "rules" in one way or another, yet still manages to keep your interest, entices you to wander around, provides clear direction, etc.? Spend some time at this site and try to put into words how it breaks the "rules" yet creates a great interface and clear navigation.

Oh boy, it's a Quiz!

Of the two examples below, which one instantly strikes you with a visual impression of a better interface and navigation? Why is that? Exactly what is going on in both of these pages that gives you your instant impressions? Put into words the problems with one and the solutions of the other, specifi cally in regard to the interface and navigation. Add other comments, if you wish.

Problems:

Solutions:

How to recognize Good & Bad Design

This chapter sums up all the concepts we've talked about in this section of the book. Bad design is easier and more fun to recognize. We find in our workshops that people love to pick apart web sites, and we are all endless critics, even of pretty good pages.

Although these bad examples were inspired by real pages, we didn't want to pick on any one in particular so we made up a bunch of bad ones. We don't feel it's helpful or necessary to point out "web pages that suck" and trash the designers of those pages. In fact, we think it's mean. Even though we might think some web pages are a bit dorky, those pages were created by someone with good intentions, a happy heart in the empowerment of this media, and with a simple lack of education in what makes for a better-designed site. No one makes bad-looking web pages on purpose. Whoever is making a web page, no matter what it looks like, is moving forward and trying new things. It's our job to help them, not to trash them.

It is certainly possible to have a web site that is worse for your business than no web site at all. We've seen lots of those. The quality of your web site should be comparable to the quality of your work, your products, and/or your philosophy. This is exactly why we wrote this book—because the initial impression from a web site can directly and concretely affect people's impression of you or your business, and many people need help in making that first impression a good one.

There is no self-guided tour at the end of this chapter, but there is a list of the signs of amateur web design and a list of several features of good web design. As you wander around the web, keep those lists handy. Take a close and thoughtful look at web pages every day and put into words why some work and some don't. Exactly what is it that creates a look of quality and sophistication, or a lack of quality and oftentimes therefore a lack of trust? The more ideas you can articulate, the more power you have to make good and interesting decisions.

Bad Design

Here are a few of the most prevalent design mistakes on the web.

BE THE SPIRIT OF BLACKSMITHS, VAGABONDS, BEGGARS, THIEVES, WEAVERS OF SPELLS, SINGERS, DANCERS OR MUSICIANS.

LIVING ON THE MARGIN OF CIVI-LIE-ZATION, JEALOUS OF THEIR ETHNIC UNITY, CONSCIOUS OF RACIAL ORIGINALITY, SATISFIED WITH THEIR NATURAL WAY OF LIFE, THE GYPSIES REPRESENT AN EXCEPTIONAL CASE. THEY ARE THE UNIQUE EXAMPLE OF AN ETHNIC WHOLE PERFECTLY DEFINED. THROUGH SPACE AND TIME FOR MORE THAN A THOUSAND YEARS AND BEYOND THE FRONTIES OF EUROPE, THEY HAVE ACHIEVED THE REMARKABLE FEAT OF PLOUGHING THROUGH THE CIVILIZED WORLD WHILE CONTINUING TO CONFORM TO THE RULES OF EXISTENCE THAT WERE USED BY THE NOMADS OF ASIA. IN THE GYPSY'S EYE THE ONLY WAY OF LIVING THAT HAS WORTH IS TO ABSORB, ELIMINATE, SELECT, REJECT, AND CONSERVE THE MAIN ROOT OF UNIVERSAL CUSTOMS AND BELIEFS, SO HE BECOMES ENRICHED AND FLOURISHES IN TIME BY CHANGING CERTAIN MEANINGS AND CONSERVING HIS VALUES.

ALL KINDS OF REAL GYPSIES, BY WHATEVER NAME THEY MAY BE KNOW, ARE UNITED IN THE SAME LOVE OF FREEDOM, IN THEIR ETERNAL FIGHT-FLIGHT FROM THE BONDS OF CIVILIZATION, IN THEIR VITAL NEED TO LIVE IN ACCORDANCE WITH NATURE'S RHYTHM, IN THE DESIRE TO BE THEIR OWN MASTERS.

FLAMENCO IS THE *TAO* OF OUR HEART'S FLAMES FLAMING INTO FREEDOM, NOT TO BE MONOPOLIZED BY ONLY ONE OR A FEW, AND ONLY TO BE REALIZED WHEN THE DUENDE APPEARS....!

FLAMENCOS LIVE IN ECSTASY IN THEIR OWN PASSIONS. THEY TRANSFORM LIFE INTO A FINE ART OF SMALL AND GREAT WISHES AND MOODS, AND INTO FREEDOM. THEY NEVER ACCEPT THE SHACKLES OF MEDIOCRITY. THEY ENJOY THEMSELVES, THEY GIVE THEMSELVES, THEY FEEL THEMSELVES, THEY LIVE!

All-caps text.
All-caps text on a black background.
All-caps text on a black background on a line length that stretches from one side of the web page to the other.

Some pumps require controllers to protect their motors and to run more efficiently. Manufacturers will specify if one is required with their pump. The size of the PV system and the type of water pump required for a given water pump application depends primarily on the daily water requirement, the total dynamic head, the efficiency of the pump and the available insolation.

Oops. Don't break your lines unless it's something like a poem. You never know how someone else has set up their text defaults—if you set line breaks and someone chooses a different font or size than you expect, the lines breaks are guaranteed to be different.

File Not Found

The requested URL /imperial/none.htm was not found on this server.

Check the links on your site regularly.

Don't tell me how to set my browser. Maybe I like it just the way it is. ESPECIALLY don't tell me to set a specific pixel width or what font and size to set my text defaults.

This site is best viewed with **Internet Explorer 3.02** or **Netscape 3.0 or higher**. Please enable your java and java script in your browser settings for better site viewing capabilities. Also, in order to catch all the action on the screen, please set your monitor pixel width to 600x800 or higher.

Statewide Delivery   Contractor's Welcome

Don't these look like buttons? They're not. They're just statements. And why are the type sizes so very different?

If you're going to use a cool, trendy font, at least make it LARGE ENOUGH FOR ME TO READ. And how about a color with enough contrast so it shows up on the page.

New version of
HyperBole
for Macintosh released!

The workgroup-ready HTML XTension for QuarkXPress gains more site management features and is ready for databases and search engines through the advanced META capability. FREE Update for current users!

If you want to link from your page to our page, the address is "http://www.contreadit.org/helpme/glasses.html"

Oh my gawd. If you're going to set type really little, PLEASE don't make it italic. And a web address does not need quotes around it.

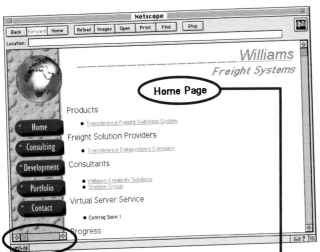

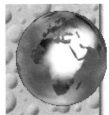

Get rid of the ~~goobers~~ I mean the anti-aliasing artifacts around the edge of the circular graphic. (See page 180 about anti-aliasing.)

Don't EVER make me scroll sideways within a frame, ESPECIALLY within one of these navigation frames.

Be consistent about the proximity of subheads to their respective heads. And try to keep the heads closer to their subheads.

Excuse me, but I know it's a home page.

Perhaps because we tend to associate large type with books for small children, large type on a web page gives a site an unsophisticated look. It's also more difficult to read because we can't see whole phrases at a time—we have to move our heads to see the sentences.

Now, you can certainly find sites where the designer has used big type and it looks great, powerful, and has an impact (as on page 150). But why does it work in that case? Put it into words. We'd bet there's contrast on the page—contrast between the large, powerful type and the smaller body copy. In this example above, it's all big; there is no contrast, just big type. Why?

Are you wondering how to make those true apostrophes you see on this page instead of the typewriter apostrophes you usually see on the web? It's easy—directions are on page 217.

Speaking of apostrophes and quotation marks (above), there is no excuse to use straight quotes and straight apostrophes in graphics. None. A straight quote is the single most visible sign of unprofessional type and graphics.

This page has a nice image and a nice logo, but the BIG buttons overwhelm the page.

Why is the subtitle in all caps? If you do insist on using all caps, DON'T ITALICIZE IT.

The text inside buttons should be CONSISTENT. Why change sizes?

Be honest. Can you read the type on your web page? If it's the least bit difficult to read, change it.

This is an animated GIF that doesn't stop. It seems to be a horse galloping with a carriage, which doesn't have anything to do with the site.

In your web authoring software, you probably see space between the left edge and the text, but in the browser that space doesn't appear. Always check your web pages in a browser before you post them.

Also, there are too many different sorts of graphics for a space this small. If you want to add the image on the right, at least put it farther down the page or on another page and allow white space to separate it from the other images and logo.

And don't make anyone scroll sideways!

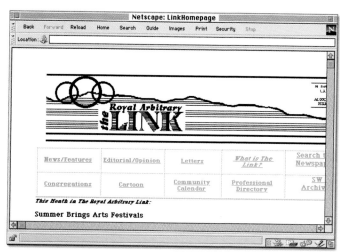

With so many great graphics on the web, a poorly scanned image guarantees a poor impression of the information on your page. Don't do that to yourself.

Keep the page within 640 pixels wide—DON'T MAKE ME SCROLL SIDEWAYS.

Don't use text links inside big table cells as a graphic element, as shown above. Line up the text links on one baseline.

It's visually annoying and a bit disturbing when a frame rolls into another frame of the same color, making it look like this: Please don't do that. Borderless frames are great, but not when a frame of the same color scrolls into it. In that case, leave the border.

Also, think about whether you really need a scrolling frame. The scroll bar in the middle of a nice clean page is like a piece of egg on your shirt.

Oops. These aren't really buttons.

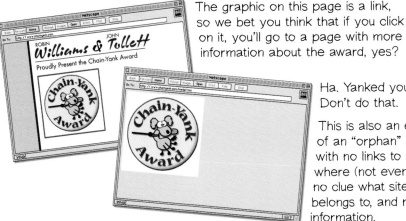

The graphic on this page is a link, so we bet you think that if you click on it, you'll go to a page with more information about the award, yes?

Ha. Yanked your chain. Don't do that.

This is also an example of an "orphan" page with no links to any-where (not even back), no clue what site it belongs to, and no information.

Good design

Notice one consistent feature of all the pages we feel show good design—they all fit within 640 x 460 pixels. One-size surfing. No scrolling sideways. No scrolling down to get to important information such as the navigation system. Of course, there may be more information to scroll to on many of the other pages in the site, but on every page *the initial visual impression* is complete within that framework. Also, the navigation is clear—it tells you where you are going, how to get there, and what you can expect.

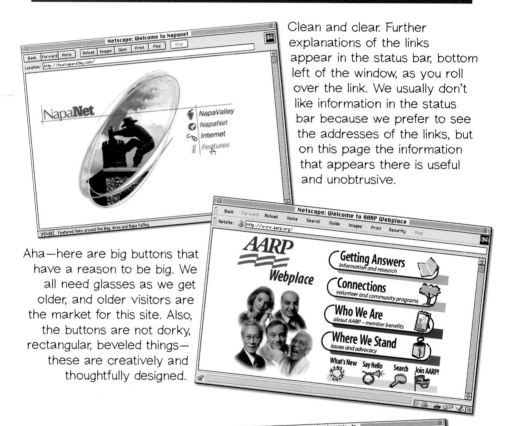

Clean and clear. Further explanations of the links appear in the status bar, bottom left of the window, as you roll over the link. We usually don't like information in the status bar because we prefer to see the addresses of the links, but on this page the information that appears there is useful and unobtrusive.

Aha—here are big buttons that have a reason to be big. We all need glasses as we get older, and older visitors are the market for this site. Also, the buttons are not dorky, rectangular, beveled things—these are creatively and thoughtfully designed.

The home page for Dayton Lummis uses type and a single visual to dominate the page while still adding visual interest with navigation icons. Simplicity can be the key to an interesting design. (This layout uses the technique of splitting a graphic into pieces, as explained on page 238.)

Consistency, or repetition, from page to page is important. The visitor should never have to wonder if different web pages belong to the same site. Exactly what elements are repeated from one page to the next that tell you you're in the same site?

The Mining Company, an incredible search tool created and maintained by humans, has a wonderfully consistent interface. You always know where you are, where you came from, and where you can go. Plus it is clean, organized (notice the alignments of elements!), and the initial visual impression is complete within 640 x 460.

What is it that makes the page so inviting? Could it be the WHITE space, the comfort of a tidy place, and the bright colors that make it colorful yet not overwhelmingly so? How did they manage to get so much information into such a tiny space? Perhaps with strong alignments and SMALL buttons?

Watch out for the following items—each one is a sign of an amateur designer. Each item can be easily corrected to make the page look so much more professional. Keep in mind that the point of eliminating bad features is not just to make the page prettier, but to communicate more effectively.

Backgrounds

- ☐ Gray default background color
- ☐ Color combinations of text and background that make the text hard to read
- ☐ Busy, distracting backgrounds that make the text hard to read

Text

- ☐ Text crowding against the left edge
- ☐ Text that stretches all the way across the page
- ☐ Centered type over flush left body copy
- ☐ Paragraphs of type in all caps
- ☐ Paragraphs of type in bold
- ☐ Paragraphs of type in italic
- ☐ Paragraphs of type in all caps, bold, and italic all at once

Links

- ☐ Default blue links
- ☐ Blue link borders around graphics
- ☐ Links that are not clear about where they will take you to
- ☐ Links in body copy that distract readers and lead them off to remote, useless pages
- ☐ Text links that are not underlined so you don't know it's a link
- ☐ Dead links (links that don't work anymore)

Graphics

- ☐ Large graphic files that take forever to download
- ☐ Meaningless or useless graphic files
- ☐ Thumbnail images that are nearly as large as the full-sized images they link to
- ☐ Graphics with "halos" of icky stuff (called anti-aliasing "artifacts") around the edges
- ☐ Graphics with no alt labels
- ☐ Missing graphics, especially missing graphics with no alt labels
- ☐ Graphics that don't fit on the screen

Tables
- ☐ Borders turned on in tables
- ☐ Tables used as design elements, especially with extra large (dorky) borders

Blinking and animations
- ☐ Anything that blinks, especially text
- ☐ Multiple things that blink
- ☐ Rainbow rules
- ☐ Rainbow rules that blink or animate
- ☐ "Under construction" signs, especially of little men working
- ☐ Animated "under construction" signs
- ☐ Animated pictures for e-mail
- ☐ Animations that never stop
- ☐ Multiple animations that never stop

Junk
- ☐ Counters on pages—who cares
- ☐ Junky advertising
- ☐ Having to scroll sideways
- ☐ Too many little pictures on the first page of awards that don't mean anything

Navigation
- ☐ Unclear navigation; overly complex navigation
- ☐ Complicated frames, too many frames, unnecessary scroll bars in frames
- ☐ Orphan pages (no links back to where they came from, no identification)
- ☐ Useless page titles that don't explain what the page is about

General Design
- ☐ Entry page or home page that does not fit within standard browser window (640 x 460 pixels)
- ☐ No focal point on the page
- ☐ Too many focal points on a page
- ☐ Navigation buttons as the only visual interest, especially when they're large (and dorky)
- ☐ Cluttered, not enough alignment
- ☐ Lack of contrast (in color, text, to create hierarchy of info, etc.)
- ☐ Pages that look okay in one browser but not in another

So-much-better Design Checklist

One of the elements of good web design is a lack of the elements that make bad web design. If you stay away from everything on the previous page, you've probably got a pretty nice web site. In addition, keep these concepts in mind:

Text
- ☐ Background does not interrupt the text
- ☐ Text is big enough to read, but not too big
- ☐ The hierarchy of information is perfectly clear
- ☐ Columns of text are narrower than in a book to make reading easier on the screen

Navigation
- ☐ Navigation buttons and bars are easy to understand and use
- ☐ Frames, if used, are not obtrusive
- ☐ A large site has an index or site map

Links
- ☐ Link colors coordinate with page colors
- ☐ Links are underlined so they are instantly clear to the visitor
- ☐ The links give the visitor a clue as to where they are, what page they are currently on

Graphics
- ☐ Buttons are not big and dorky
- ☐ Every graphic has an alt label
- ☐ Every graphic link has a matching text link
- ☐ Graphics and backgrounds use browser-safe colors
- ☐ Animated graphics turn off by themselves

General Design
- ☐ Pages download quickly
- ☐ First page and home page fit into 640 x 460 space
- ☐ All other pages have the important stuff in 640 x 460
- ☐ Good use of graphic elements (photos, subheads, pull quotes) to break up large areas of text
- ☐ Every web page in the site looks like it belongs to the same site; there are repetitive elements that carry throughout the pages

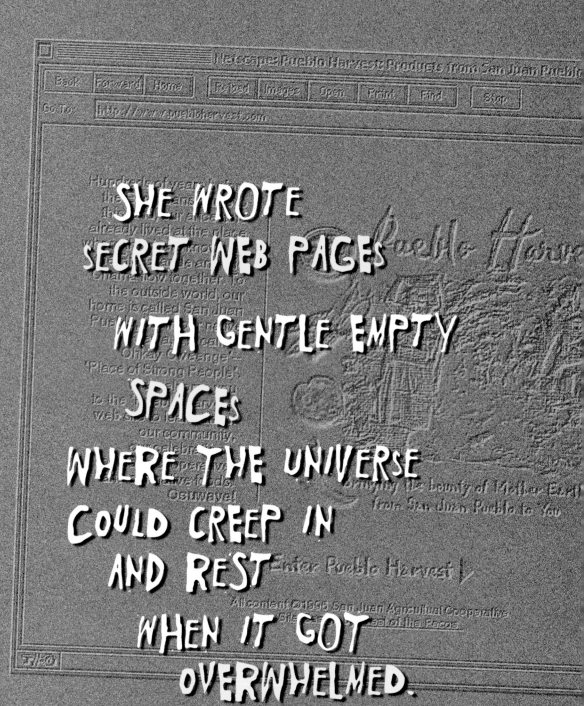

SHE WROTE
SECRET WEB PAGES
WITH GENTLE EMPTY
SPACES
WHERE THE UNIVERSE
COULD CREEP IN
AND REST
WHEN IT GOT
OVERWHELMED.

"This 'telephone' has too many shortcomings
to be seriously considered as a means of communication.
The device is inherently of no value to us."

Western Union internal memo, 1876

Color on the World Wide Web

The World Wide Web is full of color. Many of us have never had the opportunity to publish in color before because it was prohibitively expensive. Now it's free. But this means we have to know a little more about the technology of color than we've had to know before, which is the purpose of this chapter. Even if you've worked in color printing before, *color on a monitor is very different from printed color on paper.*

The aesthetics of color

A discussion of the aesthetics of color should probably include color theory, color psychology, color models, color wheels, and color management. Since there's not room here to adequately cover even one of these topics, let's count our blessings and think about color on a less scientific level. Of all the talented, brilliant designers and illustrators out there, only a very small percentage of them have made the effort (or felt the need) to study the fine points of color theory. "How can this be?" you ask, especially if you're new to design and have been torturing yourself by thinking you must be at a disadvantage because you haven't had formal color training.

Simple. Most professional designers use a combination of basic design guidelines and what they decide in their own judgment will look good. Experience certainly helps one's self-confidence in this area, but ultimately you need to learn to trust your own color judgment.

Color schemes can either be limited or unlimited. Unlimited sounds nice, doesn't it? It *can* be very nice unless you overdo the use of color to the point of making the design a visual mess.

A limited color palette, or color scheme, can be very appealing and can add more of a feeling of sophistication and organization. Using a limited color palette doesn't prevent you from using full-color photographs or deviating from the overall color scheme for occasional emphasis. Also, with a limited color scheme in mind, you have a choice of whether those colors will be very different (such as red and green), or very similar (such as red and orange). Ultimately, the colors you choose should create an overall feeling and personality for the site. As you create graphics for headlines, subheads, and navigation icons, use the colors from your color scheme as the predominant colors in your graphics. This helps give each page the same look and feel no matter how different the content is on each page.

An important consideration in working with color is contrast. Text should always have good contrast between the type color and the background color. Beautiful combinations aren't always easy to read—dark purple text on a black background may look stunning, but asking someone to read a whole paragraph of it is enough to test the patience of close, personal relationships, not to mention anonymous strangers surfing your site.

So how do you know what colors look good together? Look at the colors other designers have used in print and online. Save samples of color combinations that catch your eye. If they looked great when someone else used them, they'll look great when you use them. There's not a color combination that hasn't been used countless times, so don't worry that you're stealing someone's idea. Be careful, however, that you don't use your competition's color scheme if you're creating a commercial site.

Remember: most designers (99.9 percent, we'd bet) don't use a scientific approach to choosing color. They experiment, using trial and error until they create something they consider pleasing and effective.

Even though the color scheme uses an unlimited color palette, the simple organization of the page and the plain white background keeps the page from looking too unstructured and complicated.

Subtle contrast can be as pleasing and effective as strong contrast. Just make sure there's enough contrast that communication is easy and enjoyable.

CMYK color

The **CMYK** color model is what we use when printing in full color. It stands for **C**yan (a blue), **M**agenta (the closest thing to red), **Y**ellow, and blac**K**. In a full-color printed piece (which designers and printers call a "four-color process" piece), color images are separated into various values of these four colors, and the values are represented by little dots. These process inks are translucent, so when a light value of yellow has a light value of cyan printed on top of it, the result appears to be green. If you look at any printed color image with a magnifying glass (including the images in this book), you can see the four dots of the four colors. These four colors, in layers of dots, create every color you see in a full-color image.

These are the four process colors. You won't see any dots in these boxes because they are printed 100 percent of each color. But the image on the right is a combination of each of these four colors. You can see the dots of each of the four colors in the enlargement.

CMYK is sort of what we see the world in. That is, it's a "reflective" color model. The light comes from the sun or a light bulb, it hits an object such as a magazine page or a tree, and the color is reflected from the object into our eyes. Now, that's a very simple way of expressing a very complex color theory, but if you want a complex explanation there are lots of very large books explaining it. The important thing to understand is that this is so very different from how a monitor works. On a monitor, the light comes directly from its source, through the screen, and straight into our eyes—it does not reflect off of any object. Therein lies the big deal about color on the World Wide Web.

You may hear the term **spot color.** Spot color is not CMYK—it is ink straight from a can. That is, if you want green headlines, you get green ink from a can. When you print a flyer with two colors, such as black and green, you use spot colors. When you print a full-color brochure, you use CMYK. There is no spot color in this book. There is no spot color on the web.

RGB color

RGB stands for **R**ed, **G**reen, and **B**lue. Monitors, including television, video, and computer monitors, all create their images on the screen by emitting red, green, and blue light. These lights can be emitted in varying intensities. The colored lights overlap each other, which allows the monitor to display up to millions of different color combinations.

RGB color is not a reflective model like CMYK—the color comes straight from the light source to our eyes without bouncing off of any objects. Because of this, RGB color acts very differently from what we are used to. In RGB, red mixed with green makes yellow. Really. But you don't have to worry about that—just be aware of it.

RGB values

As you work with images for the web, you will come across **RGB values** all the time. Each individual color has a value, also called an intensity, from 0 to 255. The combinations of these values produce the various colors. Take a look at these examples:

R 172	R 25	R 255
G 155	G 178	G 255
B 69	B 115	B 76

[Of course, these RGB colors are being represented on the printed page in CMYK!]

When you see three numbers like that, understand that those are the RGB values and they indicate a particular color. Many graphic software applications allow you to enter RGB values to create the colors you want. Other software might use percentages to describe the three values. We'll go into this in greater detail on pages 167–169.

On the World Wide Web

Web pages, of course, are always displayed on a monitor, so **every image you create for a web page should be saved in the RGB mode.** You will also see colors for web images described in *hexadecimal code.* Oh boy. In fact, the HTML code that describes your web page translates any RGB color you use into its hexadecimal code. It looks something like this: `66FFCC`. You'll see it when you look at the source code for your pages.

Indexed color

You will often hear the term **indexed color** in reference to web graphics. The indexed color mode is simply a limited selection, called a *palette,* of up to 256 colors.

An image in full RGB mode can display up to millions of colors. When you convert an image to indexed color mode in a program such as Photoshop, all but a maximum of 256 RGB colors are deleted from the image. If the image needs to display a color that is not in its limited palette, the computer uses the closest approximation or simulates the color as best it can from a combination of the colors that are available. If the image has to simulate a color from existing ones, that new color usually appears *dithered,* or kind of spotty, as you can see on page 163.

When you choose to index an image, you can choose the color palette. You don't have to have all 256 colors in the palette—for instance, if your image only needs 12 colors, you can limit the palette to 12. Limiting the colors makes the file size much smaller, which is better for displaying on the web (smaller files appear on the page faster). Step-by-step directions for how to decrease the number of colors in an indexed color graphic are on pages 198–199.

Light acts like this on CMYK color.

RGB color comes right through the monitor, straight into your eyes.

Indexed color is a limited palette of RGB colors.

Bit depth

Before we go on to talk more about RGB colors and how to make sure you are using colors that are consistent on most computers, we need to talk about **bit depth,** which is also called *pixel depth* or *bit resolution.* Yes, it sounds really boring and technical, but you are going to hear that term all the time. It's not difficult to understand, and you will—we guarantee—feel really good about understanding it.

You'll often hear the terms **8-bit** and **24-bit** when people are talking about the web, as in, "We have to make it readable on 8-bit monitors," "You have to turn this into an 8-bit graphic," "I'm really cool cuz I've got a 24-bit monitor," and "I have utter disdain for people who won't spend the money to upgrade to 24-bit." So this is what it is:

A **bit** is the smallest unit of information that a computer understands. A bit is one electronic pulse. That pulse can do two things—it can be an on signal or an off signal. It can be a 1 or a 0 (that's the basis of the binary system or the "ones and ohs" you hear people talk about in reference to computers). Everything a computer does is built from these 1s and 0s, these on and off signals. Amazing.

The computer screen is divided into tiny little **pixels,** or picture elements. These pixels turn on or off, white or black, depending on the **bits** of information that are sent to them.

Long, long ago, like 1985, our monitors had pixels that weren't very smart. The monitors were called **1-bit** monitors because the pixels could only understand one bit of information at a time. With only one bit of information, a pixel could be one of two "colors"—either white or black, on or off.

Later, monitors and pixels got smarter. Let's say you have a **2-bit** monitor. That means every pixel can understand two bits of information at once. With two bits of information sent to a pixel, that pixel could be any one of four "colors." It would have these choices: 1 1, 0 0, 1 0, or 0 1. In other words, both bits could be on, both bits could be off, one on/one off, or one off/one on. (One of these colors is always black, and one is always white.)

So if you have a **4-bit** monitor, each pixel understands 4 bits of information at once. With 4 bits, you can arrange those 2 on/off signals in 16 different ways. In the illustration below, each column represents one pixel, each white box represents an on signal, and each black box represents an off signal. Each pixel can have a total of four bits. This is pixel *depth.*

Each of these combinations of on/off signals
represents a different color.

There's a math formula to figure out how many different colors a pixel can display. You're going to see this formula often, so you may as well understand it: Each electronic pulse, each bit, can provide 2 pieces of information, a 1 or a 0, right? So that's 2. If it's a 4–bit monitor, let's say, then the formula is 2 (pulses) to the 4th (four bits) power, written as 2^4. If you've forgotten your high school math (most of us have), this 2^4 means multiply 2 x 2, multiply that by 2, then multiply that by 2 (a total of four times).

So, then, let's get to the point of this whole thing: How many colors can a pixel show if it is **8-bit**? Well, 2^8 is 256. So an 8–bit graphic is 256 colors. An 8-bit monitor can only display 256 colors. An 8-bit grayscale image (black and white) can display up to 256 shades of gray.

A **16-bit** graphic or monitor can display 65,536 colors. And a **24-bit** graphic image or monitor can display 16.7 million colors. That was easy, huh?

Detail of pixels on or off.

Detail of "deeper" pixels

1-bit graphic (2 colors)
The spacing and sometimes the size of the black and white dots creates the illusion of image and shadows.

4-bit graphic
With only **sixteen** shades of gray, an image can show more detail, but it's still not smooth.

8-bit graphic
With **256** different shades of gray, an image shows well-resolved shadows and definition.

Same image, different bit depth.

8-bit graphic (256 colors)
Notice how the graduated colors appear kind of spotty and the transitions are not smooth. That's because there aren't enough colors in the 256-color palette to blend effectively. This is called **dithering.**

24-bit graphic (16.7 million colors)
A 24-bit graphic has plenty of colors to blend from one to the other smoothly. On the web, you will only see all the colors of a 24-bit graphic if your monitor can display 24-bit color (see next page).

Monitor resolution

Most of us are pretty familiar by now with the concept of **printer** resolution. We know that the greater the number of dots per inch, the cleaner the edges of the printed piece—a 600 dpi printer prints smoother edges than a 300 dpi printer, and a 300 ppi image prints smoother than a 72 ppi image.

But **monitor resolution** is completely different from printer resolution—you will get yourself in trouble if you continue to think of them in the same way. How "resolved" an image appears on the screen is a combination of the bit depth of the image itself (explained on the previous pages) and the settings of your monitor. You can change the number of **pixels** and the number of **colors** your monitor displays.

Use your control panel to change the settings for your monitor. On a Mac, it's called "Monitors" or "Monitors & Sound." On a PC, it's called "Display."

Pixels: The default number of pixels *per inch* on a Mac monitor is around 72; the default on a PC is usually 96. In your control panel you can choose to display a varying number of *total* pixels on your screen. For instance, you might have 640 pixels across by 480 down, called "640 x 480." You might choose 800 x 600 or 1024 x 768. You might have other options, depending on your monitor. When you choose the *default* setting for your monitor, you'll see 72 or 96 pixels in one inch. If you choose any other setting, the actual number of pixels on the screen will change.

Now, if your default is 640 x 480 and you change it to 800 x 600, you have *more pixels,* right? If you have more pixels, how do they manage to fit onto the screen? They get smaller. More of them fit into one inch. If you change the setting to 1024 x 768, you get even more pixels, and each one is even smaller. Changing to a higher pixel count is often called setting your monitor at a higher "resolution" because we tend to think that the more dots or pixels per inch, the higher the resolution.

When the pixels are smaller, everything on your screen looks smaller. You are looking at the same images, they are just crammed into a smaller space. It's like a bird's-eye view. When things are smaller, they can *appear* to be more highly resolved. If you want to see everything on your monitor larger, change the setting to fewer pixels, such as 640 x 480. It's like a close-up view. Whether you set it smaller or larger is your personal preference.

Colors: The most important setting, as far as how good a graphic looks on the screen (how highly "resolved" it looks), is the number of colors. If your monitor can only display 16 colors, then all of the graphics will appear to be "lower resolution," even if you have millions of tiny pixels on your screen. Even if the *graphics* are 24-bit (we're assuming you just read the section on bit depth so you know what "24-bit" means), the graphics will appear to be in low resolution because your *pixels* can't display that color depth—the monitor has to fake it.

The relationship between pixels and colors: Now, how many *pixels* you have chosen to display on your screen directly influences how many *colors* you can display. The color depth also depends on how much **RAM** (megabytes of *memory*, not hard disk) you have installed in your computer.

You remember from reading the previous pages about bit depth (color depth) that the number of colors a pixel can show depends on how many bits of information are being sent to it, right?

Well, the more pixels you have on the screen, the more bits of information the computer has to send. Sending all of these bits takes *memory.* The bigger the monitor and the more pixels you choose, the more memory it will take to put lots of color in every single pixel.

Experiment with your control panel: Watch what happens to the number of colors available as you change the pixel setting. More pixels, fewer colors. If you add more RAM or video RAM (special RAM dedicated to your monitor), you can have lots of pixels and lots of colors at the same time.

So the point is that **the number of colors your monitor can display is what gives you the impression, on the screen, of higher resolution.** On paper, a 72 ppi image looks awful, even if it's 24-bit. On the screen, a 72 ppi image can look great if you have enough colors. Examples are on the next page.

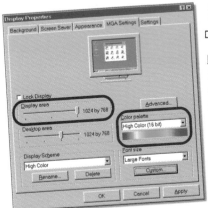

 Windows: Right-click on the Desktop background; choose "Properties."
Display

Experiment with these settings. Watch what happens to each of them as you change the other. If you want more colors, you might have to settle for fewer pixels. If you want more pixels, you might have to settle for fewer colors. If you have enough RAM, you can have both. On this computer with 16 megs of RAM, we can get only 16-bit color if we want to keep the higher pixel setting.

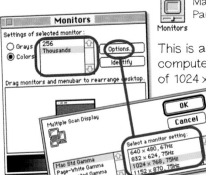

Mac: From the Apple menu, slide down to Control Panels and out to "Monitors" or "Monitors & Sound."
Monitors

This is a 20-inch color monitor connected to a computer with 48 megs of RAM. At a pixel setting of 1024 x 768, we can't get millions of colors for all those pixels on that huge screen. But if we lower the pixel count to 832 x 624, then we **can** get millions of colors. Or if we added extra video RAM, we could get millions of colors at the higher pixel setting. Experiment.

Resolution of images

Below are different screen shots (pictures of the display on the screen) of the same image. Glancing at the images quickly, which ones seem to be in the highest resolution? What is making those appear to be in higher resolution than the other two?

Read the captions carefully and you'll find that more pixels per inch in the *image* (such as 144 ppi as opposed to 72 ppi) does not mean the image looks better *on the screen.* On paper, yes, 144 ppi will look better than 72, lots better. But on the screen, the pixel count in the *image* itself isn't really a factor because the *monitor* can only display it at 72 or 96 pixels per inch.

So when you create graphics for the web, reduce the pixels per inch to 72 ppi—your files will be much smaller and the lower *image* resolution will not affect how it displays on the *screen.* (We go into detail about the importance of file size on page 181.) The low image resolution does ensure, though, that if anybody "borrows" your graphics from a web page, they won't be able to make t-shirts or posters out of those 72 ppi images.

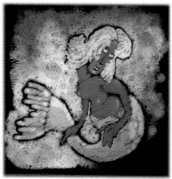

72 ppi image
8-bit monitor display
(256 colors)

144 ppi image
8-bit monitor display
(256 colors)

72 ppi image
16-bit monitor display
(thousands of colors)

144 ppi image
16-bit monitor display
(thousands of colors)

Browser-safe colors

So now you know a lot about color on the monitor. All of the previous information is important to understanding one particular concern on the web, and that is **browser-safe colors.** Even though most monitors can display at least 8-bit color (256 colors), there are only 216 of these colors that are common to the browsers and operating systems of different computers. If you use any other color outside of the common 216-color palette, the browser will convert the odd color to the closest color it can find in the system palette, or it will "mix" several colors to try to match the odd one as closely as possible. When the browser mixes colors, you get a *dithered* look, where you can see the different colors trying to blend (shown on page 163). Whether the browser chooses another color or dithers one for you, your graphics might not look so good. *This is only a problem with flat colors, as in graphics, illustrations, drawings, etc.—it's not an issue with photographs.*

A dithered graphic or background color isn't the worst thing that can happen to a web site. So if this information is overwhelming you, feel free to skip it. You can always come back when you need it. But if you are hoping to become a professional web designer, or even if you're not but you're feeling okay with all this info, learn to work with browser-safe colors in your graphics now. It's a pain to try to go back to previously created graphics and make them browser-safe.

How to get browser-safe colors

There are several ways to make sure you are using the right colors. Here are some suggestions for getting color palettes or swatches from other places. On the following page are suggestions for creating your own browser-safe colors anywhere you find a color dialog box.

- Open a browser-safe swatch palette (shown on page 169) in your graphics program or in your web authoring software and choose only from those colors. The newest versions of the software almost all have browser-safe palettes built in. For instance, Microsoft Image Composer has a 216-color palette as its default.

    If you don't have the newest version of the software you use, go to the software's web site, download the swatch palette for your program, and load it.

- In other paint programs that don't use swatches, open a GIF file that represents the colors and use the eyedropper tool to select a color from the palette. You can find GIF files on Lynda Weinman's web site (www.lynda.com) or on the CD in her book, *Coloring Web Graphics.* By the way, Lynda invented the term "browser-safe colors."

Creating browser-safe colors

On the previous page are suggestions for finding ready-made palettes or graphics from which you can pick browser-safe colors. You can also make your own colors in most graphic software, including web authoring software, simply by entering the correct values for each color.

■ On page 288 of this book is a browser-safe color chart. On the printed page, of course, the RGB colors are represented by CMYK, but there's no way around that. At least you get an idea of the colors—they are going to look a little different from monitor to monitor anyway.

In your web authoring software, the color picker for your computer comes up automatically when you choose to change the color of the background or text. In that dialog box, enter the values that will produce the color you want (shown on the opposite page).

If you're using Mac OS 8, the color picker has an HTML option (also shown on the opposite page). You can enter either the RGB values, the hexadecimal values, or move the slider bars.

■ The browser-safe colors can be represented by RGB values, percentages of each color, or hexadecimal code. Each of these representations of the same color are made from the same six different choices, as shown below, so it's actually very easy to look at the RGB values, the percentages, or the hexadecimal code and instantly tell whether the color is browser-safe or not. This is cool.

All RGB values are either 00, 51, 102, 153, 204, or 255.

All percentages of color are either 0, 20, 40, 60, 80, or 100 percent.

All hexadecimal codes are either 00, 33, 66, 99, CC, or FF.

The values are always listed in the same logical order: first red, then green, then blue. So it's easy to make a chart showing the different ways these values relate to each other.

RGB	hex	%
0	00	0
51	33	20
102	66	40
153	99	60
204	CC	80
255	FF	100

You can see that the color 51:0:204 is browser safe.

The hexadecimal code for that same color would be 3300CC.

The percentage values for that same color would be 20/0/80.

Remember, they are always in the order of red, green, then blue.

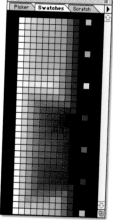

Photoshop 4 comes with a browser-safe color swatch (shown above, left). From the Adobe site (www.adobe.com) you can download a browser-safe color swatch for Photoshop 3 **or for any other program that can load swatches.** Store the swatch where you will find it again. In Photoshop, from the Windows menu, choose "Palettes," then "Show Swatches." Press the right arrow and choose "Load Swatches...." Find the swatch you downloaded and click OK.

There is a CD included in the wonderful book, *Coloring Web Graphics,* by Lynda Weinman and Bruce Heavin. On the CD they have included hundreds of browser-safe palettes, organized in very useful ways. This is an example of a palette organized by hue and saturation. These palettes are much easier to work with than the standard "disorganized" one.

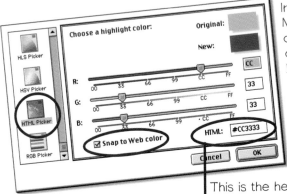

In the Color Picker on a Mac using OS 8, one of the choices is "HTML Picker." You can slide Red, Green, and Blue slider bars to create a color. This is the trick: **As long as you set the slider directly on top of the markers 00, 33, 66, 99, CC, or FF, your color will always be browser safe.**

This is the hexadecimal code that represents the color you just made.

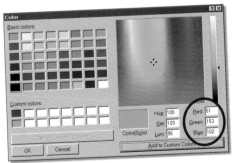

If your web authoring software gives you a place to type in RGB values, you can type in values you find in the chart on the last page of this book. This example is from Microsoft FrontPage.

Oh boy, it's a **Quiz!**

If you can answer all these questions correctly, you know more about color and resolution on the web than many professionals.

1. If you were going to **print** a full-color image, which color model would you use?

2. Which color model should you use for all graphics on the **web**?

3. Is indexed color RGB or CMYK?

4. How many colors can be in a graphic that uses the indexed color mode?

5. On the screen, what is more important to how good an image looks (how well "resolved" it is)—the pixels per inch of the image (such as 72 ppi or 144 ppi) or the bit depth of the monitor?

6. How many colors or shades of gray can an 8-bit graphic display?

7. How many colors are in a 24-bit graphic?

8. If you have an 8-bit monitor, will you ever see the full color range of 24-bit graphics?

9. How many colors can a 16-bit monitor display?

10. If you set your monitor at a very high pixel count, does everything look larger or smaller, and why?

11. Why can your monitor display more colors when you set a pixel count of fewer pixels?

12. Why do we need to bother to use browser-safe colors in backgrounds and graphics?

13. Write the RGB intensity values for a browser-safe color.

14. Write the RGB percentages that would create the same browser-safe color in your answer #13.

15. Write the hexadecimal code that would create the same browser-safe color in your answer #13.

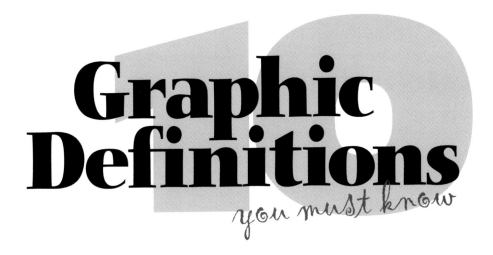

Graphic Definitions *you must know*

You must learn the definitions in this chapter, in addition to the color definitions in the previous chapter, because to make web pages you need to know the terminology of the graphics you will be making and uploading. If you are accustomed to working in print, you are perhaps accustomed to letting the printer take care of details for you—often you didn't have to be so careful. But on the web, you are uploading files to the Internet yourself. You are responsible for the files you create, so you must know what you are doing!

> **Beginners** (*this includes advanced* HTML *programmers who do not have a background in graphic design*): Use this chapter to look things up when you need them. If you are not familiar with graphic terms and technology, this chapter might be a bit overwhelming, so use it when you need it. But use it.

> **Intermediate and Advanced users** (*including professional print designers who are now designing for the World Wide Web*): Use this chapter to clear up those terms you've been hearing and didn't quite know exactly what they mean. Find out how you should do things on the web differently from printing on paper.

Before desktop publishing, getting a job published was the work of a number of specialists. With desktop publishing, many designers became one-person shops, creating and producing the job, and only sending the work out for the final mass-production printing. Now we have taken it one step further—we each "print," or publish the job ourselves on the World Wide Web. So we are all having to know more and more.

File formats

Every file on your computer is in a specific **file format.** The file format is the internal information that tells the computer what kind of file it is—a spreadsheet, a word processing document, an Encapsulated PostScript file, a bitmapped graphic, etc.

When you save a document in any application, the default choice is to save it in the **native file format,** which is the format native to, or natural to, that program. For instance, when you save in Microsoft Word, the program automatically saves the file as a Word document. Adobe Photoshop automatically saves files as Photoshop files. Many times only the original application can open or use a native file format. For instance, neither Adobe PageMaker nor QuarkXPress can use a native Photoshop file on a layout page; you must save a Photoshop file in another file format before the layout applications can use it.

In many applications you have the option to save a file in many other formats. The advantage is that other applications can then read or use that file. For instance, in Word you can save a file as a WordPerfect file; as Text Only (ASCII); for Macintosh, Windows, or DOS; for various versions of other programs; and many other file formats.

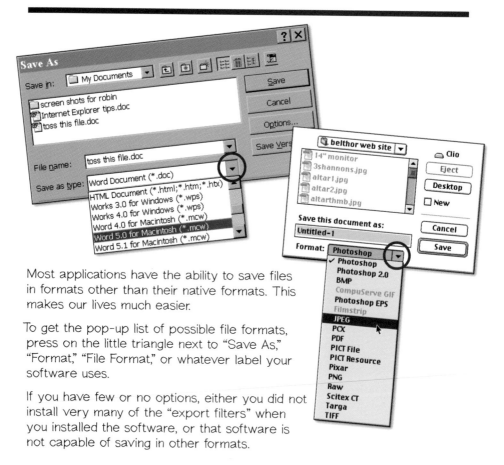

Most applications have the ability to save files in formats other than their native formats. This makes our lives much easier.

To get the pop-up list of possible file formats, press on the little triangle next to "Save As," "Format," "File Format," or whatever label your software uses.

If you have few or no options, either you did not install very many of the "export filters" when you installed the software, or that software is not capable of saving in other formats.

Terminology of graphic file formats

What we are concerned with in this section are the various **graphic** file formats, specifically the ones that can be used on the web—GIF and JPEG. Before we discuss GIFs and JPEGs, though, let's define some of the terms you'll see over and over again.

There are two basic kinds of graphics: those whose structures are based on pixels (the dots on the screen), and those based on mathematical formulas. You'll hear them called these terms:

pixel-based	math-based
bitmap	outline, object-oriented
paint	draw
raster	vector

Applications that let you use tools like paintbrushes and erasers are **bitmapped,** or **raster,** programs. You can edit individual pixels, smudge colors, make shadowed edges, etc. If the application has the word "paint" or "photo" in the name, it is a bitmapped graphics program.

Applications that draw shapes with handles on them are **object-oriented,** or **vector,** programs. If you can select an object and then click a color to change it, or grab a handle and change the object's size or shape, the file structure is based on mathematical formulas. If the application has the word "draw" or "illustrate" in its name, it is a vector graphics program.

Graphics on the web (file formats GIF, PNG, and JPEG) are always bitmapped, or rasterized. Many designers create their original artwork in a vector program such as FreeHand or Illustrator, and then open in it Photoshop or a similar program to "rasterize" it, or turn it into a bitmap.

Bitmapped graphics are created by changing the colors of individual pixels on the screen (the "bits" of information are "mapped" to the pixels on the screen).

This enlargement shows the individual pixels of a bitmap. The pixels can be edited one by one or as a group.

Vector graphics are generally smooth-edged because the shapes are mathematically defined instead of being mapped to individual pixels.

This enlargement shows one of the objects that makes the image. You can move the "handles" on the object to change its shape.

GIF file format

GIF is a graphic file format developed by CompuServe specifically for online use. It stands for Graphic Interchange Format. GIF is pronounced "giff," not "jiff"—the "g" stands for the hard "g" in "**g**raphical."

There are two very important things about GIFs. One is that they are **cross-platform,** meaning any kind of computer can view them. Many other file formats cannot be sent from one system to another, but people have been sending GIF files back and forth to each other over the Internet since 1987. And because all kinds of computers are being used to view web pages, it's critical that we are all able to view the same graphics.

The second important thing about GIFs is that they are **compressed.** Compression makes a file smaller—smaller in *file size,* not in dimensions. For instance, a 2 x 2-inch image in the graphic file format called TIFF might be 900K. The same 2 x 2-inch graphic in the GIF file format might be 5K.

Compression is important on the Internet because it allows files to be transferred quickly. If the graphics on a web page are small in file size, the page will download onto your computer much faster. You've probably been to web pages where it took a long time to see the page, and what did you do? You probably moved on without waiting for everything to appear. Large files are annoying.

The GIF compression scheme is described as "lossless," meaning the image does not lose any quality in the process. Now, when we teach you to make your GIFs really small (in Chapter 11), we are going to go beyond the natural compression scheme and *manually* reduce the colors, which might degrade the image slightly. But the compression scheme itself will not degrade the image.

GIF images use **indexed color** (you read page 161, right?), which means they can have a maximum of **256 colors,** called an **8-bit graphic** (page 163). However, very few GIFs need all 256 colors, so part of your job is to reduce the number of colors in the image down to the very minimum really necessary. Directions on how to do that are on pages 198–199. But first read and understand about this very important file format.

Advantages of GIFs

There are two kinds of GIFs, **87a,** developed in 1987 and not used much anymore, and **89a,** developed in 1989, and the current standard. The biggest difference between the two is that 89a files can have one color that is *transparent.*

Transparency is a big deal. It's what lets the background color of a page show through part of an image. You can choose one color in your image to be transparent. Without transparency, most of the graphics on the web would be set in a big white box. The other graphic file that is used on the web, JPEG, cannot have any transparent areas.

Another important feature of GIFs is **interlacing.** Have you noticed that some web graphics appear in layers, each layer adding more clarity to the image? That's interlacing. It lets you get an idea of what the graphic is going to be, just in case you might want to skip it and move on to another page. It also allows you to scroll up and down and read any text that appears while waiting for the graphic to fully resolve itself. The JPEG file format does not interlace.

A third important advantage of GIFs is that you can create **animations** with them. These are simple and fun to do—directions are on pages 210–212.

When to choose the GIF format

Because of the way GIFs are compressed, they are best used for images with large areas of solid color, such as simple illustrations, logos, text as graphics, cartoons, etc., as opposed to photographs or watercolor, pencil, or charcoal illustrations. If there are subtle changes in colors, as happens in photos or certain illustrations, it's usually best to use JPEG (next page).

You certainly *can* save everything as GIFs if you want to. It's just that most photos look better as JPEGs, and the file sizes are smaller. The one exception is a very small photo (smaller than 1.5 inches)—the "overhead" in the JPEG compression scheme is such that a small photo can be compressed much better in GIF than in JPEG, and the results are about the same. Experiment with your images and see what works best, in terms of both file size and image quality.

Also read the information on page 180 about aliasing and anti-aliasing. (Basically, an aliased graphic is jaggy on the edges; an anti-aliased graphic appears smoother on the edges.) If you anti-alias a graphic (smooth it), the GIF file will be a little larger because of the extra bits of color needed to anti-alias it. You need to choose which is more important—slightly smaller file size, but jaggy; or slightly larger file size, but smoother.

 This image, with its flat colors, would be best as a GIF file.

This image, with its subtle shades of colors, would be best as a JPEG.

JPEG file format

JPEG (pronounced "jay peg") is a graphic file format. The initials stand for Joint Photographic Experts Group. As its name implies, this format is best used for photographs, or for images that have subtle color changes, depth, lighting effects, or other gradations of color or tone.

Like GIF images (previous page), JPEG files are also **cross-platform** and **compressed.** Unlike GIFs, however, the JPEG compression scheme is "lossy," which means data is actually removed from the graphic image to make the file size smaller. It does a pretty good job at this, though, so if you do it right you generally won't notice a significant difference in quality from the original.

You can't make any part of a JPEG file **transparent.** Since all graphic files are rectangular, all JPEGs will appear with straight edges. Sometimes, however, you might put an uneven, oval, or rough border on a photograph. If you want the area outside the border to be transparent, you will need to save the photo as a GIF, which is just fine.

Progressive JPEGs

A standard JPEG is not **interlaced;** that is, you have to wait for the entire photograph to slowly work its way down the page in its full resolution. This is a good reason to make your standard JPEGs as small as possible.

However, there is a new file format called **Progressive JPEG** that is becoming more widely supported both by browsers and by graphic software that can create the format. The progressive JPEG uses a superior compression scheme (meaning you can make smaller files), it has a wider range of quality settings than for the standard JPEG, and it is interlaced.

You can make a progressive JPEG in Photoshop 4. In Photoshop 3 you can use a plug-in called ProJPEG from BoxTop Software. (We visited BoxTop's offices in the small town of Starkville, Mississippi—*hello, Travis!*) Get the plug-in at their web site: www.boxtopsoft.com.

Advantages of JPEGs

Whereas GIF files are limited to a maximum of 256 colors (called 8-bit), JPEG files can contain 16.7 million colors (called 24-bit). This is why they are better for photographs, watercolor images, pencil or charcoal drawings, and other such images where there are subtle transitions between colors.

You can also choose from a variety of compression levels; the more compression, the smaller the file and the more degradation of quality. How much degradation occurs at a "low" setting depends on how that software interprets a term such as "low" or "high." For instance, in Photoshop, the settings of low, medium, high, and max refer to *quality*, not to the amount of *compression*. You can usually get a perfectly acceptable image using the "low" setting in Photoshop 3 or the "1" setting in Photoshop 4. In Windows 95 Paint, however, the settings refer to the amount of compression, so the "low" setting creates a totally unusable image. The lowest setting in the ProJPEG plug-in, where you have a range from 100 to 0, is also unusable. So experiment with your software. Experiment on a *copy* of the photo.

When to choose the JPEG format

The JPEG format does not compress areas of solid color very well. It works best on photographs and those other kinds of images we keep mentioning. There are times when you might want to save a *photograph* as a GIF. You might want to animate it, make an area transparent, or interlace it (if you don't have the tools to make a progressive JPEG). But there are no good reasons to save a *graphic* (such as a headline or button) as a JPEG. Leave JPEGs to photos and similar images.

These kinds of images usually are best saved as JPEG files because of their subtle gradations of tones.

"Looking for America"

If you have a white background on your web page, you can easily put an irregularly shaped JPEG on the background and have it appear to "float."

PNG file format

PNG stands for Portable Network Graphics (unofficially, it stands for "PNG's not GIF"). Pronounce it "ping." It's a new file format that was developed in direct response to the legal problems ensuing from CompuServe and Unisys demanding, as of 1995, licensing and royalty fees from developers who use GIFs in their products.

Like GIF and JPEG files, PNG files are **cross-platform** and **compressed.** They use a totally "lossless" compression scheme, like GIFs, meaning no data is removed or lost from the image. In fact, they can compress even smaller than GIFs, even though a PNG can have more color.

It will be a little while before this format completely replaces the GIF format (which it is expected to do, and it may even replace JPEGs) because the browsers need to be updated to display PNGs, and software needs to be updated to create this new file format. Already, though, Photoshop 4 can make PNGs, and there are plug-ins that allow most browsers to display them.

Advantages of PNGs

GIF files have a maximum of 256 indexed colors; PNG files can be either indexed 256-color images, they can have 16.7 million true colors, or they can be 16-bit grayscale (see page 162 if you're confused about "bits" and how they relate to color). In a GIF you can choose only one color to be transparent; in a PNG you can have 256 levels of transparency.

Like GIFs, PNG files are **interlaced** so you will see a low-resolution image on the page immediately, which gradually develops into the detailed version. Better than GIFs, the first low-res image you see is clear enough to tell what it is, so you can make a decision about whether you want to stick around to see the rest, or take off and go to another page.

Another important feature of PNGs is that they include "gamma" information. "Gamma" refers to the brightness of an image. The built-in gamma correction in PNGs means the image will somehow correct itself according to the monitor it's on and display itself at the brightness level it was originally intended. As we discussed before, Macintosh monitors are brighter than PC monitors. So images created on Macs tend to appear darker on PCs, and images created on PCs tend to appear washed-out on Macs. A PNG file will supposedly correct for this.

You can adjust the brightness of the image by clicking your mouse and choosing the Brightness option (shown below). You can zoom in to look at the image closer (although it will be very bitmapped) and move the image around within its space. You can invert the image (make it look like a negative), smooth it, or sharpen it. We're not quite sure yet what the advantages are to letting web site visitors do this. Maybe it's one of those technology things we'll find uses for as it grows on us.

For more information on PNGs, see the PNG page at:

www.wco.com/~png

Also check out the site of Thomas Boutell, who created PNGs:

www.boutell.com/boutell/png/

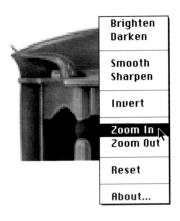

Once you are using a browser that can view PNGs, you can access the menu shown above on each image.

On a Mac, hold the Command key down and press on the image.

On a PC, click the left mouse button.

If you zoom in, you can then press on the image and move the enlarged version around within its space.

Anti-aliasing

You'll often hear the term **anti-aliasing** when people talk about web graphics. It refers to the apparent smoothness of the edge of a graphic.

These orange shapes (whether they are text or graphic objects) have not been anti-aliased. They have the "jaggies." The inset is an enlarged view of an edge of the orange object. Notice the "stair-stepping." This is aliasing.

To anti-alias an edge, the software (such as Photoshop) changes the colors of the pixels along the edges—it blends the color of the object with the color of the background. This tricks our eyes into seeing the edge as smoother.

Because of the extra colors necessary to create the blend, file sizes of anti-aliased GIFs are a bit larger. Some designers believe it is better not to anti-alias graphics and text and thus keep the file size smaller. Other designers believe the slightly larger file size is a worthwhile trade-off to get a graphic that looks better on the screen. There are times when one or the other approach works better for a particular project.

Personally, we prefer anti-aliased graphics in almost all cases, except when creating very small type as graphics (see page 233). There are other ways to reduce the file size that don't compromise the quality of the image, such as reducing the physical size of the image, reducing the number of colors in the GIF to the bare minimum (see pages 198–199), and creating a common color palette for the entire site. Unless you have a good reason not to, click the "anti-alias" button whenever you see it.

This type is not anti-aliased. It's mathematically defined, like vector graphics.

This type is anti-aliased because it's actually a bitmapped graphic (as explained on page 173).

Type printed on paper is not usually represented by pixels—the only time type is anti-aliased for print is when it is part of a larger image, such as type set within a photograph, or when type is created as a graphic to achieve a special effect, such as on the title page of this book.

File size of images

When web designers talk about the "size" of a graphic, they're usually not talking about the dimensions, such as 3 x 4 inches or 250 x 435 pixels. They're usually referring to the "file size." The file size is measured in kilobytes or bytes, and it refers to how much disk space the file takes up. The larger the file size, the longer it takes to send it over the lines, and the longer it takes to appear on the browser page.

A little lesson on bits and bytes

The smallest unit of information on a computer is a **bit.** One bit is one electronic on or off pulse. One bit doesn't tell the computer much. But eight bits strung together make one byte. One **byte** of information can put a letter, such as "A," on your screen. Put 1024 bytes together and you have a unit of information called a **kilobyte.** Put 1024 kilobytes together and you have a **megabyte.** (Most floppy disks hold around 1.4 megabytes of information.) And guess how many megabytes make a **gigabyte?** Our hard disks are typically 500 megabytes to 1 or 2 gigabytes.

Most web graphics are measured in **kilobytes.** Small graphics such as buttons or small headlines might be only **byte**-sized. That's good.

How to find the correct file size

When you are making web graphics in a program such as Photoshop, don't believe the file size it displays for your images. The graphic program is usually telling you how much space the program itself needs to work with that graphic, not the literal file size of the image. To find the real size of your files, see below.

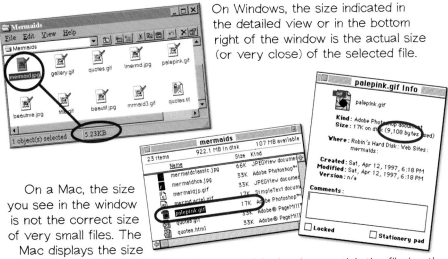

On Windows, the size indicated in the detailed view or in the bottom right of the window is the actual size (or very close) of the selected file.

On a Mac, the size you see in the window is not the correct size of very small files. The Mac displays the size of the smallest "cubbyhole" on the hard disk that it can stick the file in—the bigger your hard disk, the bigger the individual cubby. To see the actual size of the file, select the file (click once on it). From the File menu, choose "Get Info." The **Size** in **parentheses** is the true size.

Image maps

An **image map** is just a fancy name for one graphic that has several different links on it. A graphic with only one link is just called a graphic, or maybe a linked graphic. But an image map graphic has several "hot spots," or different invisible buttons, you can click on.

Image maps are useful in several ways. If you have a photograph of a classroom or family, you can put a hot spot on each person's face that links to that person's personal page. If you have an illustration that represents the front office of your business, you could have different items in the graphic link to different aspects of your business. Sometimes image maps are created just to have fun, to prevent a potentially boring lineup of standard links.

Some people, especially those with slow modems, do surf the web with their graphics turned off. What happens if a visitor comes to your page and cannot see the graphic that is your image map? They can't click the links. So if you make an image map, you must also make sure to do two other things: provide a set of the same links in text format, and provide alternate labels (explained on the following page) within the image map for the links.

Server-side vs. client-side image maps

Say what? Well, until recently the only way to create an image map was to set up the graphic, define the hot spots, create an image map file with information like the site map format (NCSA or CERN), the line break preference, the path to the site's root directory on the server, etc., then hire someone to write a "CGI script" to make it work. It was awful. Forget everything you just read in this paragraph. That procedure is for a **server-side image map,** one that is dependent on the server doing the work.

A **client-side image map** is created as easily as creating any other link on your page: on the large graphic, you draw a shape that you want to be an invisible link button, tell that button where to link to, and it's done.

Which kind of image map would *you* choose to do?

There are people who say that because very old browsers can't read client-side image maps, everyone should do server-side maps. But the vast majority of browsers that are being used now are perfectly capable of reading client-side, so that's what we recommend.

Just be sure that you are following the appropriate steps in your web authoring software to make client-side image maps! For instance, in PageMill, use the image editor to make *server-side* maps; double-click the graphic and use the toolbar buttons to make *client-side* image maps.

You can usually tell if a graphic is an image map by positioning the pointer over the graphic. If there is any link at all, of course, the pointer becomes the little hand. If there are several hot spots within the graphic, you might see the browser hand switch from pointer to hand as you move over the graphic. If not, check the status bar at the bottom of the window. If the graphic is one link, there will be one address in the status bar. If it's an image map, you'll see the status bar information changing as you move the pointer.

Notice the text links that go to the exact same places as the links in the image maps. If anyone is cruising without graphics, they will still be able to link to other pages in the site.

In this example, the four buttons below the image map (Index, Peachpit Press, Feedback, and Credits) are individual graphics. Each one has an "alternate label" (see next page) that will appear if the graphic doesn't.

Alternate labels

When you create a web page, you have an option to add an **alternate label** (called "alt label" for short) to every graphic. You don't have to do this, but alt labels are a sign of a thoughtful and well-designed site.

If a graphic has an alt label, the visitor will see the label as the page loads so they know what to expect. If someone is surfing with the graphics turned off, the alt labels tell them what they are missing. In some browsers, the alt label will appear when the mouse is positioned over a graphic.

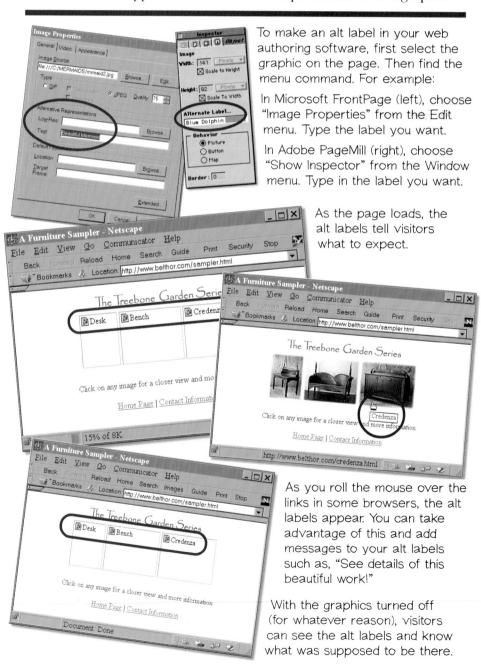

To make an alt label in your web authoring software, first select the graphic on the page. Then find the menu command. For example:

In Microsoft FrontPage (left), choose "Image Properties" from the Edit menu. Type the label you want.

In Adobe PageMill (right), choose "Show Inspector" from the Window menu. Type in the label you want.

As the page loads, the alt labels tell visitors what to expect.

As you roll the mouse over the links in some browsers, the alt labels appear. You can take advantage of this and add messages to your alt labels such as, "See details of this beautiful work!"

With the graphics turned off (for whatever reason), visitors can see the alt labels and know what was supposed to be there.

Thumbnails

A **thumbnail** is a small, "thumbnail-sized" version of an image. When you click on it, you jump *to another page* with a larger version of the same image. This way a visitor can see a lot of different, small images on the first page without having to wait for larger files of the larger pictures to load. As you know, if a page takes too long to appear, many visitors will leave your page. But if visitors *choose* to see the enlarged image, they can—and they know ahead of time that it will take longer to download. They are *choosing* to wait for it.

To make the thumbnail process work, you have to make **two separate files** for that one image! The smaller image file will be displayed on the first page; it links to another page that holds the larger image.

- In your **image editing software** (such as Photoshop, Adobe PhotoDeluxe, or Paint Shop Pro), fix up the original "source" file— do all those things you need to make it look nice.

- Save **two copies** of the image (*copies*—don't do this to your original source file!).

- Open one of the copies. Make the dimensions small, like one inch across. Make it a 72-ppi GIF (see pages 174–175 and 198–199). Even if it's a photograph, images with very small dimensions (less than about 1.5 inches) are usually better as GIFs rather than JPEGs—they look just as good and the file size is much smaller.

- Put this file on the first web page.

- Open the second copy of the image.

- Make this second image file as big as you want (within reason).

  If you think the visitor might want to print the graphic or download it to their computer for some reason, then go ahead and keep this graphic at a higher resolution (something like 100 or 144 ppi). It won't look any different on the screen, but it will be a clearer image if they print or download it.

  If you don't think people will be printing or downloading the image, or if you want to discourage anyone from "borrowing" it, leave the resolution at 72 ppi.

- Make note of the size of the larger file (see page 181).

- Put the larger file on a second web page.

- Link the small graphic on the first page to the large graphic on the second page.

It's a nice touch to tell the visitor just how large the larger image will be, both in file size and in inches. Put this information right next to the small thumbnail so a visitor has a clue of what to expect when they click that link. On the larger page, be sure to put a title on the page, a headline or at least a caption, and a button taking the visitor back to the thumbnail.

A very common problem we see on amateur web pages are thumbnail images that lead to "orphan" pages, pages that have nothing on them except a larger image. Not only is that boring for the visitor (at least provide a new piece of information along with the larger image), but it's bad planning.

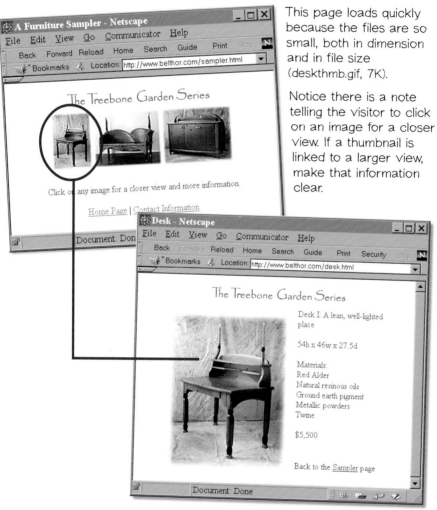

This page loads quickly because the files are so small, both in dimension and in file size (deskthmb.gif, 7K).

Notice there is a note telling the visitor to click on an image for a closer view. If a thumbnail is linked to a larger view, make that information clear.

So here is a larger view. The graphic, of course, is a **completely different file** (desk.jpg, 28K), even though it looks like exactly the same image.

Notice there is new information so visitors don't feel like they wasted their time coming here. There is a link back to where the visitor came from. And there is identifying information so they know they are still in the same site.

Self-Guided Tour
of the World Wide Web

Find an example of each of these graphic items. This tour includes concepts from both the color and the graphic definitions chapters.

☐ A graphic or background with colors that dither.

(If you have a monitor with fewer than 256 colors, everything is probably dithered. If you have a monitor displaying thousands or millions of colors, you probably won't find anything dithered. In that case, change your monitor to 256 colors or less so you can see what others might see with a typical monitor.)

☐ An interlaced GIF image. How do you know it is interlaced?

☐ A JPEG image. What makes you think it's a JPEG?

☐ A graphic with text that is not anti-aliased, or a graphic image that is itself not anti-aliased.

☐ A thumbnail image that is linked to a larger version of the same image. Did the designer tell you how big the larger file is?

☐ An image map. Did the designer include an alternate navigation bar in case the image map wouldn't work on your browser, or in case you are browsing with your graphics off?

☐ A graphic file that takes so long to download you don't have the patience to wait for it.

☐ A useless graphic that doesn't add to the content, the communication, or the aesthetic value of the page.

☐ Turn off the graphics in your browser. Go to some new pages you haven't seen yet. Are there alternate labels that tell you what the unloaded graphic is? If the unloaded graphics are links to other pages, are there alternate labels that tell you where the link will take you?

☐ Keep your eyes open for PNGs and progressive JPEGs. You have to be using Netscape Navigator 3.0 or Internet Explorer 4.0 or above to see them. As of this writing, there aren't very many PNGs or progressive JPEGs on the web.

Oh boy, it's a Quiz!

For questions 1 through 4, choose which of the following images would be best saved as JPEGS or as GIFS—circle your choice. State the reason why.

1.

GIF   JPEG

_____
why

2.

GIF   JPEG

_____
why

3. _Local Sites of_ **Native American** _information_

GIF   JPEG

_____
why

4. **Hat Collection**

GIF   JPEG

_____
why

5. Which of the following is **not** an advantage of a GIF file?
   a. unlimited color
   b. lossless compression
   c. transparency
   d. interlacing

6. Which of the following is **not** an advantage of a JPEG file?
   a. millions of colors
   b. lossless compression
   c. variety of compression levels
   d. maintains subtle color changes

7. Name two reasons to use alt labels.
   1. . . . .
   2. . . . .

8. Which of the following is **not** an advantage of anti-aliasing?
   a. appearance of smooth edges
   b. smaller file size
   c. nicer-looking graphics
   d. looks better on a screen than on paper

9. Which of the following is **not** an advantage of a PNG file?
   a. easy pronunciation
   b. lossless compression
   c. lots of color and transparency
   d. lots of software support

10. How many separate graphic files does it take to create the thumbnail-to-larger-image concept? **1 2 3 4**

How to Prepare Image Files *for the Web*

This chapter is all about how to prepare graphics for the World Wide Web. The first part tells you how you can get graphics to put on your page if you don't know how to draw or use drawing or illustration programs. This segment also tells you how to get photographs onto your pages, and it includes information about how to scan a photograph so your can get it into the computer.

The latter part of the chapter tells you how to use your software to make your graphics work for the World Wide Web, and how to make GIFs and JPEGs. It assumes you know how to use the software to create the graphic in the first place, or how to bring a scanned image into your program. (Chapter 13 has lots of tips and tricks for more advanced users.)

On the very next page are the **web graphic specifications** for those of you who know how to create graphics already and just want to know the bare minimum of information to make graphics for the web.

Web graphic specifications

These are the specifications for graphics on the web. If you're making the graphics yourself, follow these rules. If you have someone else make graphics for you, make sure they understand the images must follow these specifications. The actual GIF and JPEG file formats are explained in detail in Chapter 10.

- ☐ **JPEG:** Photographs, as well as other images that are similar to photographs, such as scans of paintings with lots of color gradations, pastel drawings, charcoal or pencil drawings, etc., should usually be saved in the **JPEG** format, as we discussed in Chapter 10. JPEGs can display 24-bit color as discussed in Chapter 9. Save as:

    72 ppi (pixels per inch when referring to the resolution on the screen; when printed, it's *dpi,* or dots per inch)

    Lowest quality level (depending on the software; experiment to see what is acceptable)

    RGB color

- ☐ **GIF:** Illustrations, type, images with flat color, are best saved in the **GIF** format (or keep an eye on PNG). GIFs are 8-bit. Save as:

    72 ppi

    Indexed color mode

    Reduce the color palette to the minimum necessary to maintain the image

- ☐ Before you save it as a GIF or JPEG, make the image the **size** you want it on the web page. You *can* reduce it once it is on the page, but that's bad planning and will result in a longer download time than necessary (see page 181). You *can* physically enlarge the image on the web page, but it will look bad because of the low screen resolution (as shown on page 83).

If you don't want to make your own graphics

It's just a fact that even the simplest of graphics, such as tiny little bullets or colorful headlines in a nice typeface, make such a difference in the visual impression of a web page.

If you don't want to make your own graphics, there is plenty of ready-made art, called **clip art,** available to you. If you don't have or know how to use any graphic program at all, make sure you get clip art that is created specifically for the web. You can get backgrounds, bullets, rules (lines), buttons, and more. If you know how to use just about any graphic program, you can get any kind of clip art and adapt it for the web. All of the examples shown below are from ImageClub Graphics. ImageClub can be found at www.imageclub.com—they have a phenomenal amount of great clip art available, as well as lots of fun and inexpensive fonts that make great web site headlines. Also, most of the web authoring software packages come with a collection of web clip art—look on your disks. And Robin's book *Home Sweet Home Page and the Kitchen Sink,* published by Peachpit Press, has a CD-ROM with John's great clip art.

Lots of people have created web graphics and put them on the web for you to use for free—dig down through Yahoo to the World Wide Web sections, and you'll find lots of links to free graphics. Hire a friend or relation to make you some graphics, or ask your kids and grandkids. Check the local college for art students who can do graphic stuff for you. Buy books of copyright-free clip art and have someone *scan* the images for you (details on following pages). Oh, with a wee bit of ingenuity you can make your web site sparkle with a few well-placed graphics.

If you don't have Adobe Photoshop

If you plan to be creating many web sites, you'll probably end up investing in Adobe Photoshop. It's an indispensable tool for designing and manipulating graphics, and for changing files into the proper file formats. At the time of this writing, Photoshop LE (Limited Edition) is included in the package when you buy Adobe PageMill. SiteMill, which is a great program for managing a whole web site, whether it was created in PageMill or not, is also included in the Mac version, and all this, plus over a thousand pieces of web clip art, animations, and sounds, for $99! But if you don't have Photoshop at the moment, here are some alternatives for converting graphic files into the GIF or JPEG formats you need.

Inexpensive software

Many of the less expensive software packages, such as the paint or draw portions of ClarisWorks, Adobe PhotoDeluxe, Jasc Paint Shop Pro, or Microsoft Image Composer (which comes with FrontPage), can do a great deal of image creation and photo manipulation. Most graphic software now lets you save in a variety of formats, including GIF or JPEG. Adobe PhotoDeluxe is a delightful and incredibly simple program in which you can edit photographic images, and it has the same export features for making GIFs and JPEGs that you'll see on pages 198–201.

Let your web authoring software convert images

If your graphic software does not have the option of saving as a GIF or JPEG, then save the file on a Mac as a PICT; on Windows, save the file as a BMP. Just about every web authoring software will automatically convert those graphics to the correct file format when you paste or insert them on the web page (file formats are explained on page 172). Some web authoring packages will convert other file formats as well. Read your manual!

Before you add a graphic to a web page and allow the software to convert it, you must tell your program *where* to put that converted copy! For instance:

- **Adobe PageMill:** From the Edit menu, choose "Preferences...."
  - Click the "Resource" icon on the left side of the dialog box.
  - Click the folder icon under "Resource Folder."
  - From the resulting dialog box, find and choose your web site folder, or the folder within your web site in which you are storing all of your graphics. Click OK.

- **Claris Home Page:** From the Edit menu, choose "Preferences...."
  - From the menu in the Preferences dialog box, choose "Images."
  - Next to "Converted Images Folder," click the "Set..." button.
  - From the resulting dialog box, find and choose your web site folder, or the folder within your web site in which you are storing all of your graphics. Click OK.

- **Microsoft FrontPage:** Put the graphic on the page.
  - If the graphic was not a GIF or JPEG, or if it came from a folder other than your web site folder, then when you Save the page, the program asks if you want to "Save this image to a file?" Click "Yes" and the converted file will be placed in your web site folder.
- **GoLive CyberStudio:**
  - From the Edit menu, choose "Preferences…."
  - Click the "General" icon.
  - Under the section called "Picture Import," click the "Select…" button.
  - From the resulting dialog box, find and choose your web site folder, or the folder within your web site in which you are storing all of your graphics. Click OK.

Shareware software for converting files

From www.shareware.com you can download shareware to convert existing graphics, such as clip art that was not already converted to a web format. On a Mac, check out GraphicConverter or GIFConverter. On Windows, try BMPtoGIF, Paint Shop Pro, or any of the multitude of other programs available online. Open a graphic file in one of the programs, then choose "Save As" from the File menu. Choose to save as a GIF or JPEG.

Unfortunately for this technique, most clip art from commercial sources is in the EPS format, which some graphic converters might have trouble opening. Try it and see. Some software will tell you how to enhance the program so you can open EPS files; for instance, you might need to go to their web site and download something extra—follow their directions.

Photoshop is an investment in your future

If you plan to do lots of web page design, either for yourself or others, you will want to buy and learn to use Photoshop. You don't even have to know a great deal about the program to make nice graphics. And remember that Peachpit Press has lots of Photoshop books to help you get started.

How to get artwork or photographs into your computer

If you have photographs or artwork you want to put on your web pages, they must be *scanned*. A scanner is a piece of hardware that makes a copy of anything you put on its glass top. It's kind of like a copy machine, but instead of making a copy of the image on a piece of paper, it makes a digital copy on a disk. A computer can understand and display this digital version of the image. Some small scanners are handheld—you roll the scanner over the image.

Do you want a photo of yourself? Check the local Internet cafe or copy shop. They often have little cameras sitting on top of the computers that can grab a photo of you and put it on a disk.

Send your film to a digital processor

Ask around for a local film processor who can send your film out for digital processing. Your photos will come back on a CD, usually in a variety of resolutions (you can also ask for prints). You can then open these digital photos in your graphic software, fix them up, and save them as GIFs or JPEGs, ready for placement on your web pages.

You can send your film to a number of companies that will produce GIF or JPEG files of your images. They post your files on a web page, and from there you can download them using a password or using the posting site address, which only you know. The files are ready for you to place on the web—you just might need to crop them or clean them up.

One business that does this is Seattle FilmWorks at www.filmworks.com. Send them your film and they will either post your photos on the Internet for you to download, send them to you on floppy disks, or send you prints, contact sheets, negatives, or any combination of possibilities. They even send you free film every time you use their services! For similar companies, check the ads in computer magazines or search the web. Dig down through Search.com or Yahoo.

What to tell someone who is scanning for you

If someone is going to scan images for you, be sure to tell that person the images are for the World Wide Web. If the person scanning is not accustomed to making web graphics, give them a copy of page 190 and ask them to follow those specifications.

How to scan it yourself

If you have lots of photographs and/or artwork you want to put on your web page, it might behoove you to invest in your own scanner. For web quality graphics, the inexpensive scanners you can buy at Sears or office supply stores are great. When you buy one, keep in mind that the biggest thing you can scan is what will fit on the glass top of the scanner.

When you scan, follow these guidelines:

- Physically size the image (as in inches or picas) to approximately the finished **dimensions** you will want it on the web page.

  If you plan to work on the scanned image in a program like Photoshop or Paint Shop Pro, you might want to size it a little larger, then reduce it to the web page size in your image editing program (Photoshop or Paint Shop Pro).

- You will eventually change the **resolution** of the image to 72 ppi before you put it on the web page. If you do not plan to work on the image, you can go ahead and scan it at 72 ppi. But if you plan to clean up the image or change it in any way, it will be easier to work on if you scan it anywhere from 100 to 150 ppi.

  If possible, choose a scan resolution that is built into your scanner. That is, if you have a menu choices of (for instance) 72, 100, 133, or 150, then use one of those.

  If you don't have choices but just a place to enter a number, enter 144 pixels per inch. Then when you reduce the resolution to 72 (half of 144), you get the cleanest image.

  If you just have a choice of Low, Medium, or High, choose Medium (unless you have a lot of work to do on the photo, in which case you might want High).

- Always save scanned images in the **TIFF file format**—TIFFs were invented for scanning. (If you scan directly into Photoshop, though, save as a Photoshop file.) Later you'll change it to GIF or JPEG.

  If the image is strictly black and white, like a logo, choose Bitmap or Line Art.

- If you have a choice of how many **colors,** don't bother scanning for more than "thousands" of colors (although some high-end scanners only offer "millions" or "billions").

  If you really want a high-quality scan of a photograph or similar art, then go ahead and scan for millions of colors. You will eventually convert that photographic image to a JPEG which *can* contain millions of colors.

  If the image is not a photo and has lots of broad, flat colors, you can get away with scanning for only 256 colors, since you will eventually reduce the color palette to even less than that anyway.

Use a digital camera

If you plan to take and use lots of photographs yourself, investing in a digital camera will make your life much easier. You can get great digital cameras for less than a thousand dollars now, and some cost only a couple hundred dollars. You take the pictures, the camera stores them on a little hard disk inside the camera, you hook the camera up to your computer and pull the pictures from the camera right onto your own hard disk. No scanning. No film to buy or pay for. No waiting for film to be developed. No worries about the kids wasting film. It's great.

A digital camera is the best solution if you're going to do something like make a family web site, a corporate site with photos of all of your employees, or a site for your dog kennel with lots of photos. It's also perfect for those times when you want to update your web site daily, perhaps for updating during a conference to show people who can't attend what's going on, for posting photos during the school fair or at camp to show parents at home what their children are doing that very day, to show grandparents the new baby as she grows, to keep friends and relatives apprised of what is happening on the cross-country bike trip, or to add the cameo and personal shots to the school yearbook.

There are many companies making digital cameras now. Check your local photography store, or if you get computer magazines, check the ads. There are always articles in computer magazines comparing the various models of cameras. Ask around at the computer user groups, or go online and search for information. We've been using a Kodak DC40 for over a year now and we've been very happy with it.

These images were taken with a digital camera.
We made no enhancements.

Step-by-Step
Directions

In this next section we provide step-by-step directions for saving your graphics into the appropriate web file formats. We've also included lots of information about how to make background graphics, since everybody likes to do that, as well as some advanced tips on how to make the background of your graphic match the background of the web page. In Chapter 13 we go into step-by-step detail on a number of more advanced techniques—this chapter contains the basics. Most of these steps assume you are using Photoshop, or at least Adobe PhotoDeluxe.

Make a GIF

Graphics that consist of areas of flat color, such as type or stylized illustrations, are most effectively saved as GIF files. The results are almost always clean and smooth, especially if the original art is created using browser-safe colors (see pages 167–169). The following example shows the development of a headline graphic from its creation to the final conversion into a GIF file. **If you already have a graphic that you just want to turn into a GIF, or if you are using Adobe PhotoDeluxe, skip to step 6.**

1. In Photoshop we created a new file with a transparent background. Even if you don't want a transparent background, make sure your graphics and type are all on separate layers so you can easily manipulate them.

2. We drew the graphic swoosh on the left of the example with the pen tool and filled it with a browser-safe color. We set the type on another layer, also using a safe color. Since each element is on its own layer, it's easy to experiment with color: select a layer, pick a different color, and press Option Shift Delete (Mac) or Alt Shift Backspace (Windows).

3. A Gaussian Blur shadow is always a temptation (see Creating Drop Shadows on pages 243–244), but we chose to make a simple, flat-color drop shadow to keep the file size down and to ensure a clean, crisp graphic.

Tip: GIF files that contain blurs and gradual color gradations look great on monitors that can display thousands of colors, but on 256-color monitors, the blurs and gradations appear banded or dithered.

Blends and Gaussian blurs look great on monitors that can display thousands of colors.

But blends and Gaussian blurs degrade quite a bit on monitors that can only display 256 colors. Too many subtle colors are required to create smooth blends and blurs, forcing the computer to simulate the missing colors by dithering, as shown here.

Since this graphic uses flat, browser-safe colors, it looks the same in 256 colors, shown here, as it does in thousands of colors.

4. The graphic's background looks white because in Photoshop's Preferences we set the "Transparency & Gamut" Grid Size to "None."

If we change Grid Size to "Small," the Photoshop file looks like this:

5. If we export the file now, it will have a transparent background, regardless of how our Preferences settings make it look on the screen. Because transparent backgrounds can be problematic, we usually prefer to make the background of the GIF file match the color or texture that's used as a background on the web page (see pages 210 and 211). But the background color for this page will be white, so we created another layer, dragged it to the bottom of the Layers palette, and filled it with white. Of course, you could fill this layer with any color or pattern.

6. To export a graphic as a GIF: From the File menu, slide down to "Export…" and choose "GIF89a Export…." If you don't have this option in your menu, you probably don't have the GIF89a plug-in. Download it from the Adobe site and put it in the Photoshop/PhotoDeluxe plug-ins folder.

7. In the GIF89a Export dialog box, choose the "Adaptive" Palette and set "Colors" to the smallest number available (8) or type in "4." Click the Preview button to see what the file will look like. If it doesn't look good enough, close the Preview window and try a higher number of colors. Keep adding a few colors until you've chosen the lowest number of colors that make the image just barely acceptable. Click OK.

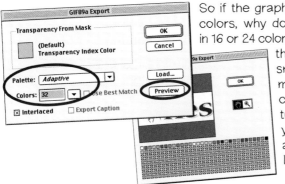

So if the graphic has three browser-safe colors, why does the GIF file look better in 16 or 24 colors? Because the anti-aliasing that Photoshop applies to smooth the edges creates many variations of the main colors. The alternative is to turn anti-aliasing off when you're creating the graphic and try to ignore the "jaggy" look.

8. Click the **Interlace** checkbox (see page 175 for an explanation of interlace). Click OK. (If you don't interlace the image in your graphic program, you can usually do it in your web authoring software.)

9. In the **Save** dialog box, the file name appears with ".gif" automatically added. Edit the name if necessary, following the file naming rules (see page 71), but leave the ".gif" extension on the name. **Make sure you save the file into the same folder that all your final web graphics are in.**

Make a JPEG

JPEGs are the best format to use for photographs or graphics that have many colors and shades and very few, if any, areas of flat color. Because JPEGs can support more colors than GIFs, photographs usually look much better as JPEGs than as GIFs. Monitors that support only 256 colors will dither the image (make up colors that are *close* to the ones it doesn't have) to compensate for not being able to display all the colors, but monitors that are capable of displaying thousands or millions of colors will show the image in all its glory.

1. To make a JPEG, open an image in Photoshop, PhotoDeluxe, or any other image editing program that can save files as JPEGs. Make any adjustments desired, such as in Hue/Saturation, Levels, and Sharpening. Retouch the file if necessary.

2. Save the image in the program's "native" file format (whatever the program automatically saves its files as; see page 172). Save this file along with your other original graphics in a folder named "Source Files."

   Tip: If possible, save this file in larger dimensions and at a higher resolution than you anticipate needing at the present time. Then later, if necessary, you can use the same photo at a larger size without loss of image quality.

3. Make a copy of your source file and open the copy. In preparation for saving this as a JPEG, resize the image and change its resolution to 72 ppi. For this example, we saved the file at 300 pixels wide (about 4 inches) at 72 ppi.

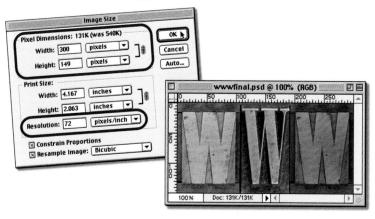

4. Now save the file as a JPEG: From the "File" menu, choose "Save as...."

In the "Save" dialog box, name the file with a web-safe name and add ".jpg" to the end of the file name.

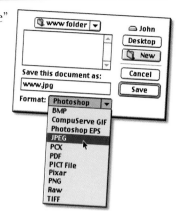

5. From the "Format:" menu, select "JPEG." Click "Save."

6. After you click "Save," the **JPEG Options** dialog box appears.

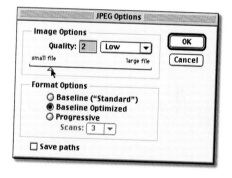

The **Image Options** slider lets you choose the quality of the image. The higher the "Quality" setting, the larger the file will be (in kilobytes, not dimensions).

Most JPEGs look just fine at the lowest setting. An exception is when the image is of a person's face. In that case, we usually move the quality setting up to at least the "Medium" range.

Under **Format Options,** choose "Baseline Optimized" for best color quality. Or choose "Progressive," which enables the file to load progressively, from low resolution to high resolution, similar to the "interlacing" feature available in GIF files. Click OK.

Tip: Don't be misled by the image on your screen that you just saved. Photoshop won't show you how the file has changed until it's closed and then opened again. You might want to save several variations of the JPEG in different quality settings. Programs other than Photoshop or PhotoDeluxe have different standards for quality settings; that is, the low setting in Photoshop might be equivalent to the medium setting in another program, so be sure to experiment with your software to find the best quality level that creates the smallest file.

Note: The JPEG compression scheme throws away some digital information—that's what makes the files smaller. If you *resave* a JPEG file, it will throw away even more information during the compression process. The amount of degradation depends partly on what settings were used in the "Image Options" of the JPEG Options dialog box. If you didn't keep the original, uncompressed file, you can sometimes rework and resave a JPEG and retain fairly reasonable quality, but don't count on it. Always keep an original, high-resolution source file in case you need to make changes.

Make an image map

Break out of the buttons-for-navigation rut and have fun with image maps. This technique allows you to define certain areas, or hot spots, of a graphic image as links to other pages or sites.

Be sure to read the information on page 182 about the important difference between server-side and client-side image maps. Web authoring software makes creating image maps extremely fast and easy, but you do need to read your manual to learn how your software distinguishes between client-side and server-side. For instance, in Adobe PageMill, using the tools in the toolbar makes a client-side map; using the tools in the image editing box makes a server-side map. The directions on this page describe how to make a client-side image map in PageMill or Claris Home Page, but your software will be very similar.

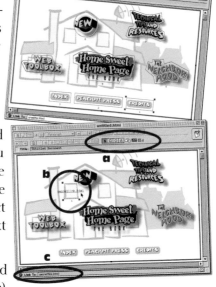

The Home Sweet Home Page illustration features icons that represent the main sections of the site, as well as several buttons beneath the house that refer to other internal and external links.

1. Place the image file (JPEG or GIF) onto the web page.

2. In PageMill, double-click the image, and the image mapping tools in the menu bar become active (**a**). In Claris Home Page, select the image, then from the Window menu choose "Show Object Editor." Click the "Edit..." button next to "Client-Side Image Map."

3. Select one of the tools and draw around the area you want to define as a link (**b**).
   While the path is selected, type the URL you want to link to in the "Link to:" field at the bottom of the window (**c,** PageMill) or in the dialog box that appears (Home Page). Press Return or Enter and the URL appears inside the drawn shape. That shape, or button, is now called a "hot spot." After you've made the link, the hot spot looks like this: `credits.html`

You can even put a secret link on a page, as shown above. No one will know the link is there unless they notice the pointing hand as it passes over the house window. Make the link connect to a surprise page of useful or entertaining content. Also use image maps to make hot spots on playful graphics that would otherwise be difficult to define.

Make background graphics

Web page backgrounds can be black, white, a color, or any GIF or JPEG graphic that repeats (tiles) to fill the screen. Besides plain colors or patterns, you can also use images that create a vertical edge along the left side of the page, or a horizontal space across the top, or one giant image.

Your web authoring software offers a simple way to place or insert a graphic as a page background. Try the "Insert" command, or look in the dialog box where you change the color of the background. Or read your manual.

Readability should be your main consideration when choosing a background graphic. Many sites have beautiful backgrounds that make the pages unreadable and thus annoying. Good contrast between the text and the background is the safest way to go. *You* might be awestruck by the background you created, but the person visiting your site would probably rather be able to read the darn text. Sure, there are exceptions to every rule—you may be designing an online skateboard magazine or a web site for a heavy metal band, in which case readability might not be your primary goal. Most of the time, however, readability is a good thing (although you wouldn't know it by cruising around on the web).

Left-edge graphic as background

One of the most popular backgrounds is a graphic that creates a bar or stripe down the left edge. This not only dresses up the page with color, but also acts as an organizing element for the page.

The background on this page is actually this long, skinny graphic that repeats itself over and over.

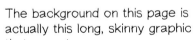

1. To make a simple horizontal background, open a new file approximately 1000 pixels wide by 50 pixels high. (If you make the width too short, scrolling to the right on the web page will make the edge of the graphic appear again, making your page look . . . well, dorky.)

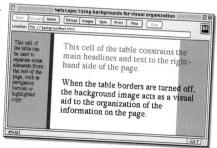

2. Select the first couple of inches of the file and fill the selection with a color. Choose a browser-safe color  (see pages 167–169) so it won't dither and lessen the text readability.

3. Select the rest of the image area: from the "Select" menu, choose 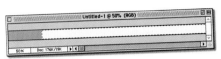 "Inverse." Fill this with black, white, or another color.

4. Now add a small stripe of accent color between the two colors.

5. For this simple background, you can crop away most of the height of the image. The dimensions in this  example are now 1000 pixels wide and 10 pixels high. The file size is 250 bytes (.25K).

6. Export the image as a GIF file (see "Making a GIF" on pages 198–199) and place it on the web page as a background.

Here is an example of a left-edge background used in combination with a table to organize information. Below right, the table borders are off.

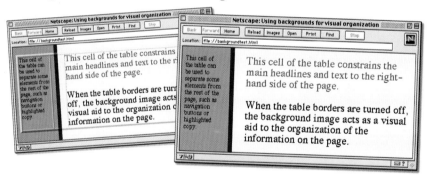

Top-edge graphic as background

Top-edge backgrounds work just like left-edge ones except they're ... hmmm, across the top instead of down the left edge. To 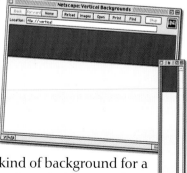 ensure that the design at the top of the vertical strip doesn't repeat too soon and show up on the page as you scroll down, make the graphic file taller than the scrollable content area. Using a top-edge background works best on pages that don't need to scroll or that scroll very little. To make this kind of background for a long scrolling page would require an extraordinarily long graphic.

This vertical, top-edge background was created the same way as the horizontal, left-edge background above.

Giant-image backgrounds

Backgrounds don't have to be tiny little slivers of graphics. If you have a fairly large image that works well (the readability thing again), you can put it in the background and still have the page load in an acceptable amount of time. Limit the number of colors in the image to keep the file size down as much as possible, and plan the colors to contrast with the text on the page.

1. Open an image in your image editing software and experiment with different ways to change the file to make it a pleasing background against which text can be read.

2. We used a dark color theme for the background and light colors for the text. We sized the art to 700 pixels wide and 500 pixels high so it fills the window space of 640 x 460 pixels that we like to design within.

3. We exported the file as a GIF with 16 colors. Because most of this large image is one flat color, the GIF compression scheme is able to compress the file to just 16K. Not bad, unless you compare it to typical file sizes for vertical and horizontal background GIFs—from .5K to 3K. Even though the file size is small for a graphic this large, it will still take a little more time to load than if you used a tiny, repeating file.

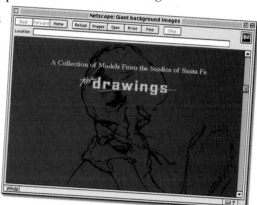

4. Place the GIF file onto your web page as a background image.

There's another example of a large background on page 140, on the web page for the Computer Book Cafe from Studio B.

Tip: We created the headline in this example in Photoshop with anti-aliasing turned on to give the edges of the type a smooth appearance. We created another layer below the type layer and filled it with the same browser-safe blue as the page background. Then we used the pencil tool to erase the blue background almost all the way up to the letterforms of the headline. This prevents "artifacts," or unsightly pixels, along the edge.

The type now has a transparent background so it can sit on top of the large graphic, but the anti-aliased type edges are protected by the aliased background color around them. (See page 208 for an example of how anti-aliased edges and transparent backgrounds can mess up your page.)

Create a seamless, textured background

You can create a beautiful, textured background pattern easily and quickly by simply adding "noise" to a solid color. This is only one way to make a gently patterned background—experiment with the other filters.

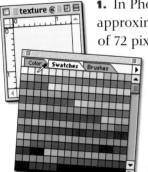

1. In Photoshop, create a new file whose size is approximately 100 pixels x 100 pixels, with a resolution of 72 pixels per inch.

2. Select a color from the browser-safe color palette (explained on pages 167-169). Choose either a light pastel so that dark type will read easily against it, or choose a dark color so pastel or white type will read easily.

3. Press Option Delete (Mac) or Alt Backspace (Windows) to fill the window with the foreground color.

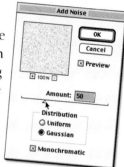

4. Add "noise" to the color: From the "Filter" menu, select "Noise," and then "Add Noise...." The "Add Noise" dialog box will appear and you can choose the settings you like.

5. Since you probably want this background to be soft, subtle, and easy to read against, apply a Gaussian Blur to the texture image: From the Filter menu, choose "Blur," then "Gaussian Blur." When working on files that are low resolution (72 ppi, in this case), small adjustments in filter settings go a long way. Try a Gaussian Blur setting between .3 and .5.

6. To test the texture as a background, go to the "Select" menu and choose "All" to select the entire image area. Then:

7. From the "Edit" menu, choose "Define Pattern." You won't see anything happen, but the background pattern you just defined is now ready to be placed in a test file as a tiled pattern.

8. Create a new file that's two or three times larger than the texture file (300 pixels by 300 pixels, for instance).

9. From the "Edit" menu, choose "Fill...." The "Fill" dialog box appears. From the "Contents" pull-down menu, choose "Pattern," then click "OK." Make sure "Opacity" is set at 100% in this dialog box, unless you want a lighter version.

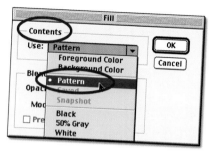

10. If you like the appearance of the tiled pattern in the test file, export the small texture file as a GIF89a file (as explained on pages 198–199). You can then place it as a background image on your web page.

Have fun experimenting with combinations of filters. For instance, after you've added Noise and Gaussian Blur to a flat color, return to the "Filter" menu and choose "Blur," then "Motion Blur...." Move the "Distance" slider to the right for a streaked, woodgrain effect.

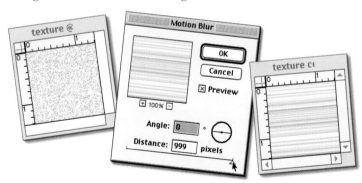

Graphics with colored backgrounds that match the background color of your web page

When you make the background of a GIF file transparent, the image quality varies depending on the background color or texture of the web page it's on. For instance, your graphic may have a soft shadow that you want to blend seamlessly into a page's textured or colored background. In this case, creating the *illusion* of transparency is better than using an actual transparent file.

In the example to the left, we created the original illustration in Adobe Illustrator. Then we opened that illustration in Photoshop to *rasterize* it (change the mathematical formula of the Illustrator file into pixels) and to create the soft shadow on a separate layer.

If we export this as a GIF89a file with a transparent background and place it on a page with a textured background, the shadow appears hard-edged and opaque (and dorky).

We can avoid this hard-edged effect by creating a background for the graphic that will match the web page background.

1. If the background is a flat color, create a new layer in the Photoshop file (if the background's not a flat color, see the next page).
2. Fill this new layer with the exact color that is being used as the background color of your web page (white or a color). If you don't know how to match colors, read the section on browser-safe colors.
3. Make sure all three layers are visible (the illustration layer, the shadow layer, and the background layer).
4. Export as a GIF89a file.

Now, when the GIF file is placed on the web page, the background color of the web page and the background of the GIF match perfectly to create an effect of the illustration floating on the page.

But what if the background of the web page is a colored texture?

The technique on the previous page works great on a background that's a flat color. But if your background is one of the lovely textures you just made, you'll have to do this extra step to make the background of your graphic match that of your web page.

1. Open the original texture file you've created (see "Create a seamless, textured background" on pages 206–207).

2. From the "Select" menu, choose "All."

3. From the "Edit" menu, choose "Define Pattern." This loads the texture into memory.

4. Now, in the graphic file, select the background color layer in the "Layers" palette.

5. From the "Edit" menu, select "Fill...." The "Fill" dialog box appears. From the "Contents" section pull-down menu, choose "Pattern." Make sure "Opacity" is set at 100%. Click OK.

   The background of the illustration is now filled with a tiled texture pattern that will match the background of the web page.

6. Make sure the correct three layers are visible (the illustration layer, the shadow layer, and the textured background layer).

7. Export as a GIF89a file. When you place this file on a web page that has the same background pattern, the graphic will blend seamlessly into the texture of the web page.

Now, it's usually pretty easy to match the graphic to the background when the pattern is some vague, noisy texture. Other background patterns or textures may be harder to match, such as checkerboards or snakes or other clearly repeated patterns. In fact, if the background is something like stripes, it is practically impossible to match the graphic background to the page background across all platforms and all browsers. Find another solution besides an exact match of stripes.

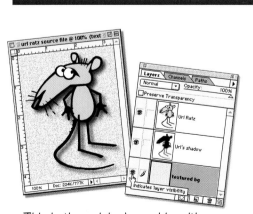

This is the original graphic with the web page texture applied.

This is the GIF placed on the web page with the background.

Make an animated GIF

Simple animations can add interest to a page without adding a lot to the page size. To make animated GIF files, you need to download shareware software such as GIFBuilder for the Mac or GIF Construction Set or GIF Animator for the PC. Find them at www.download.com or www.shareware.com.

Then you have to make the separate graphic files, or frames, that will be composed into the animation sequence. Try to keep animations to a minimum number of frames—animations that have large numbers of frames can be irritatingly slow to download. The final animation file in this example weighs in at 9.8K.

After you make the individual pieces, you'll put them together in the animation software you downloaded. This will make one compact GIF file that you can place on your web page just like any other GIF. When you post your site on the World Wide Web, you'll send this one GIF file along with it. Here's what we did to create an animated GIF of Browser the Net Hound wagging his tail.

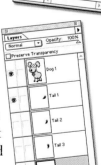

1. Initially we created the art in Adobe Illustrator. Then we opened it in Photoshop with a resolution of 72 ppi. We saved the dog's tail as a separate file so we could place it on its own layer in Photoshop.

2. We duplicated the tail layer two more times so we could rotate it to a different angle on each of its three layers.

3. To serve as a white background when we export different versions of the image as GIF files, we created a layer filled with white and dragged it to the bottom of the stack of layers. We've found we have fewer problems with solid color backgrounds than with transparent ones.

4. We made sure to turn on the visibility of the dog layer, the first tail layer, and the white background layer (click on the boxes to the left of the layers so the eyeball icons appear), and we turned off the visibility of the other layers.

   Then we exported those three layers as one GIF89a file (see pages 198–199).

   Do not check the "Interlaced" checkbox. The animation file, once loaded, will play so quickly that interlacing won't be noticeable.

So this is what the first exported file looks like. Notice the position of Browser's tail here and in the other two GIFs.

5. Next, we turned off the visibility of the "Tail 1" layer and turned on the "Tail 2" layer. We kept the dog and background layers visible and exported this as another GIF89a file.

6. Then we turned off the "Tail 2" layer, turned on the "Tail 3" layer, and exported this combination as a GIF89a file.

Now that we've created the necessary GIF files, we can place the GIFs in an animated GIF application. For this example we used GIFBuilder on the Mac; Construction Set or GIF Animator on the PC operate in a similar fashion.

1. Open GIFBuilder. From the Window menu, select "Frames Window."

2. Again from the Window menu, select "Preview Window."

3. On your Desktop, open the folder that holds the GIF files you just made and position it on the right side of your monitor. Position the Frames window on the left side of your monitor. Drag the newly created GIF files from your folder into the Frames window.

4. From the Options menu, slide down to "Colors" and choose "Best Palette."

5. Again from the Options menu, slide down to "Loop...." From the "Looping" dialog box, set the number of times you want the animation to repeat (loop). "Forever" means the animation will go on forever, which drives people nuts. "No" means it will animate once, then stop. Please enter a number instead of choosing "Forever."

6. In the Frames window, set the amount of delay (how much time each frame should stay on the screen before jumping to the next frame): Double-click on the column of numbers under the "Delay" heading in the window. You'll get the "Interframe delay" dialog box. Choose a delay. You can preview the animation (see step #7), see if you like the delay, then change it if necessary.

7. To preview the animation, pull down the "Animation" menu to "Play." It's cute, huh?

8. Go back to the Frames window and readjust the "Delay" settings if necessary.

9. Save the animation file. Make sure you add ".gif" on the end of the file name. The animation made of three separate GIF files is now one compact file that can be placed on a page just as you place any graphic! You do not need to place any of the separate GIF files that were used to build this one.

wagtail.gif

Below are the same three GIF files placed into Microsoft GIF Animator, which comes with the Bonus Pack of FrontPage. Just drag the GIF files from your folder into the little frames of GIF Animator, set the Duration (Delay) for each frame, and set the number of loops. Click the Preview button. In this example, we added the GIF version "tail2.gif" in the fourth frame, as well as the second frame, to smooth the transition of the tail wagging.

When you are happy with the preview, save the file.

wagtail.gif

wagtail.gif

Put the composite animated GIF in your web site folder, then drag it onto the web page. You won't see it animate until you go into Preview mode.

Typography on the Web

Frankly, typography on the web is a mess. There are so many variables as to how the type can appear, and so many limitations to what we can do. There are certain basic typographic rules web designers should adhere to and we should be as intelligent and thoughtful as possible in presenting type on web pages, but we can only go so far on our end.

If the type on your screen looks particularly terrible when *you're* surfing the World Wide Web, it might be your own fault. Is most of the type too small? Blurry? Chunky? Letters bumping into each other? Many of these things can be fixed on the user's end, and as you fix your own screen, you'll get a clue as to the number of variables other users might be fiddling with that will affect the look of the web pages *you* design.

To add to the problems, several different corporations are each competing to create typographic web standards. It will be years before the dust settles (if it ever does), and in the meantime we have to contend with the mess as best as possible.

The web is all about reading information, so our goal is to make reading as easy as possible for the visitor (and for ourselves on our own computers as we browse). In this chapter we'll go over the basics of good typography. We'll discuss the ways we have to adjust the traditional rules to fit this new medium. And we'll talk about the new things coming up that might or might not make everything better and easier.

Readability vs. legibility

First of all, let's get straight about readability and legibility—they are not the same thing. **Readability** refers to how easy it is to read a *lot* of text, extended text, pages and pages of text. In print and in lengthy web pages that are text heavy, a clean serif face is the most readable.

Serif, Readable

Legibility refers to how easy it is to recognize shorts bursts of text, such as headlines, buttons, signs, etc. In print and on the screen, sans serif faces are more legible.

Sans Serif, Legible

Readability

There are a number of guidelines to follow that are guaranteed to make type *more* readable, and a number of factors that make type *less* readable. You don't have total control over the type on a web page, however, so these guidelines are a bit different from the time-tested rules of printed material. Be sure to read the following pages regarding the default font and type size built into browsers so you understand what you can and can't control. Of the things you can control, follow these guidelines:

- Generally, use a serif typeface for extended text. On the screen, however, sans serif type can actually be easier to read in shorter amounts of text, such as a couple of paragraphs, or paragraphs that are separated by graphics. This is only a concern if you are choosing to force a typeface to override the visitor's browser default, or if you are setting paragraphs of text as graphics. Otherwise, let the visitor set their own default—they will choose the face they feel most comfortable with.

- Not too big (not above 14 point).

- Not too small (not below 10 point).

- Never set large amounts of text in bold, italic, caps, small caps, script, etc. Small amounts of these are okay when necessary.

- Avoid very long lines of text—never let your text spread out across the entire browser window. Long lines make it difficult for the reader's eye to find the beginning of the next line, especially on a screen. Keep your type in columns, or at least block indents, rather than flowing across the page.

- On the screen, shorter lines are better than longer lines, but avoid very short lines of text. We read *groups* of words, not one word at a time, so very short lines break up the thought patterns too much.

- Make sure there is enough contrast between the type and the background. Black text on a white background is best; other combinations can work if there is enough contrast. Never set red text on a bright yellow background, or dark blue on black, or orange on pink, etc.

Legibility

As with the concept of readability, there are general guidelines that make type more or less legible. These guidelines apply to short bursts of text, remember, such as the text in buttons, lists, signs, etc.

- Generally, use a sans serif typeface.
- Avoid typefaces like **Antique Olive**, where the ascenders (the parts of the letters that rise above the body of the lowercase, such as the tops of the d, f, or h) are hardly bigger than the bodies. That feature makes it difficult to tell "**h**" from "**n**" or "**i**" from "**l**." **Avoid faces like Hobo, that have no descenders in p, j, q, or other letters that should have them.** Avoid faces like Peignot, which mix capital and lowercase letters together. All of these kinds of things make words less legible because you have to spend extra time figuring them out. Save those faces for very special occasions, and compensate for their inherent lack of legibility.
- Don't set type in all caps, unless you really need the rectangular look of an all-caps word. All caps are much more difficult to read because every word has the same rectangular shape. Look at the different shapes of the words **cat** and **dog**. We recognize those shapes when we read. But in all caps, **CAT** and **DOG** have the same shape. Be careful.
- Use the techniques on page 232 to make small text easier to read.

Breaking the rules

As with all rules, you can break them with glee. But you have to know the rules before you can break them, and then have a clear, conscious reason—in words—why you are breaking the rule and why it is okay in that case. Do it consciously and thoughtfully. Make up for it. For instance, reverse type (light type on a dark background) makes text appear smaller, but if you really want to use reverse, compensate for it by making the type a little larger and the lines a little shorter. If you really want to set the credits in a small size, don't make them unreadable by also setting them in italic, bold, a silly face, or on a long line.

To create great type on a web site, you must be well grounded in great type in general. We suggest you read *Beyond The Mac is not a typewriter*, by Robin. There are a few Mac keyboard shortcuts included, but everything else applies to any type, regardless of the computer platform. Also read *A Blip in the Continuum*, by both of us. It's about breaking the rules with gusto.

Be conscious

If it looks hard to read, it is. If your page needs the designer look of a special typeface that isn't perfectly readable or legible, go ahead and use it. Just follow the guidelines to compensate for the reduced readability as much as possible. Be sensible. Don't push it so far that people will get annoyed or not spend the time to read it. Critique other pages for readability and legibility. Notice what works and what doesn't, and why.

Good, clean type (right) in a column that is not too long and not too short makes easy and pleasant reading. About eight to ten words per line seems to be a good setting for on-screen reading.

If you really need small type, consider specifying Arial or Geneva (both sans serif) for easier on-screen reading.

This week:
Driving in Europe.

If you really like driving, you'll like driving in Europe.

Much is made of the American love affair with the car but I think that's mistaking dependency for love. Americans count on the independence and flexibility a car gives them. Many do, indeed, dote on the automobile itself, but to appreciate true car love one must be, for instance, in Italy during the running of the Mille Miglia. Now that's a love affair with the automobile.

There are Europeans, of course, who look upon their cars as household appliances on a long tether as most Americans do. However, after many years of observation and thousands of miles of driving in Europe and the US, I've concluded that more Europeans than Americans looks upon driving as a sport.

If you are of like mind, and you've planned a European trip then look forward to your time at the wheel on the Continent and in Great Britain.

Santa Fe Stages, The International Theatre Festival is the place to be this summer! Two World Premieres and four U.S. Premieres highlight our summer season. Stages is challenging the traditional performing arts scene by demanding the impossible and delivering the unexpected.

Drive She Said
A syndicated newspaper column by Denise McCluggage.

In this web site a sans serif font was specified for the headlines (as in "Drive She Said"), since headlines need to be read easily and quickly—visitors often scan the heads to see if they want to read the article. To scan quickly and easily, the type needs to be as legible as possible, so a sans serif face is a good choice. The sans serif face also makes a good design contrast with the serif body copy.

Watch for examples of where other designers have broken the "guidelines" of perfect readability and legibility. Put into words why the design looks good and why it's still readable and/or legible. Is it the size, contrast, color, length, limited number of words, alignment, or what?

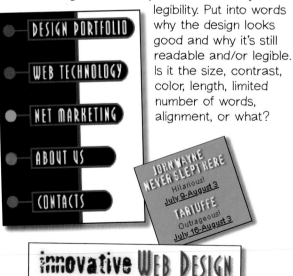

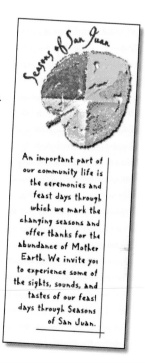

An important part of our community life is the ceremonies and feast days through which we mark the changing seasons and offer thanks for the abundance of Mother Earth. We invite you to experience some of the sights, sounds, and tastes of our feast days through Seasons of San Juan.

Quotation marks!

You've probably heard that it's impossible to use real quotation marks and apostrophes on the web and that you should just get used to seeing and using typewriter quote marks. That's not quite true. You *can* set real quotes and apostrophes—it just takes a little extra time. Instead of "typewriter quotes," you can set "curly, professional quotes." You have to edit the HTML code, but it's really easy: you simply replace the existing quote mark or apostrophe with the correct code from the chart below. Some web authoring software and most HTML editors can search-and-replace, which would obviously make this process faster than doing it manually. You might not want to spend the time to do this to all of your body copy, but definitely use real quotes and apostrophes in your headlines. Please.

opening single quote	'	*&*#145;
closing single quote, apostrophe	'	*&*#146;
opening double quote	"	*&*#147;
closing double quote	"	*&*#148;

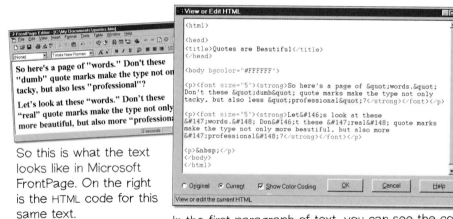

So this is what the text looks like in Microsoft FrontPage. On the right is the HTML code for this same text.

In the first paragraph of text, you can see the code for the typewriter quotes (") and you can see the apostrophes ('). We replaced each of these with the appropriate code from the chart above.

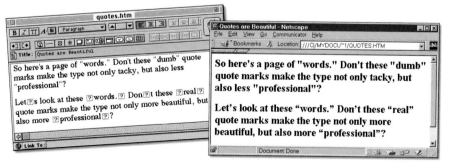

Some web authoring software, such as Adobe PageMill, won't display the quotes while you create the page. As you can see on the left, the quotes appear as question marks—each of the question marks stands for HTML code that PageMill doesn't understand. But the page will look fine in the browser, as shown on the right.

Default fonts and sizes

Every browser has a default type and size set in it when you install the browser on your computer. The default is usually 12 point Times, but you can change it to anything you prefer. Before we talk about changing the default, let's talk about how that default affects the text on web pages.

When you create the text for a web page in your web authoring software, you have the following three general options. How each of these options appears on a user's monitor is relative to the default font and size set in their browser. You cannot depend on the type looking the same on anyone else's computer as it does on yours.

1. You can set the text in the "Paragraph" or "Normal" style. (This applies a size to the *entire paragraph*.)

   Whatever is set as "Paragraph" or "Normal" will appear on someone else's computer in their browser's default size and font.

2. You can apply a "Heading," labeled either 1 through 6, or Largest to Smallest. Each heading appears in the browser's default font. (The heading style applies to the *entire paragraph*.)

   The heading size will appear on a web page in relation to the default browser size. If the browser default is larger than 12, then headings 1, 2, and 3 will be relatively larger than 12, and headings 5 and 6 will be relatively smaller (heading 4 is the same as the default size).

3. You can select certain characters and apply something like +1 or -2, or perhaps you click a button that makes the selected text larger or smaller. (This applies only to the *selected characters,* not to the entire paragraph.)

   The selected text will display several point sizes smaller or larger than the default browser point size.

Most of the time when you see fancy text on a web page, that text is a graphic. Making text a graphic is the only way you can guarantee that the visitor sees the font and size you want.

Bottom line: let go of total control

There is no way for you to know what the defaults are in someone's browser. It is possible for you, as a web page designer, to specify certain fonts and point sizes and those specifications will usually override the user's defaults (see page 245), but don't overdo it. Accept the limitations of the World Wide Web and let go of total control. Don't create designs that are dependent on text being a certain font, size, or in a certain place. Don't tell the visitor how to set their defaults—maybe they like their defaults the way they are. It's not their problem to make their system match your ideal—it's your problem to work around the variables.

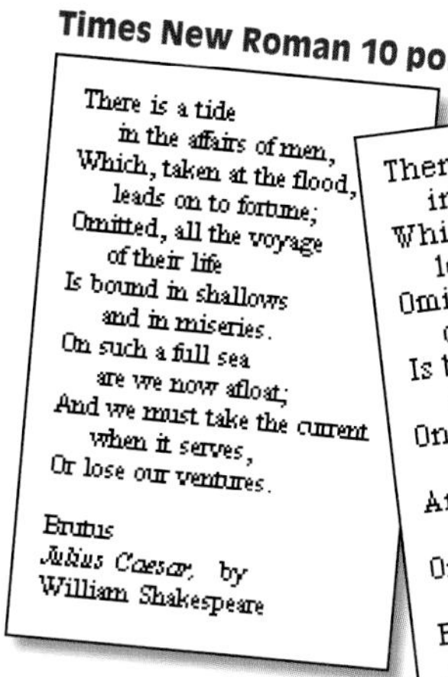

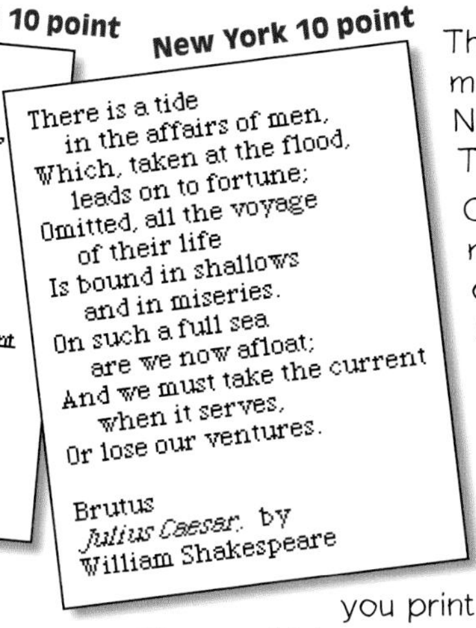

Times New Roman 10 point

There is a tide
in the affairs of men,
Which, taken at the flood,
leads on to fortune;
Omitted, all the voyage
of their life
Is bound in shallows
and in miseries.
On such a full sea
are we now afloat;
And we must take the current
when it serves,
Or lose our ventures.

Brutus
Julius Caesar, by
William Shakespeare

New York 10 point

There is a tide
in the affairs of men,
Which, taken at the flood,
leads on to fortune;
Omitted, all the voyage
of their life
Is bound in shallows
and in miseries.
On such a full sea
are we now afloat;
And we must take the current
when it serves,
Or lose our ventures.

Brutus
Julius Caesar, by
William Shakespeare

The standard default on most browsers is Times New Roman (PC) or Times (Macintosh).

On a Mac, New York is much more readable and legible on-screen than Times because New York was originally created specifically for the resolution of the screen. We suggest you try changing your default from Times to New York. But before you print a page, change it back to Times, which was created specifically for printing.

Arial (PC) and Helvetica (Mac) are the two sans serif typefaces that are almost always installed on computers.

On a Mac, Geneva is much more readable on the screen, for the same reason New York is more readable than Times. If you specify a sans serif to override a visitor's default, please specify Geneva for Mac users.

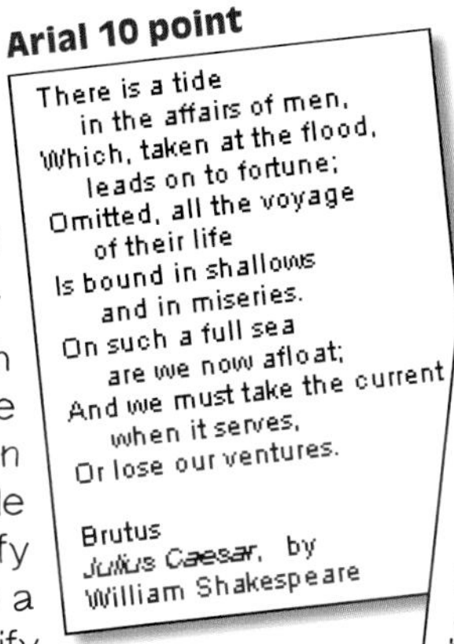

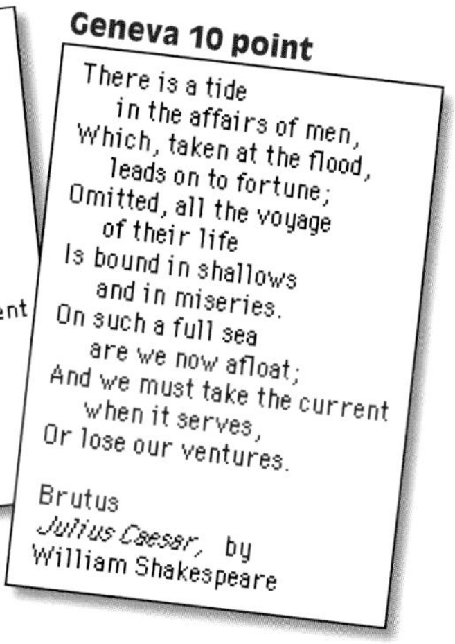

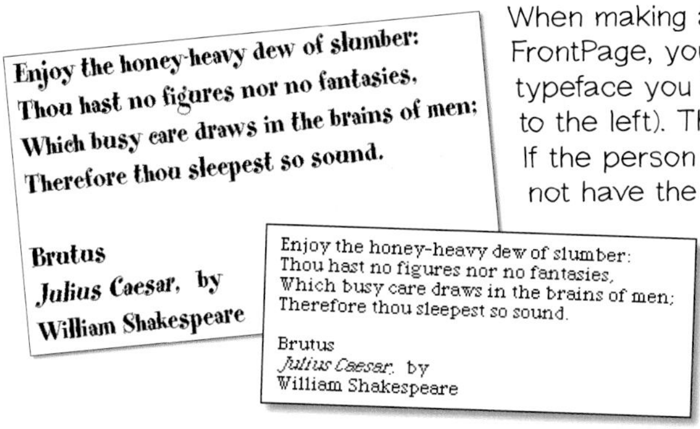

Arial 10 point

There is a tide
in the affairs of men,
Which, taken at the flood,
leads on to fortune;
Omitted, all the voyage
of their life
Is bound in shallows
and in miseries.
On such a full sea
are we now afloat;
And we must take the current
when it serves,
Or lose our ventures.

Brutus
Julius Caesar, by
William Shakespeare

Geneva 10 point

There is a tide
in the affairs of men,
Which, taken at the flood,
leads on to fortune;
Omitted, all the voyage
of their life
Is bound in shallows
and in miseries.
On such a full sea
are we now afloat;
And we must take the current
when it serves,
Or lose our ventures.

Brutus
Julius Caesar, by
William Shakespeare

Enjoy the honey-heavy dew of slumber:
Thou hast no figures nor no fantasies,
Which busy care draws in the brains of men;
Therefore thou sleepest so sound.

Brutus
Julius Caesar, by
William Shakespeare

Enjoy the honey-heavy dew of slumber:
Thou hast no figures nor no fantasies,
Which busy care draws in the brains of men;
Therefore thou sleepest so sound.

Brutus
Julius Caesar, by
William Shakespeare

When making a web page in Microsoft FrontPage, you can choose any typeface you have installed (as shown to the left). This is a serious delusion. If the person viewing the page does not have the exact typeface installed that you chose when you made the web page, your fancy text turns into their default face (as shown to the left).

The variables

One of the most difficult aspects of web design is the number of variables that influence how the type appears on a user's monitor. One or all of these factors can make the type on the web page you design appear ten different ways on ten different computers. These are the variables.

- **The browser's default font:** When you download and install a browser, it opens with a default typeface already set. Every user can change their own default.

- **The browser's default font size** (if it has one), or the "Enlarge text" and "Reduce text" command or button: Netscape allows you to set the point size that you want the default text to display in, plus you can enlarge or reduce type from the View menu. Internet Explorer has a button to make the default text larger or smaller on every page.

- **The resolution of the monitor:** The monitor resolution you choose will make everything on your entire screen, including type, larger or smaller. See pages 164–165 for details on monitor resolution (which is very different from printer resolution!).

- **In Windows 95, the custom font size setting in "Display":** This setting also changes the size of everything else on your screen. (Since we like to keep the monitor resolution at 1024 x 768 on our PC, we find that the type setting of 125 percent makes the text much more readable on web pages, as well as on the screen in general.)

- **The font specified in the HTML file by the web designer:** Many designers specify a font in the HTML code; this generally overrides the default. See page 245 on how to specify a font and size.

- **The font size specified in the HTML file by the web designer:** Many designers specify a larger (or sometimes smaller) font size for selected text, especially for headings or to make the first word in a paragraph stand out. This size is relative to the default size.

In Internet Explorer, you can set a default font for browsing. From the View menu, choose "Options." Click the "General" tab if it's not already showing. At the bottom right, click the button "Font Settings...." Then choose a font from this dialog box.

To change the default font size, click the "A" button on the browser tool bar (shown below). It will cycle you through five sizes.

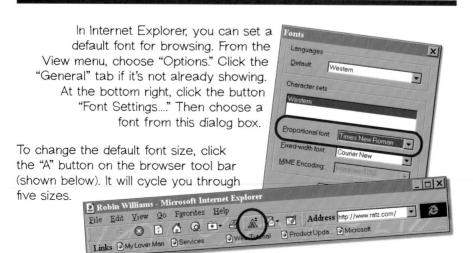

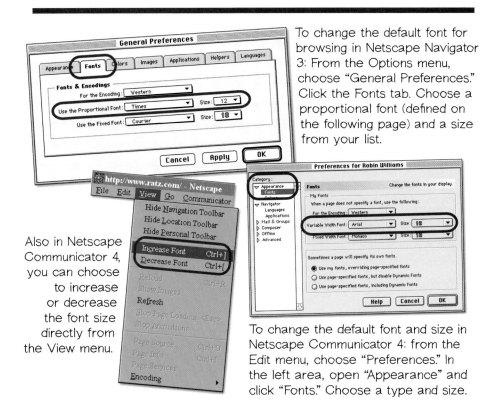

To change the default font for browsing in Netscape Navigator 3: From the Options menu, choose "General Preferences." Click the Fonts tab. Choose a proportional font (defined on the following page) and a size from your list.

Also in Netscape Communicator 4, you can choose to increase or decrease the font size directly from the View menu.

To change the default font and size in Netscape Communicator 4: from the Edit menu, choose "Preferences." In the left area, open "Appearance" and click "Fonts." Choose a type and size.

The numbers (640 × 480, 1024 × 768, etc.) refer to the number of pixels displayed on the monitor, width by depth, and is often called the "resolution." The more pixels, the more you see on your screen, but everything is smaller. The fewer pixels, the less you see on the screen, but everything appears bigger.

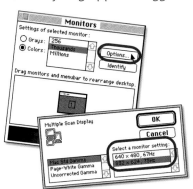

On a **Mac,** you can change the resolution of your monitor from the Monitors Control Panel. Click the "Options..." button, then choose a monitor setting. You do not have to restart if you switch resolutions, so you can experiment easily.

In **Windows 95,** use the Display Control Panel to change the resolution: click the "MGA Settings" tab. Use the "Display area" slider bar. To change the relative size of the type (which changes the size of everything so the new type fits in), click the "Custom..." button. Experiment to find a combination you like best. You may have to reboot.

Other things to know

Here's the scoop on some other type topics we know you will come across.

Proportional vs. monospaced type

You've probably noticed in your browser preferences that you have two font choices to make: one for a **proportional,** or **variable-width,** font, and one for a **monospaced,** or **fixed-width,** font.

In a proportional, variable-width font, each character takes up a "proportionate" amount of space—a capital "W" takes up much more space than a lowercase "i" or a period. Almost everything you read in print is proportional type. *The proportional font you choose in your browser will be your default text.* This paragraph is proportional.

```
In a monospaced, fixed-width font, every character takes
up exactly the same amount of space—a capital "W" takes
up the same amount of space as a period. You can draw
lines through the columns of letters. Courier, Monaco,
and OCR are monospaced typefaces. When a web designer
uses the style "Preformatted" or "Teletype," it appears
in the browser in the chosen monospaced font. This
paragraph is monospaced. duh.
```

Logical vs. physical styles

In your web authoring software, some formatting applies to selected characters, and some applies to entire paragraphs.

Some styles are "physical," and some are "logical." All browsers interpret physical styles the same way; if you choose "Bold," it will appear Bold in every browser. But different browsers might interpret logical styles differently; if you choose "Emphasis," it might be italic in one browser, bold in another, and underline in another. Very few designers use logical styles.

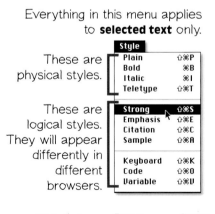

Everything in this menu applies to **selected text** only.

These are physical styles.

These are logical styles. They will appear differently in different browsers.

Everything in this menu applies to the **entire paragraph,** whether you select every character in the paragraph or not.

This is how Adobe PageMill interprets the logical styles.

This is how Netscape interprets the logical styles, using the defaults set for proportional and monospaced fonts.

Other special characters

Besides quotation marks (as we discussed on page 217), you might want to insert other special characters on a web page, such as © or ™.

On a **Mac,** you can enter many of these characters directly on your web page simply by using the same keystrokes you usually use. For instance, to type the © symbol, press Option G. (There is a complete list of the keyboard shortcuts for alternate characters in *The Mac is not a typewriter* and *The Little Mac Book,* both by Robin.) Check to make sure your software converted the symbol to the proper HTML code before you post your page!

Below are a few of the most common special characters you might want. Open the source code for your document and type the sequence for the character directly into the text in the HTML code, as shown in the example on page 217. If you've used DOS or old Windows software, you might recognize these numbers from the standard ANSI character set.

•	&#149;	©	&#169;	¢	&#162;	–	– (en dash)
é	&#233;	™	&#153;	£	&#163;	—	— (em dash)
ñ	&#241;	®	&#174;	¥	&#165;	…	… (ellipsis)

The curse of the underline

In print, it is against the law to underline text. Absolutely forbidden. You will go to jail. The underline is a proofreader's mark that tells the typesetter to set the underlined words in italic; the typesetter removes the underline in the process. Underlining italic text is truly redundant.

On web pages, however, we are accustomed to seeing links underlined. So on web pages, the underline has become very important. If you take away that visual clue, we have to manually slide our cursor over every piece of colored text to see if it is a link or merely a different color. Some designers advocate always turning off the underline, but we feel the clue is important to the clear communication of what is happening on the page.

Features of TrueType & OpenType
Learn about the features of TrueType including hinting, font smoothing, embedding and multilanguage support.

Developer information
Includes articles and specifications for those developing TrueType, OpenType and applications that use fonts.

Links and contacts
Constantly updated, this section now includes over 300 links to type and typography related sites on the Web.

In the example to the left (from Microsoft's typography page), breaking the rules doesn't work. How many links do you see? There are actually eight links, but it's not clear whether the colored text indicates links or simply special words that the designer wants to highlight. Go for clear communication.

In the works

These are several of the new typographic features of web pages that will be appearing soon.

Cascading style sheets

You'll be hearing a lot about cascading style sheets (abbreviated "CSS"). They allow you to define specific parameters, or styles, for text, and with more control. You can embed fonts and set the spacing, leading, margins, colors, and other details. This information is stored in an outside file, and the designer can call on it and apply that style to other pages or to specific sections of text. The "cascading" part means you can create a series of style sheets, and the appropriate one will automatically be used. You might create a style sheet based on the visitor using a fast connection, large monitor, and lots of colors, and other style sheets for successively lower-end use. The style sheet, browser, and server determine what the visitor is using and the style sheet cascades down through its list to find the one appropriate to that visitor. This allows every visitor to see the site at its best. For details on cascading style sheets and how to create them, visit www.w3.org/Style or www.w3.org/TR/WD-css1.

TrueDoc and Dynamic Fonts

Netscape and Bitstream have joined forces to offer a new font choice, Dynamic Fonts, based on Bitstream's TrueDoc technology. Dynamic Fonts only display in Netscape Communicator 4.0 and later. You need to use "TrueDoc-enabled" web authoring software to create your web pages, and the server who hosts your site must declare a TrueDoc PFR MIME type (you don't need to know what that means—that's their job). None of these things is a big obstacle. Dynamic Fonts can be used in cascading style sheets, and if a user doesn't have the latest browser, the fonts will revert to the user's defaults. For more information and to see the fonts in use (if you have Netscape 4), check the Bitstream site at www.bitstream.com.

> Bitstream Chianti Extra Bold in a Headline *
> *Bitstream Cataneo in a Headline* *
> Typical Typeface in an H2 Head
> * if viewed in Netscape Communicator PR4 (and later)

OpenType

Microsoft and Adobe have joined forces to create a new font file format, OpenType, which includes font embedding—building the fonts right into the web page. For details, see www.adobe.com/type/opentype.html.

Free fonts for web pages

Microsoft offers a number of **free fonts** on their web site. It seems that the goal is to eventually flood the world with these free fonts and everyone will use them on every web site. Feel free to download the typefaces and use them, but keep in mind that a significant portion of the world sees Microsoft as the Dark Side and will never own those fonts. If you insist on using them, make sure your site looks just as good to those visitors who do not use Microsoft typefaces. Find the free fonts at www.microsoft.com.

Self-Guided Tour of the World Wide Web

With new thoughts in your mind, take a closer look at the typography on the World Wide Web:

☐ Find a page where the text bumps up against the left edge. Do you find your eye bumping into that edge every time you go back to the next sentence?

☐ Find a page that is set in all caps. Read it, pretending you didn't notice it was all caps. Did you read all the way through? Or did something make you not continue? Did you notice how you have to work harder to read lots of all-cap text?

☐ Experiment with the default font in your browser. Find a font and size you feel most comfortable with.

☐ With your default set, keep an eye out for a page where the designer has specified the font to be smaller than your default. What do you think?

☐ Change the resolution on your monitor and notice how it affects the size of the type on web pages. Remember as you design that many people have their monitors set at a smaller resolution so they can see more on the screen (but everything is smaller) or larger resolution so everything is bigger (but they see less at one time).

☐ Keep an eye open for a web site where you think the designer has broken the standard rules of typography, yet the site "works"—it's clear, you know what is going on, the type contrasts help structure the hierarchy of information, you can read it, it even looks good. Put two things into words: 1) What "rules" were broken, and 2) Exactly what is it that makes the typography still work? Spacing? Line lengths? Size? Control of your eye flow (how?)? Typeface design? If you can put it into words, you gain the power to incorporate the discoveries into your own work.

Oh boy, it's a Quiz!

Go through this list and decide whether the concept suggested should *never* be applied, or can perhaps be applied *sometimes.* "Never" means just that—it is not an option. "Sometimes" means you can sometimes get away with it, but you must be conscious; you'll probably have to compensate for the technique in some way, but the design effect can be worth it. If you choose "Sometimes," explain what you would do to make the suggested effect most readable or legible.

Never **Sometimes**

☐ ☐ **1.** Choose any old typeface on your hard disk and set really cool default headlines (not graphic ones) with it.

☐ ☐ **2.** Let the text stretch the entire width of the web page.

☐ ☐ **3.** SET LOTS OF TEXT IN ALL CAPS SO PEOPLE WILL BE SURE TO SEE IT.

☐ ☐ **4.** Put red text on an orange background because the subtle yet "dazzling" color combination looks artsy.

☐ ☐ **5.** Make the type really large so people won't miss it.

☐ ☐ **6.** In the code, specify that none of the links should be underlined.

☐ ☐ **7.** Make the main text smaller than the visitor's default so it will look really small and trendy.

☐ ☐ **8.** Use a busy background even if the type can't be read because it is more important for visitors to see that you know how to make cool backgrounds.

☐ ☐ **9.** Use italic on the entire web page because it is pretty and gives an extra flair.

☐ ☐ **10.** Use really grungy typefaces, not only in your buttons and graphic headlines, but throughout the entire text because who cares if people read it or not—you're going for a "look" on this site.

☐ ☐ **11.** Make some text very, very small, but set it in all caps to compensate for the small size.

Advanced Tips & Tricks

Don't feel like you have to already be an advanced sort of web creator to read this section—the "Advanced" label just means that what you will be doing in this section puts you into the Advanced category.

Nothing in this section is difficult or even tricky. These are just tips and techniques to make your graphics look better and act better, and to make some interesting and useful things happen on your web pages. Most of the techniques are ones we use in Photoshop, although you can use the same concepts in several other applications. We do assume you have a basic, working knowledge of your software. If you are new to Photoshop, we recommend *Photoshop: Visual QuickStart Guide,* by Elaine Weinmann and Peter Lourekas, published by Peachpit Press. It's available for Photoshop versions 3 and 4, and for Macintosh or Windows. They'll get you up and running very quickly so you can take advantage of these advanced tips.

Fun with tables

Tables can do a lot more than just put your text in columns. Here are several examples. Also check out pages 236–237 about slicing graphics into pieces and putting the separate pieces into different cells of a table for more layout options.

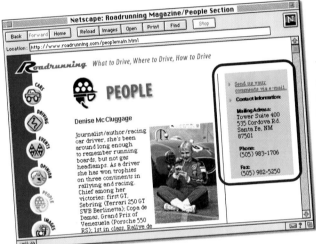

This simple table with a colored background makes a perfect sidebar. This is actually a small table within a cell of the larger table that fills the page.

Below are variations of tables used as sidebars. Each separate color is a separate cell in the table.

This table has a graphic in the top and bottom cells.

This is a one-cell table set within a one-cell table. The inner table has a border of 1.

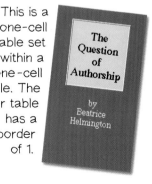

Instead of turning the borders on, this table uses varying cell colors and a little cell spacing to separate items.

This is also a one-cell table set within a one-cell table. The outer table has been moved in close to the inner table, so it appears as simply a border. If visitors change the size of the text in their browsers, the tables expand together automatically to fit the text.

Typographic Tip: Notice this example has more space between the lines. We forced this extra linespace by applying a larger size type to several spaces between words on each line. The larger size is least obtrusive if you select spaces after commas or periods.

This might look like an image map, but it is actually a collection of individual graphics. Each graphic is placed in a cell of the table. Links are applied as usual.

Read the text in this screen shot to see how this table arrangement was made. You probably won't see the wrapped text in your web authoring software (as shown below, middle), but it will appear correctly in the browser (left). Most software lets you add extra code (as shown below, right) to make special things like this happen.

For an explanation of the code, see pages 245-247.

Richer color

When preparing photographs as JPEGs, don't be timid about enhancing the image. In Photoshop you can use several techniques to enhance the color of images.

Most scanned images respond well to increasing the **saturation,** which refers to the strength or purity of the colors. Overdoing this technique can have some pretty bizarre effects, so use some restraint.

1. From the "Image" menu, pull down to "Adjust," and from the submenu select "Hue/Saturation...."

2. Move the Saturation slider in the "Hue/Saturation" dialog box to the right until the image looks the way you want it to.

Also experiment with making a **duplicate layer** to see how the two layers affect each other. To make another copy of the same layer, select the layer and from the Layers palette menu (**a**), select "Duplicate Layer."

1. Select the top layer.

2. From the Layers palette, click on the Mode pull-down menu (**b**) and select "Multiply."

3. If the effect is too strong, move the opacity slider (**c**) at the top of the Layers palette to the left.

Most photographs will look clearer with some **sharpening,** although keep in mind that sharper images are also slightly larger files.

1. From the Filter menu, slide down to "Sharpen...," then to "Unsharp Mask...."

2. Experiment with the "Amount" and "Radius" sliders until you have the look you want. Press on the preview image to see the before-and-after change.

Pre-load graphics

How would you like to have a large image load onto a page really fast? You can do it by **pre-loading** the graphic on another page. You put the graphic on an early page, resize it really small, and it loads while the visitor is reading. The visitor doesn't even know it's there. The browser puts the image in its cache (browsers just do that automatically). When the visitor gets to the page with the large image, it appears very fast because the browser is not downloading it at that minute, but simply bringing it up from its cache. This is how to do it:

1. On one of the first pages of your site, create some interesting content that will hold the reader there for a minute or so.

2. On that same page, place the large graphic that you want to appear fast. We know, you really want that graphic on another page.

3. In the HTML code, resize the graphic to 1 pixel wide by 1 pixel high: Find the `<img src>` code for the graphic. It will look like this:

   `<img src="webwork.gif">`

   Add size code directly after that img src info, so it looks like this:

   `<img src="webwork.gif" width="1" height="1">`

   This resized version (1 pixel by 1 pixel) of the image is barely visible, but it does show up as a dot on the page. Place the tiny image at the bottom of the page, several scrolling clicks beyond the content area of the page and no one will realize its there.

4. While this early page is being read, the image is being loaded onto the visitor's hard drive. As soon as the visitor goes to the page with the full-sized version of the graphic, the graphic appears instantly.

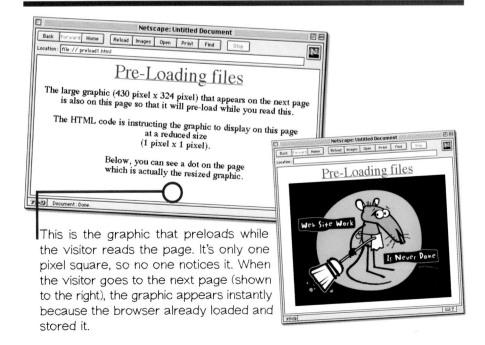

This is the graphic that preloads while the visitor reads the page. It's only one pixel square, so no one notices it. When the visitor goes to the next page (shown to the right), the graphic appears instantly because the browser already loaded and stored it.

Easier-to-read small type

It's easy to set large type such as headlines and subheads in custom fonts and turn them into good-looking graphics. But **very small type** sometimes gets so soft and fuzzy from the anti-aliasing process that it's difficult to read and looks really bad.

Sometimes you can work wonders on a graphic with small type like this by creating **duplicate layers** of it in Photoshop.

1. Make a copy of the type layer by dragging it on top of the "New Layer" icon (the page symbol) at the bottom of the Layers palette.

2. Now, with one layer positioned on top of the other, the type seems twice as opaque. Before you export this graphic as a GIF file, be sure the visibility of both layers is turned on (the eye icon is showing).

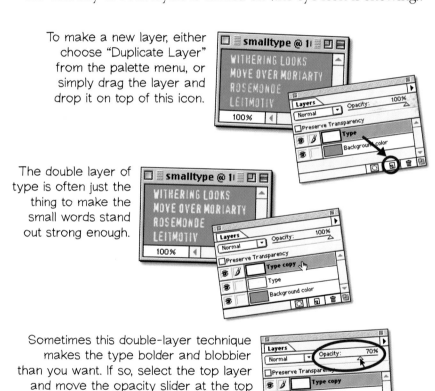

To make a new layer, either choose "Duplicate Layer" from the palette menu, or simply drag the layer and drop it on top of this icon.

The double layer of type is often just the thing to make the small words stand out strong enough.

Sometimes this double-layer technique makes the type bolder and blobbier than you want. If so, select the top layer and move the opacity slider at the top of the Layers palette to a lower percentage until the type looks lighter.

Sometimes you need to make **even smaller type as a graphic.** The same anti-aliasing that makes large graphics and type look so nice can make small type look like mush. You can solve this problem by turning off the anti-aliasing feature when you set the type. On a Macintosh, you can go one step further toward legible type and choose a city-named font that was originally designed for the lower resolution of the monitor—a font like New York, Geneva, or Monaco. You may still want to use the technique on the previous page to beef up the type.

The anti-aliasing makes this type too fuzzy to read.

Don't anti-alias the type. And on a Mac, choose a font with a city name.

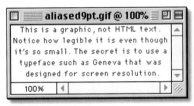

This screen shot above shows how legible small type as a graphic can be.

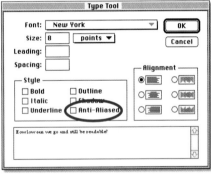

In Photoshop, uncheck the "Anti-Aliased" checkbox.

As a last resort (it can be time consuming), **manually retouch** the letterforms.

1. Enlarge the image to at least 200 percent.

2. Use the pencil tool to manually retouch the areas of type that have turned to mush. Be careful, though, because too much retouching can look worse than none. Keep checking to see how it looks at the smaller size.

When you retouch, choose "New View" from the View menu. This gives you a duplicate version in a separate window so you can see how the changes look at actual size as you make the changes in the enlarged view.

Low-source proxy

If you need to have a large graphic on a page that will take a while to download, you can make a quick-loading, **low-quality** image load first, then let your **higher-quality,** slow-loading image come in on top of it. This lets people see what is coming and make a decision whether to stay or not, instead of instantly leaving because of the wait. (Unfortunately, Internet Explorer ignores the low-source proxy. Use Netscape.)

The HTML code instructs the browser to display an image by calling upon one *source.* The code looks like this: `<img src="car.jpg">`, where "car.jpg" is the source.

But an image can have *two* sources. If the code calls for an additional source and refers to it as *lowsrc,* that image will load first. Typically, the low source image is lower quality and contains fewer colors, which is what makes it load quickly. Sometimes you may want to use this low source technique more for effect than for practical reasons. Here's how we did it:

1. For a "high source" image, we saved a copy of the original Photoshop file as a medium-quality JPEG file and named it "carhi.jpg."

This is the JPEG image. We made all of the images from *copies* of the original high-resolution file.

2. On another *copy* of the original Photoshop file, we first converted the image to Grayscale mode, then to Bitmap mode.

3. In the Bitmap dialog box, we set the "Output Resolution" to 72 ppi and set the "Method" to "Diffusion Dither." This method isn't the only one you can use, but it does create a nice mezzotint effect.

4. Return to the Mode selections (under "Image") and choose "Grayscale."

Return once again to the Mode selections and choose "RGB Color."

5. Finally, export the image as a GIF89a file with 2 colors (as explained on page 198).

6. Now we can manually change the source part of the code so that it looks like this:

```
<img src="carhi.jpg" lowsrc="carlow.gif">
```

The low-source will automatically appear first. The high-source will load right over the top of the low-source, giving the viewer a treat instead of the pain of a slow-loading image.

This is how the page looks as the high-source image is loading on top of the low-source image.

Variations on a theme

The low-source image doesn't have to be black and white, nor does it even have to be the same picture as the high-source image. Here are a couple of other files we could use for the low-source image.

Instead of converting the original file into a Bitmap with Diffusion Dithering, we chose Image, Adjust, Posterize... and in the Posterize dialog box we chose 5 levels.

In this example, the low-source image is a totally different graphic from the high-source image. The low-source was saved as a GIF file, and the high-source is a JPEG. Again, the high-source image loads over the low-source image.

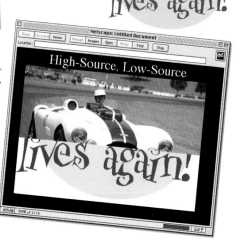

Splitting files into pieces

Why would you want to split a perfectly good JPEG or GIF into two or more separate pieces? Just two reasons (if you don't count "because it's fun"). First, some animated GIFs can be split into sections so that only a small portion of the file requires animation; this keeps the file size so much smaller, which means it will download so much faster. Second, splitting a graphic into sections can create additional layout and design options.

Splitting a GIF file for animation

In this example, the client wanted to animate his logo by having a shooting star move across the sky. We wanted the graphic to be fairly large, but an animated GIF this big would be much too slow to download because each frame of the anima-tion would be as large as the entire graphic. A solution was to split the file into sections and animate only the area that required movement. Then we placed the separate pieces into the cells of a table to hold them seamlessly together.

1. We opened the original illustration file in Photoshop at the desired size and resolution.

2. We created a new Photoshop layer for each frame of animation (see "Make an animated GIF" on pages 210–212).

3. We set the "Airbrush Options" dialog box to "Dissolve." In each frame, we used the airbrush tool to paint the star's trail.

4. With all of the layers visible (so we can see which parts of the file to separate), we dragged guidelines across the image to mark the places where we will cut it apart.

   At this point we saved the file so later we'll have the guidelines in exactly the same place.

5. We made a copy of every section that was to be cropped and turned into a separate file. This graphic was being split into four sections—three smaller pieces across the top, and one bigger piece across the bottom. So we made three copies of it (from the "File" menu, select "Save a Copy…"). So now we had four identical files, counting our original one.

6. We cropped in on a different section of each file, according to the guidelines, and saved each file as "section1," "section2," etc., so we'd know what they were later. We turned on "Snap To Guides" under the "View" menu to ensure perfect alignment later.

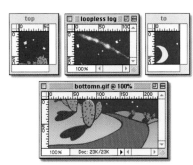

7. Three of the sections will not be animated (the top left, top right, and bottom), so we flattened those and exported them as GIF89a files.

8. In the remaining file (the top middle section), we made each layer visible, one at a time, and exported each individual frame of the animation as a GIF89a file. Now we had four separate GIFs, each one showing the star in a different position.

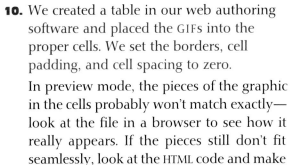

9. We placed these four GIFs into GIFBuilder to create one animated GIF file.

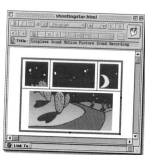

10. We created a table in our web authoring software and placed the GIFs into the proper cells. We set the borders, cell padding, and cell spacing to zero.

In preview mode, the pieces of the graphic in the cells probably won't match exactly— look at the file in a browser to see how it really appears. If the pieces still don't fit seamlessly, look at the HTML code and make sure the sizes of the table cells are identical to the sizes of the GIF files within them. If not, change the table cell sizes to match the GIF file sizes. Then view the file in a browser and the table should be holding the pieces of the file together seamlessly.

On the left is the split graphic as displayed in the web authoring software. On the right is the same graphic in the browser window.

Splitting a graphic for layout freedom

Sometimes splitting a graphic into pieces and reassembling the pieces in a table can give you great freedom in layout and design, as shown here.

Web pages usually have photos, headlines, and text that each occupy their own unique space. But in this case we want to create the illusion that our headline is part of the photo and that it's breaking out of the graphics space into the white space of the page. Ordinarily the entire graphic is a rectangle, and we wouldn't be able to tuck regular text underneath a graphic headline like this.

1. We set the main headline on a curve in Adobe Illustrator, saved it, then opened that file in Photoshop on its own layer. We set the subhead on its own layer. Placing the subhead in this file helped us determine how wide we would have to make the table later (as shown below). The subhead layer was exported as a GIF.

2. We placed guidelines where we wanted to split the file. With "Snap To Guides" chosen under the "View" menu, we selected the upper left section of the file with the marquee tool, cropped and exported it as a JPEG file. We reopened the original file, then cropped and saved the other sections in the same manner.

3. On the web page, we created a two–column, two–row table and placed the three JPEG files into the appropriate cells. In the fourth cell we added the GIF subhead file and typed the body text. We set the table border, cell padding, and cell spacing values to 0 (zero).

4. If you place graphics in table cells that are larger than the graphics, make sure the alignment commands (left, right, top, bottom, middle, center) for each cell are set appropriately to push the graphic files towards each other.

5. We prefer to make the table cell sizes the exact sizes of the graphic files. Once the graphics are in the table, we check the HTML code to make sure the cell dimensions are the same as the graphic dimensions. If not, the pieces of the split file will not align seamlessly in the browser.

```
<TD width="43%"><IMG SRC="upperleft.jpg" width="248">
```

This HTML code shows you the parts of the code that should match— find the width of the graphic, and replace the cell (TD) width with the exact width of the graphic. Remove the percent symbol, if there is one:

```
<TD width="248"><IMG SRC="upperleft.jpg" width="248">
```

Quick Photoshop tips for web designers

Even if you use Photoshop everyday, you never stop finding new tips and tricks that make you wonder how you survived without them. Here are a few of the techniques we use most often. There are many more key commands and techniques available in Photoshop than the few we mention here, but these are our favorites. Some are keyboard shortcuts, some are options for working, and some are techniques we use in creating graphics.

Keyboard shortcuts

Guidelines
Press **Command ;** (Mac) or **Control ;** (Windows) to show or hide guidelines.

Show the Layers palette
Press the **F7** key to show or hide the Layers palette.

Show the Brushes palette
Press the **F5** key to show or hide the Brushes palette.

Pick a smaller brush
Press **[** (left bracket) to choose the next smallest brush than the one you are using. Press **Shift [** to pick the smallest brush in the palette.

Pick a larger brush
Press **]** (right bracket) to choose the next largest brush than the one you are using. Press **Shift]** to choose the largest brush in the palette.

Show or hide all palettes
If you want to clear all palettes out of the way so you can see your image better, press the **Tab** key to hide or show all of the open palettes.

Hide all palettes except the Tools palette
Even more useful than hiding all palettes is being able to hide all palettes except for the Tools palette. In Photoshop 4 only, press **Shift Tab.**

Update the font menu on the fly
If you've used your font management software to open new fonts while Photoshop is open, you won't see the new fonts in the menu. But if you select the Type tool, then hold the **Shift** key down and click, your font menu will be updated (Photoshop 4 only).

Select tools with letter keys
You can select the various tools by typing a letter. This is really handy. (The shortcuts in parentheses are ones that are different in Photoshop 3.)

Marquee	**M**	Magic **W**and	**W**	**B**rush	**B**	**H**and	**H**
Lasso	**L**	**A**irbrush	**A**	Pencil	**Y (P)**	**Z**oom	**Z**
Crop	**C**	**E**raser	**E**	**P**en	**P (T)**	Switch colors	**X**
Move	**V**	Rubber **S**tamp	**S**	**T**ype	**T (Y)**	**D**efault colors	**D**
Gradient	**G**	Paint Buc**K**et	**K**	Li**N**e	**N**	Eyedropper	**I**

Fill a selection or layer with color

To fill a selection or a layer with the current *foreground* color:

- Press Option Delete (Mac) or Alt Backspace (Windows).

To fill with the current *background* color:

- Press Command Delete (Mac) or Control Backspace (Windows).

Color the pixels on a layer while preserving the layer's transparency

This technique is particularly useful when you've created anti-aliased type on a layer and then decide to change the color of the type. It's similar to the tip above, but in addition to filling the selection, this also preserves the transparency of the layer and retains the subtle color variations created by the anti-aliasing,

- To color all the pixels on the layer with the current *foreground* color, press Option Shift Delete (Mac) or Alt Shift Backspace (Windows).

- To color the pixels with the current *background* color, press Command Shift Delete (Mac) or Control Shift Backspace (Windows).

 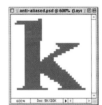 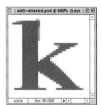 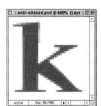

When type is anti-aliased, pixels along the edges are blurred to soften the hard edges and eliminate the "jaggy" effect of pixels.	If you select the type with the Magic Wand and fill the selection with a new color, the results are awful.	If you select the type by choosing "Load Selection" from the "Select" menu and then fill it with a new color, the results are better, but still dreadful.	Instead of selecting anything, just use the tip above and the results are beautiful (on the screen, not in print).

Customizing features

Tool cursor appearance

Photoshop lets you determine how you want your brush tools to appear on the screen. In the General Preferences dialog box, you can choose Standard, Precise, or Brush Size.

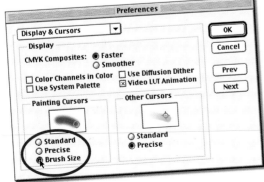

The **Standard** setting displays the Airbrush tool as an airbrush icon, the brush tool as a brush icon, etc.

The **Precise** setting displays the tool as a crosshair, useful for exact placement of the brush.

The **Brush Size** setting is the one we use most often because it indicates how large the brush is before we start spraying pixels everywhere.

Create custom brushes

- Double-click a brush in the Brushes palette to adjust its size and behavior.

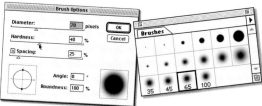

Show the options for a tool

If you're using a tool (the Airbrush, for instance) and you want to change a setting in the Options dialog box (such as the Pressure setting in the Airbrush Options dialog box), you don't have to go all the way over to the tool box to double-click the selected tool.

- Select the tool. Press Return or Enter, and the Options dialog box for the selected tool will appear.

Techniques to help make your work easier

Retouching on transparent layers

When you're painting or airbrushing objects on a layer, sometimes you want to have the brush affect only the pixels that are on the layer and not the surrounding background area.

- Click the "Preserve Transparency" box on the Layers palette. This acts as an instant mask, and whatever you paint or spray will affect only the pixels already on the layer.

Finding the right layer

Sometimes a layered file has so many layers that you can't remember which elements are where. If you haven't named each one with an identifiable name (or even if you have), here is an easy way to select the layer:

- Select the Move tool (you can type V to select it).
- Control-click (Mac) or right-click (Windows) on an element. The layer that contains that element will be selected in the palette.

Resetting values in dialog boxes

When you have a dialog box open and you're experimenting with lots of different settings, you may want to return to the original settings that were there before you went crazy with the sliders. Rather than click the Cancel button, hold down the Option or Alt key and the Cancel button turns into a Reset button—click it to get back to where you started.

Use multiple layers to create navigation buttons

By putting all the variations of the navigation buttons in one Photoshop file, the task of creating many similar buttons is simplified, and it's easy to keep alignments and sizes consistent. When you need to make a change, everything you need is in one place.

To create each individual version of the button, make sure the "eyeball," or visibility icon, is showing for each of the appropriate layers specific to that button. With only the desired layers visible, export the file as a GIF. Since exporting a graphic leaves the original Photoshop file open and unchanged, you can turn off the visibility of the layers for the button you just exported and turn on the visibility of a new set of layers representing another button.

Use the same base art for all versions of the various buttons (the layers named "Yellow button" and "white outline," in this case), so you know that all the files will align perfectly and be the exact same size on the page. Having each element on its own layer also allows you to experiment with variations, such as whether or not to include a drop shadow.

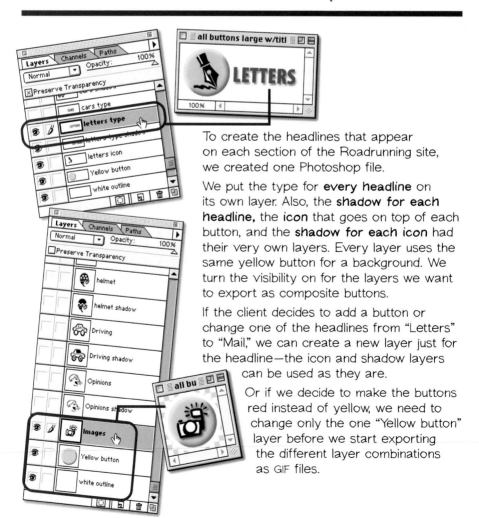

To create the headlines that appear on each section of the Roadrunning site, we created one Photoshop file.

We put the type for **every headline** on its own layer. Also, the **shadow for each headline,** the **icon** that goes on top of each button, and the **shadow for each icon** had their very own layers. Every layer uses the same yellow button for a background. We turn the visibility on for the layers we want to export as composite buttons.

If the client decides to add a button or change one of the headlines from "Letters" to "Mail," we can create a new layer just for the headline—the icon and shadow layers can be used as they are.

Or if we decide to make the buttons red instead of yellow, we need to change only the one "Yellow button" layer before we start exporting the different layer combinations as GIF files.

Make a drop shadow

Drop shadows are everywhere and some critics think they've been over-used and are sick of seeing them. We prefer not to discriminate against an effect that adds beauty and interest just because so many people have discovered it. As with any graphic technique, use common sense concerning how much you apply it. You don't want to become a visual bore.

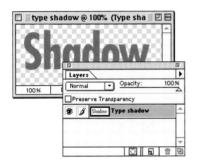

Set some type on its own transparent layer. Double-click on the layer in the Layers palette. This brings up the Layers dialog box in which you can change the name of the file. Name this layer "Type shadow." Click OK in the dialog box.

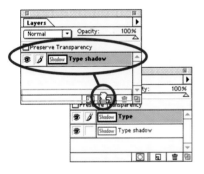

Duplicate the layer by dragging the layer in the Layers palette to the New Layer icon at the bottom of the Layers palette. The new layer that appears in the layers palette will automatically be named "Type shadow copy." Change the name to "Type."

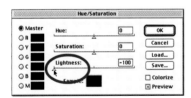

Select the layer named "Type shadow." From the Image menu, choose "Adjust," then "Hue/Saturation...." Move the bottom slider (the Lightness setting) all the way to the left so the color of the type is black. Click OK. You might not see the effect because the other layer is on top.

From the Filter menu, choose "Blur..." and select "Gaussian Blur...." In the Gaussian Blur dialog box, set your desired radius setting by looking at the preview. To see the original unblurred version again, position your mouse over the Preview window and press. Make your adjustments; when you like it, click OK.

Select the Move tool from the Tools palette and position the shadow where you want it. Or you can select the Move tool and use the arrow keys to move the shadow.

Since the shadow is on its own layer, you can easily change its color by using the technique mentioned on page 240: select a foreground color and press the keyboard shortcut to color the shadow and retain the layer's transparency.

If the shadow is darker than desired, select the shadow layer and move the Layer palette's Opacity slider to the left to lighten it.

This is the finished image.

Shadows with transparent backgrounds

Drop shadows can look great, but if you save a graphic with a shadow as a GIF file with a transparent background, the shadow edge can look really bad (unless you place the graphic on a white background). When we create shadows to be placed on colored or textured backgrounds, we avoid making them transparent. Instead we make the background layer of the file match the color and texture of the page it will be placed on, as we explained on pages 208–210.

Easy HTML enhancements

HTML stands for Hypertext Markup Language. HTML code uses plain ol' text to describe a page's appearance, deliver text content, instruct the page which images to display, and provide links to other web pages on the Internet. HTML pages can be understood by any browser on any computer.

So, the Big Question is: do you have to learn code? No. Not if you're using web authoring software that writes the code for you, such as Adobe PageMill or Claris Home Page. But if you learn just a little bit of HTML, you can add some things to your pages that your authoring software may not know how to do. A little code-hacking is useful—and fun.

HTML commands, called tags, are contained within <angle brackets.> The code can be all caps, lowercase, or any combination. You can type these commands directly in the code that your web authoring software creates. Or check your manual for directions on where to add extra code.

If you find you enjoy writing HTML, get Elizabeth Castro's book, *HTML for the World Wide Web: Visual QuickStart Guide,* published by Peachpit Press. It's clear, easy, and fun.

HTML code to specify fonts

Making text bold or italic is easy, but what if you want to make sure that certain text appears on a visitor's web page in a sans serif face such as Arial or Geneva? Put this code *in front of* the text that you want to change:

```
<font face="arial, geneva">
```

and put this code *after* the text you're changing: `</font>`

The final code looks like this:

```
<font face="arial, geneva">This type is sans serif.</font>
```

Everything between `<font>` and `</font>` will be in the typeface you specify. Both Arial and Geneva are included in this code because Arial is common on PCs and Geneva is common on Macintoshes (and much easier to read on the screen than Helvetica). You could specify any typefaces you want. On the visitor's computer, their browser will look for the fonts in the order they're listed and display the first one it finds.

If you want the text to be bold, italic, a different size, or in color, change those specifications on your web page using your software as usual. When the text appears in a browser, it will retain all that formatting, plus it will be displayed in the font you specified in the code.

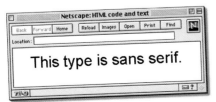

Instead of the default browser font, this page is displaying Arial.

Adding space around a graphic

If text is getting too close to a graphic or if several graphic images are crowding each other, you can add space (measured in pixels) around the image vertically, horizontally, or both.

The navigation icons in the example below are crowding each other. The code for the arrangement is shown below, where "img src" refers to the "image source," and "icon1.gif" is the name of the graphic:

```
<img src="icon1.gif">
<img src="icon2.gif">
<img src="icon3.gif">
<img src="icon4.gif">
<img src="icon5.gif">
```

Space the images apart by adding **horizontal** space, called "hspace" to the code: `hspace="20"`. Change the measurement of "20" pixels to the measurement you need. The code now looks like this:

```
<img src="icon1.gif" hspace="20">
<img src="icon2.gif" hspace="20">
<img src="icon3.gif" hspace="20">
<img src="icon4.gif" hspace="20">
<img src="icon5.gif" hspace="20">
```

This command adds the designated amount of space to *both* sides of the graphic. Therefore, the *total* amount of space between the icons is 40 pixels.

If the icons are stacked **vertically** instead of side by side, the code would look like this:

```
<img src="icon1.gif"><BR>
<img src="icon2.gif"><BR>
<img src="icon3.gif"><BR>
<img src="icon4.gif"><BR>
<img src="icon5.gif">
```

The `<BR>` command forces a "Break" that sends the next item down to the next line without any space between. This is different from a "Paragraph" command `<P>` which adds a fixed amount of vertical space to separate paragraphs or items (see page 113).

To add the desired amount of space between vertically aligned graphics, use the `vspace` command:

```
<img src="icon1.gif" vspace="10"><BR>
<img src="icon2.gif" vspace="10"><BR>
<img src="icon3.gif" vspace="10"><BR>
<img src="icon4.gif" vspace="10"><BR>
<img src="icon5.gif" vspace="10">
```

Align left or right

Some web authoring software, such as PageMill, will let you select a graphic and then click an "Align" button to align the text to the left, right, top, or bottom of the graphic. But it won't let you align text to a table. Other programs, such as Claris Home Page, don't have Align buttons even for graphics. But you can add the command to the code (that's how we created the table within a table, on page 228, with wrapped text in PageMill).

This is what the code looks like when an image does *not* have text wrapping around it:

```
<img src="dog.jpg" width="144"
height="216">
```
Here is the text. It starts at the bottom of the graphic, as shown in the example to the left.

To make the text wrap around the image, add `align="left"` (or `"right"`) to the `img src` command:

```
<img src="dog.jpg"
width="144" height="216"
align="left">
```

Next, add some vertical space around the image so the text doesn't get too close:

```
<img src="dog.jpg" width="144" height="216"
align="left" vspace="10">
```

Make a link open in a new window

Typically when you click on a link on Page A, you jump to Page B and Page A disappears. But if you want one of your links to open a *new* window so a visitor doesn't lose *your* site, add an extra piece of code to the link.

This is what a regular link looks like in the code. Notice it's just the URL preceded by A HREF.

Visit`<A HREF="http://www.cowboysindians.com">`Cowboys and Indians Magazine.`</A>`

To force the linked file to open in a new window, just add `target="_new"`:

Visit`<A HREF="http://www.cowboysindians.com"`
`target="_new">`Cowboys and Indians Magazine.`</A>`

It's possible, with JavaScript, to force a link to open the new window at a specific size (like smaller than yours) and in a certain position. But you'll have to get a book about JavaScript.

Forms

Web forms consist of a number of elements, such as text fields for people to type information into; checkboxes, radio buttons, and pull-down menus for making choices; Submit and Reset buttons, and more. Forms are very easy to create in web authoring software—you just click buttons and the various elements appear. If it's not clear what to do with an element, check your manual—each software program does the same thing in a slightly different way.

The important thing to know about forms is that once all the elements are laid out on the page, the form still won't work. That is, you can create a lovely and complex form very easily, and you can put the Submit button right there on the page, but if you just post that page on the web as is, the Submit button will do nothing. Someone must write a **CGI script,** which is an actual program that compiles the information from the form and sends it to your e-mail address. Ask your service provider for the name of someone who can do that for you. Not all servers can deal with forms, so talk to your host provider before you spend a lot of time creating a form.

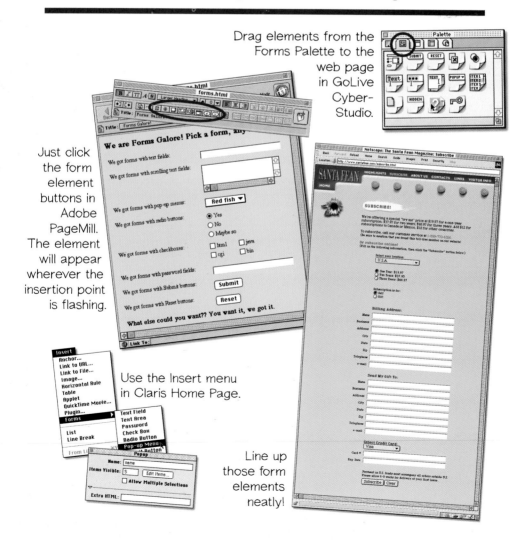

Drag elements from the Forms Palette to the web page in GoLive CyberStudio.

Just click the form element buttons in Adobe PageMill. The element will appear wherever the insertion point is flashing.

Use the Insert menu in Claris Home Page.

Line up those form elements neatly!

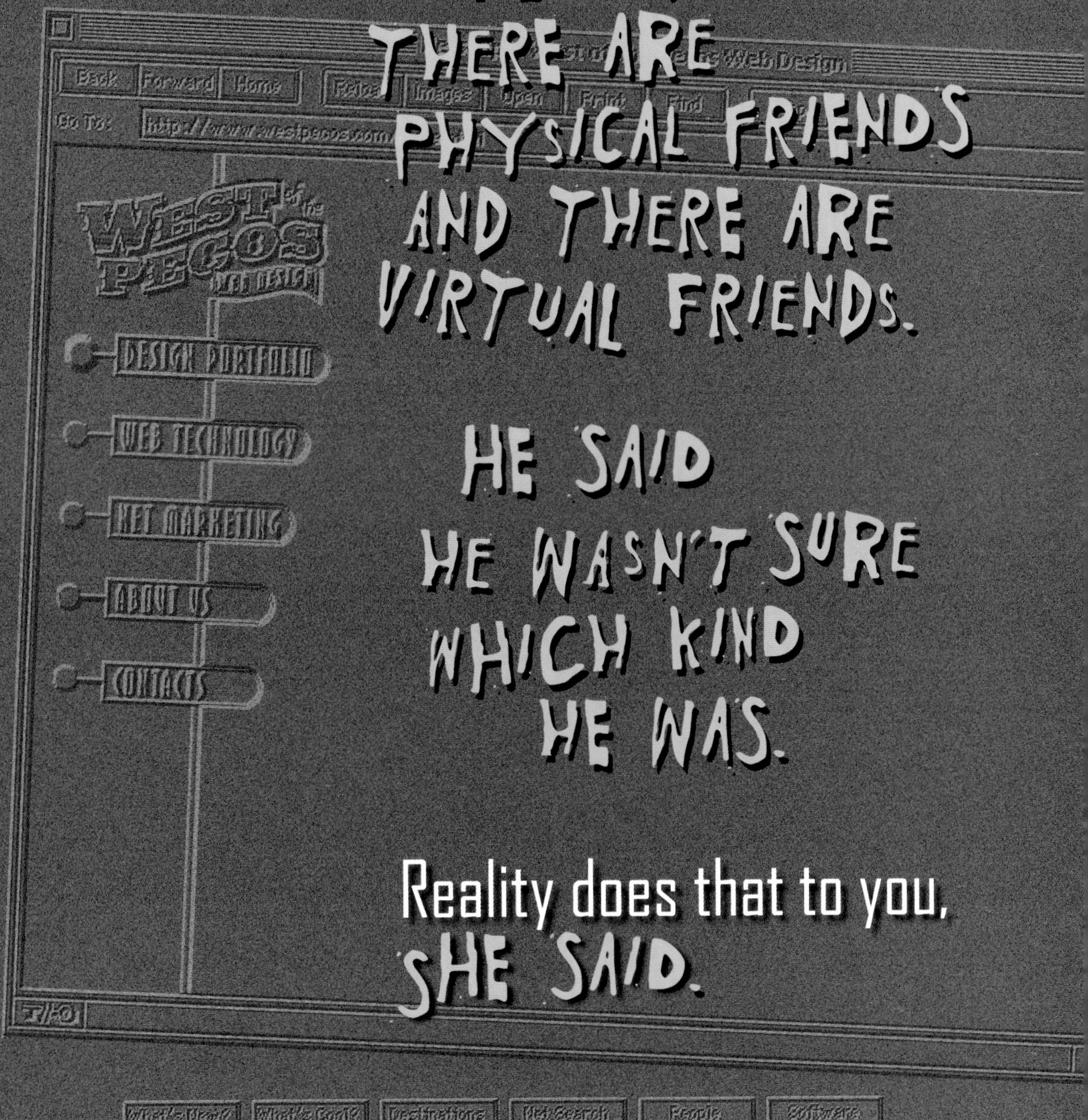

HE SAID,
THERE ARE
PHYSICAL FRIENDS
AND THERE ARE
VIRTUAL FRIENDS.

HE SAID
HE WASN'T SURE
WHICH KIND
HE WAS.

Reality does that to you,
SHE SAID.

WEST of the PECOS WEB DESIGN

DESIGN PORTFOLIO

WEB TECHNOLOGY

NET MARKETING

ABOUT US

CONTACTS

Back Forward Home Reload Images Open Print Find Stop

Go To: http://www.westpecos.com

West of the Pecos Web Design

What's New? What's Cool? Destinations Net Search People Software

"The wireless music box has no imaginable commercial value.
Who would pay for a message sent to nobody in particular?."

David Sarnoff's associates in response to his urging for investment in radio, 1920s

Test & Fix Your Web Site

You have one last thing to do before you send that web site off to the world: you must test it to make sure it works. We guarantee it is a rare web page that you upload and say to yourself, "Perfect. That's perfect." In this chapter we'll talk a little about site management software that helps you keep track of all the various parts of the web site. And we'll walk you through the process of testing your pages and fixing simple things. This is probably the most frustrating part of creating a web site—getting all those details right just before posting it. But it has to be done.

Web Site Work

Is Never Done

©1997 ballyhoo.inc

Site management software

All through this book we've been on your case to make sure your graphic files are in the web site folder *before* you put them on the page, and warning you *not* to move files to another folder after you've linked them, *not* to rename files, etc. The purpose of this is to prevent you from having to relink pages and graphics later. Let's say you made a graphic called "home.gif" and it's on every single page. If you move that graphic file to another folder or rename it "gohome.gif," you will have to go to every page with that link on it and relink the graphic with its new name. This is not a big problem if your site consists of only five pages, but if you have a 30- or 50- or 120-page site, this is a problem. Or perhaps you *plan* on having a site that's only 5 pages deep, but you get so involved that it becomes 120 pages and you need to reorganize things, make new folders for various sections, etc. To fix everything manually would be incredibly time-consuming. And boring. That's where **site management software** comes in.

Site management software does just what it says—it helps you manage your site. A good package looks at all your links and tells you which ones won't work. You can change the name of a file and the software will relink every applicable link with the new name. It will also tell you if any of the graphics are not located where they are supposed to be.

Many individual web authoring packages have some sort of site managment features built in. Claris Home Page has a feature to help reconnect graphics that were originally linked from the wrong place. Microsoft FrontPage has several features in its FrontPage Explorer component. NetObjects Fusion and GoLive CyberStudio have more powerful management features and control over the whole site.

BBEdit (pronounced "bee bee edit") is the favored Macintosh HTML editor. Luckman's WebEdit Pro and Sausage Software's HotDog Pro are popular Windows HTML editors. Many people use these to create web sites with straight code. You can search through your whole web site folder full of files and globally replace text, including link addresses, but these editors won't *tell* you what's wrong. Find BBEdit at www.barebones.com, WebEdit at www.mwtech.com/webedit, and HotDog Pro at www.sausage.com.

The most powerful package is Adobe SiteMill (Mac only at the moment), which does nothing but site management, therefore it does it best. SiteMill is currently included with the Mac version of PageMill. The best thing is that **SiteMill can manage entire sites no matter how you created them**— from straight HTML or any web authoring software. Within SiteMill you can make new folders, move or rename files, and SiteMill will update all the links. It tells you where you have links that go nowhere, pages that are not linked to anything else, and much more. Check it out at www.adobe.com.

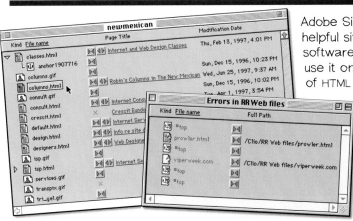

Adobe SiteMill is the most helpful site management software. And you can use it on any collection of HTML files, regardless of how you originally created the pages (even if you originally created them on a PC).

NetObjects Fusion has good site management features built in.

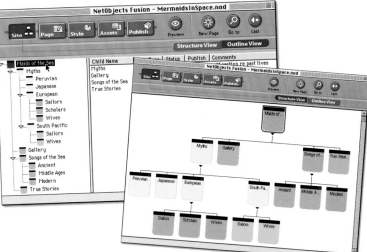

GoLive CyberStudio has easy-to-use features that help manage the files in a web site.

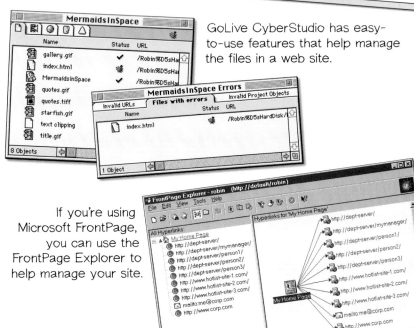

If you're using Microsoft FrontPage, you can use the FrontPage Explorer to help manage your site.

For Help, press F1

Testing your site

Before you upload your site to the world, it's important to test it to see how it works. Make sure all the graphics are in place and showing up, all of the links work, and that there are no formatting and layout problems.

You really should test your web site in different browsers, on different platforms (at least Mac and Windows), on different monitors, with different monitor settings, with graphics turned off, and with a variety of default fonts and point sizes. All of these variables make designing web pages both fun and frustrating, and they exert such influences that sites with more flexible layouts stand a better chance of appearing as you expect.

If you're creating a small site at which you don't expect much traffic, don't worry too much about testing with all these different parameters. But if you're creating a small business, corporate, international, or culturally important site, you had darn well better test it everywhere.

First, move your folder

To get the best test of your site, first move your entire web site folder into some other folder on your hard disk. Open your first page and follow your links to check all the other pages. If you had placed an item on a page while it was stored in some other folder, this procedure will reveal the mistake (the graphic will be missing). If you have a missing graphic, *make sure you find it and put that graphic into your web site folder before you fix the link!*

Offline browser check

Now, along the way of developing your web site you should be checking to see what the pages look like in a browser. This helps prevent really bad surprises at the end. So if you haven't done it before now, do this:

1. On a Mac, make an alias of your browser icon.
   On a PC, make a shortcut of your browser icon.

2. Put the alias or shortcut on the Desktop where you can see it.

3. Do not connect to the Internet (well, you certainly *can* do this if you are connected, but you don't *have* to be connected).

4. Drag the icon of one of your web pages and drop it on top of the alias or shortcut icon of the browser. This will open the browser and display your page, but the browser won't try to connect.

5. The page as displayed by the browser will probably look a little different from the page as displayed in your web authoring software.

If you see problems, open the page in your authoring software. Position that page next to the page displayed in the browser—side by side, if your monitor is big enough.

> **Fix** the problems in your web authoring package.

> **Save the page.** This is very important. You won't see the changes in the browser unless you save the page.

> Go to your browser. Click the **Reload** or Refresh button, or choose Reload or Refresh from the View menu. You will see the changes on the page. (If you don't, you probably forgot to save the changes in the web authoring software.)

6. You can also check the remote links before you actually upload the site to the server. Most web authoring software lets you choose which browser to open external (remote) links with—find that preference setting and make your choice. Connect to the Internet, then click those external links and make sure they work. Even while you're connected, you can still continue to open the web pages that are stored as files on your hard disk, view them in the browser, make changes in the web authoring program, and then reload them into your browser.

Watch someone else browse your site

Tape your mouth shut and tie your hands behind your back as you watch someone else go through your site. No fair explaining, apologizing, pointing out features, or telling the user where to go. Watch how they navigate, where they get stuck, where they spend the most time, what they miss, what works, what doesn't work. Untie your hands and make notes of places where you see the site needs improvement. Untape your mouth and ask the person what they thought as they traveled through the site. Retape your mouth and listen. Make any necessary adjustments and improvements.

Different browsers for different folks

Even a simple page will look a little different when it's viewed in different browsers, on a Mac or on a PC, in several different pixel settings, or with a couple of different font and point size choices. Expect the differences—just make sure the differences don't make the page look awful.

Netscape is the highly preferred browser. Microsoft Internet Explorer, as is common with many Microsoft products, does not always follow the established rules. Thanks to Bill Gates, designing web pages is more difficult than it needs to be (Robin's Opinion). There are many people who feel that if it doesn't look so good in Internet Explorer, that's too bad—fixing the pages to look perfect in Internet Explorer can be more trouble than it's worth, depending on how you feel about Microsoft. Get Netscape.

Fixing your site

There are often a bunch of little details that surprise you when you open your pages in a browser—you might find that spaces are not where they were on the original page, line breaks are different, the space after a graphic is not what you expected, things don't line up like you planned, tables look funny. And you thought you were finished, hmm?

- **Spacing problems.** Remember, the browser cannot see any *extra* spaces you created with the Spacebar—the code can only deal with one space between words. And often the paragraph returns you put in (especially before or after graphics) won't act the way you expected them to. You need to use the colored period or transparent GIF tricks to force space where you need it (see next page).

- **Tables are out of whack.** You have to go back to the table in your authoring software and make sure you conscientiously told every cell, as well as the entire table, to be the appropriate mix of relative and absolute values (page 62). Also check each cell to make sure you have set up the proper arrangement of alignment, both horizontal and vertical. And also check the border and cell spacing. Fun, huh. Cell colors won't show up in older browsers. And your web authoring software might show you more space between the cells than appears in the browser.

- **Graphics don't show up.** If not a single one of your graphics appears, check your browser Options or Preferences to see if you have turned off your graphics. If the preference says they are supposed to appear, perhaps you moved or renamed the graphic after you put it on the web page. Go back to your web authoring software and make sure the graphic is in the correct folder—either the same folder as the rest of the web pages, or at least in a graphics folder *inside* of the web pages folder. If you moved or renamed the graphic, delete the existing graphic on the page and drop in the one that is now stored (right?) in the web site folder.* Even if your software package can fix the link, you must have that graphic in your web site folder before you upload it to the server!

- **Page links don't work.** If you renamed or moved any page after you linked it, the link will be broken. Go back to your web authoring software and make a new link. Of course, first make sure the page is in the correct folder—the same folder as the rest of the web pages for that site.*

*On page 75 there is a tip for editing the HTML code to fix the links for graphics and pages. Of course, editing the code only works if you have first made sure the graphic or the page are in the correct folder before you edit!

Other fix-it tips

One of the biggest problems in web design is making space appear where you want it. There are two simple tricks to help solve this problem. One is very easy and handy when your background is a solid color. The other is useful when your background is a pattern.

Solid color background: Insert extra periods or letters (such as "xxx") where you want to force space, such as between, before, or after graphics, between text links, to indent paragraphs, etc. Then select and color those periods or letters with the same color as the background (shown below).

Patterned background: Make a tiny little transparent GIF—it can even be one pixel by one pixel. Either make it transparent in your graphics program, or let your web authoring software turn it transparent.

Use this transparent GIF to force space between words. For instance, if you want a line of text links to have space between each link, insert the transparent graphic between the first two links (as shown below). Stretch it to the width you want. Copy and paste that graphic between the other text links. If you need space above or below an image, insert that transparent graphic and resize it to give you the space. Use it to indent paragraphs.

Any background: To add more space *between* lines of text, select the space between two words and make that space a larger type size. It will be least noticeable if you use the space after periods and commas. You should do this to more than one space per line because you never know how the lines are going to break on someone else's browser.

transpix.gif

Make a transparent GIF.

Drop that GIF between words to force space.

home history gallery literature

To force extra linespacing, as shown below, select several spaces on each line and enlarge the type size.

Since once I sat upon a promontory,
And heard a mermaid on a dolphin's back
Uttering such dulcet and harmonious breath,
That the rude sea grew civil at
And certain stars shot madly
To hear the sea-maid's music

William Shakespeare
A Midsummer Night's Drea

To indent, you can use the transparent GIF.

Since once I sat upon a promontory,

And heard a mermaid on a dolphin's back

Uttering such dulcet and harmonious breath,

That the rude sea grew civil at her song,

And certain stars shot madly from their spheres,

To hear the sea-maid's music.

William Shakespeare
A Midsummer Night's Dream

This space is a size larger than the text. Also see the example on page 229.

Or if your background is a solid color, type several extra characters and apply the background color to those characters to make them "invisible."

Oh boy, it's a Quiz!

On the left, below, is the page as it appears in the web authoring program. On the right is the page as it appears in Netscape. Point out five differences between the two pages. State which differences are problems and how to fix those problems. Why would you let the other differences go?

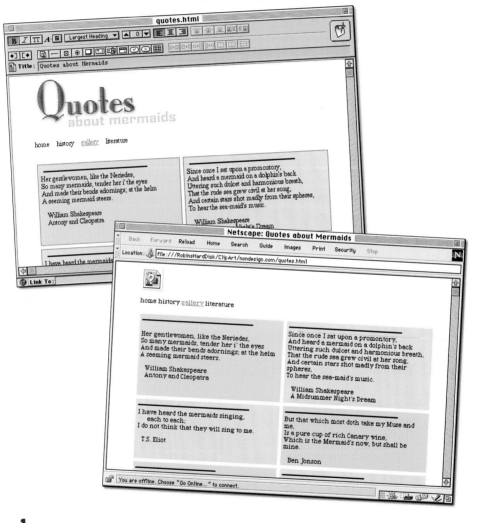

1 ....

2 ....

3 ....

4 ....

5 ....

How to Upload & Update Your Site

Your web site is finished!! Hooray!! So now what?? If you leave your site on your home or office computer, no one but you will ever see it (well, there is a limited way to serve it to the Internet from home or office, but that's another story). Your site must be posted on a *server*, a computer that's connected to the Internet 24 hours a day. To post your site on a server, you must get the files to it. When you send something from your computer to another computer, that is called **uploading files.** You'll hear the term **ftp** often—it stands for file transfer protocol, which is one way of transferring files from one place to another. You are going to ftp your files to a server.

In this chapter we'll discuss exactly what should be in the web site folder you need to upload. Then we'll show you how to upload your folder to the server. Once your site is on the server, you need to test it again and fix any problems. Then we'll show you how to **update** your own pages from your home or office in just a matter of seconds. It might seem confusing at first, but after you do it once or twice you'll realize it's actually pretty easy.

Before you upload

Before you can even think about uploading your files to a server, you must first establish a relationship with a provider (relationship = pay them money). We are assuming you did this long ago, because you were supposed to ask them how they wanted the files named (.htm or .html, index or default for the first page). Just in case you haven't, you must now call your Internet service provider (or any other hosting service) and arrange for them to **host,** or store, your site. Be sure to ask them if you can have "ftp privileges" to upload and update your own site. If they say, "No," that you must e-mail your site as an attachment and they will post it themselves, then you can skip this chapter. Remember that you don't have to post your site to a service provider in your city—you can post it anywhere in the world. So if your provider doesn't give you a good deal, ask around and see what other people in your area are doing, whom they are using as a host. But before you try to post your site, find a host!

Gather your files

In the previous chapter you did a lot of testing and fixing. We hope you were able to fix all or at least most of your problems, and that the only things you couldn't change were those things you have to live with, like text fonts and line breaks, etc.

Now you need to gather all your files to send to the service provider or wherever you have decided to post your site. All of your files might already be organized because you should have been doing that as you went along, and in the last chapter you should have discovered any missing links or graphics in the wrong place. So at this point there are three critical points to remember:

1. Send every file your site needs.
Your folder should contain every HTML file, GIF, and/or JPEG used in your site. If you got really fancy and made movie clips or sound files, of course they should be in your folder as well.

2. Don't send any files your site doesn't need.
Your folder should not have any TIFFs, PICTs, BMPs, EPSs, PNTs, PCXs, WMFs, or any other graphic files in it. Nor should there be any text files, such as word processing or SimpleText files, or even text clippings.

3. Make sure all your files are named properly.
Remember the naming conventions you learned on pages 71 and 72? Make sure you followed them:

- Every file name should have an extension: *.html* or *.htm* for web pages, *.gif* for GIF graphics, and *.jpg* for JPEG graphics.
- All lowercase letters (this is not critical—just good form).
- Only letters and numbers—no odd characters like apostrophes, colons, slashes, etc.
- Never use a space in a file name.
- The only characters you can have in a file name besides letters and numbers are periods, the underscore (_), created by typing Shift Hyphen, or the tilde (~), created by typing Shift ~, usually found in the upper-left corner of the keyboard.

If you created folders within your primary web site folder, check each one of those as well.

Very important! If you changed any of the file names or moved any files from one folder to another, you will have to go back to the web pages and replace the graphics whose names or placements have changed, and relink any files whose names or placements have changed! Do that first and test it on your computer before you upload.

ratz

This is the folder (above and to the right) that contains the entire web site.

Every web page and every graphic (and even some sound files, .wav and .aiff) are in this folder. This is the folder that was uploaded to the server.

On the Macintosh server this web site was sent to, the first page had to be titled "default.html," as shown. When a visitor enters the URL "www.ratz.com," the browser looks in this folder, finds the "default.html" file, and displays it. The URL of all other web pages in this site would be "www.ratz.com/whatever.html."

Notice the other folders at the bottom of the window. In this example, each of those folders contains another web site. Each of those web site folders contains a file called "default.html." The URL for Jimmy's web site, then, would be "www.ratz.com/jimmy/." The browser knows to look inside that "jimmy" folder, find "default.html," and display it.

shotglass

This web site, a display of Robin's Cheesy Shotglass Collection, is going to a Unix server that wants the first page to be named "index.htm."

Notice there are no superfluous files in this folder—everything is either a web page or a GIF.

Uploading files

After you prepare your web site folder, you need to do two more things in preparation for uploading.

1. **Get the free software for uploading files.** This type of software is called an "ftp client."
    - For a Macintosh, get Fetch.
    - For Windows 95, get WS_FTP95.

    There is other software you could use for this, and if your service provider recommends or gives you something else or you have something else that works great, then use that. This is just a recommendation of the software clients most people use. If your provider doesn't give you the software, go to www.shareware.com—it's easy to find and it's easy to download. If the thought of searching for and downloading the program makes you nervous, have a friend do it for you.

2. **Ask your provider or host for your ftp information.** Write down the data they tell you, which should be info like this:
    - Your **host name,** which will be something like ftp.domain.com. Or it might be a string of numbers, like 198.59.279.2.
    - Your **host type,** which describes the kind of server you will be posting to (not always required), such as Ipswitch or MAC Peter Server.
    - Your **user ID,** which will probably be your name or something equivalent, such as robin.
    - Your **password,** which you help decide. It will appear as bullets or asterisks when you enter it: ******
    - The **directory path** where your site will be stored. It will look something like this: /WebSTAR 2.0/studiox/robin/

Once you have that set up, start your connection. Then:

1. Double-click the Fetch or WS_FTP95 icon. It will open a dialog box as shown on the opposite page.
2. Type in the data the service provider gave you. Click OK.
3. Check the Preferences or Options: you want the data format to be sent as **raw data,** and you do *not* want a **.txt** suffix added.
4. The ftp client takes you to the actual server—you are now looking inside that other computer! Notice the folder name your provider gave you is open and available, waiting for you to put files into it. If you position your windows so you have the ftp client on one side of your screen and your web site folder open on the other, you can just select and drag files (not the folder itself) from your web site folder into the ftp window, drop them, and they land on the other computer (the server).

Your pages are instantly on the World Wide Web!

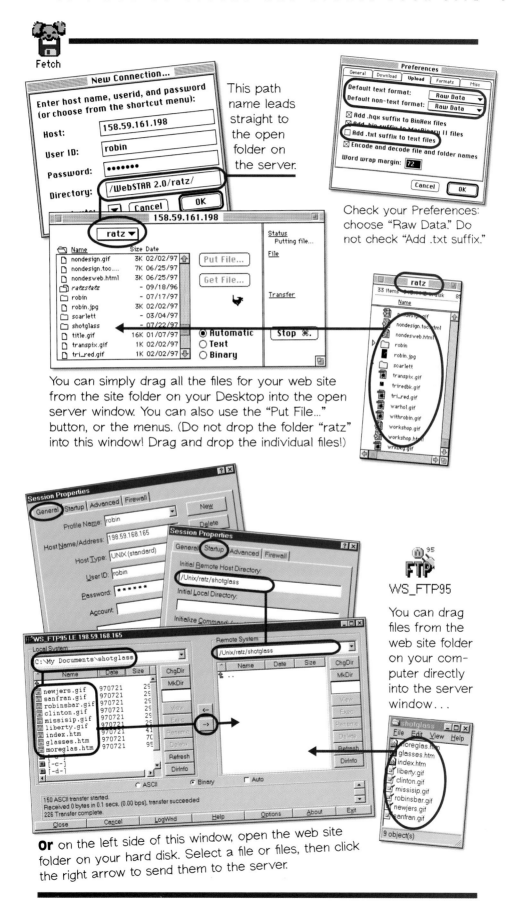

Fetch

New Connection...

Enter host name, userid, and password (or choose from the shortcut menu):

Host: 158.59.161.198

User ID: robin

Password: •••••••

Directory: /WebSTAR 2.0/ratz/

Cancel   OK

This path name leads straight to the open folder on the server.

Preferences

General   Download   **Upload**   Formats   Misc

Default text format: Raw Data
Default non-text format: Raw Data

☒ Add .hqx suffix to BinHex files
☒ Add .bin suffix to MacBinary II files
☐ Add .txt suffix to text files
☒ Encode and decode file and folder names
Word wrap margin: 72

Cancel   OK

Check your Preferences: choose "Raw Data." Do not check "Add .txt suffix."

158.59.161.198

ratz ▼

Status
Putting file...

Name	Size	Date
nondesign.gif	3K	02/02/97
nondesign.too....	7K	06/25/97
nondesweb.html	3K	06/25/97
ratzstatz	-	09/18/96
robin	-	07/17/97
robin.jpg	3K	02/02/97
scarlett	-	03/04/97
shotglass	-	07/22/97
title.gif	16K	01/07/97
transpix.gif	1K	02/02/97
tri_red.gif	1K	02/02/97

File

Put File...

Get File...

Transfer

● Automatic   Stop ⌘.
○ Text
○ Binary

ratz

33 items

Name

nondesign.gif
nondesign.too
nondesweb.html
robin
robin.jpg
scarlett
transpix.gif
triredbk.gif
tri_red.gif
warhol.gif
withrobin.gif
workshop.gif
workshop.htm
wrkbkg.gif

You can simply drag all the files for your web site from the site folder on your Desktop into the open server window. You can also use the "Put File..." button, or the menus. (Do not drop the folder "ratz" into this window! Drag and drop the individual files!)

Session Properties

General Startup | Advanced | Firewall

Profile Name: robin

Host Name/Address: 198.59.168.165

Host Type: UNIX (standard)

User ID: robin

Password: ••••••

Account:

New

Delete

Session Properties

General **Startup** Advanced | Firewall

Initial Remote Host Directory:
/Unix/ratz/shotglass

Initial Local Directory:

Initialize Command:

FTP

WS_FTP95

You can drag files from the web site folder on your computer directly into the server window...

WS_FTP95 LE 198.59.168.165

Local System
C:\My Documents\shotglass

Name	Date	Size
newjers.gif	970721	29
sanfran.gif	970721	29
robinsbar.gif	970721	29
clinton.gif	970721	29
missisip.gif	970721	29
liberty.gif	970721	29
index.htm	970721	41
glasses.htm	970721	70
moreglas.htm	970721	95
[-c-]		
[-d-]		

ChgDir
MkDir
View
Exec
Rename
Delete
Refresh
DirInfo

Remote System
/Unix/ratz/shotglass

Name	Date	Size
↑ ..		

ChgDir
MkDir
View
Exec
Rename
Delete
Refresh
DirInfo

←
→

○ ASCII   ● Binary   ☐ Auto

150 ASCII transfer started.
Received 0 bytes in 0.1 secs. (0.00 bps), transfer succeeded
226 Transfer complete.

Close   Cancel   LogWnd   Help   Options   About   Exit

shotglass
File Edit View Help

moreglas.htm
glasses.htm
index.htm
liberty.gif
clinton.gif
missisip.gif
robinsbar.gif
newjers.gif
sanfran.gif

9 object(s)

Or on the left side of this window, open the web site folder on your hard disk. Select a file or files, then click the right arrow to send them to the server.

Test your site online

As soon as you upload your files to the server, they are on the World Wide Web and anyone in the world can view them if they know the address. Don't just post them and leave, though! Open the home page in your browser, *online,* and test the entire site. Go through every page and click every link. Make sure every graphic is there. Make sure all e-mail forms work. Make sure animated graphics are moving (and stopping), and that any sound files you created are loading and playing.

If you followed the directions in the previous chapter, you probably don't have much left to fix, if anything. Once again, position your pages side by side on your screen—the page you created in your web authoring software next to the same page on the web in your browser. Leave your ftp client open and ready. If you need to make a page change, follow these steps:

1. Make note of what went wrong in the browser.
2. Open the page in your web authoring software.
3. Make the changes, and **save** the page.
4. You must now upload that page again! Follow the same procedure as when you uploaded your whole site—drag the file or files *that have changed* into your folder on the server. If you made a change in a graphic, upload the graphic, of course. If you made a change that affected three pages and two graphics, upload all five files.

    When you drag those files with the same names into the same folder on the server, *the newer files will simply replace the older ones, as long as the new files have exactly the same names as the old ones.*

5. Click on your browser window to make it active. To see the new changes, you have to **reload** the page. But some browsers store the old page in their memory cache, so if you reload and don't see the changes, you must force the browser to go back to the server and get the new page instead of displaying the one in its memory cache. Doing this is called a **force reload.**

    - **To force reload on the Mac,** hold down the Option key. While the Option key is down, click the Reload button or choose "Super Reload" from the View menu. (In Netscape Communicator 4, you can force reload with either the Option key or the Shift key.)

    - **To force reload in Windows Netscape,** hold down the Shift key. While the Shift key is down, click the Reload button or choose Reload from the View menu.

       In **Internet Explorer,** the Refresh button is supposed to act as a force reload button. It doesn't always work. If the Shift key doesn't work in your browser, try the Alt key.

6. Continue checking all pages, fixing things, uploading corrected files, and reloading the new ones to see how they look.

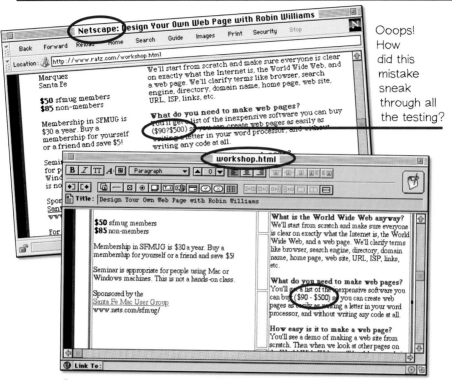

Ooops! How did this mistake sneak through all the testing?

Open the page in your web authoring software and fix it. Save it.

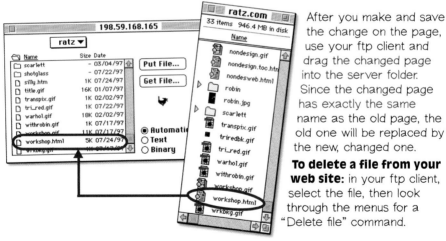

After you make and save the change on the page, use your ftp client and drag the changed page into the server folder. Since the changed page has exactly the same name as the old page, the old one will be replaced by the new, changed one.

To delete a file from your web site: in your ftp client, select the file, then look through the menus for a "Delete file" command.

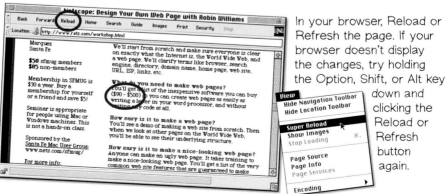

In your browser, Reload or Refresh the page. If your browser doesn't display the changes, try holding the Option, Shift, or Alt key down and clicking the Reload or Refresh button again.

Updating files

You are going to want to update your files regularly. You will especially want to update them once you see how easy it is—in fact, you already went through the updating process on the previous page, while fixing your web pages. It's simply a matter of making changes on the page, then uploading them into the same server folder, replacing the older page.

Let's say you want to change your family newsletter every two weeks. The page is already created and every two weeks you change the text. If nothing changes but the text and/or graphics on this one page, then all you have to do is upload this new page and the new graphics directly into your server folder (just like you uploaded the fixes, as shown on the previous page). As you've discovered, if this *new* newsletter web page has the exact same HTML name as the *existing* newsletter web page you want to change, then this *new* one will drop in and *replace* the existing page.

But let's say you add an entirely new section altogether. Let's say you add a "New Babies" section to your family web site because suddenly seven of your grandchildren are having babies. This means you'll have several *new* files for the new section. This also means your home page and probably other pages will have changes—*any page on which you add a new link to this New Babies section must be replaced.* So every page that has any change on it, plus the new pages for the new section, need to be uploaded. The new pages will be *added* to the collection. The changed pages will be replaced. We recommend you keep a list of files that need to be added and replaced, or use your site management software to help manage this sort of task!

Additional web sites on your site

If you want to add a whole new web site, all you need to do is upload the entire web site *folder* into your folder on the server. Let's say you (your name is Matilda) have a web site address like this: www.coyote.com/matilda. You have paid for 5 megabtyes of web site storage space, but you only use 1.5 MB, so you want to put your son's web site up with yours.

Your son creates his web site and puts it all in one folder. His folder is named wilford. You upload his folder, wilford, and drop it inside of your folder, matilda. His web address will then be: www.coyote.com/matilda/wilford. Each slash tells the browser to look down one more level, into another folder. So this address tells the browser, "Go to the domain coyote.com. Look there for the folder matilda. Look inside matilda for the folder called wilford." The browser knows, when it looks inside wilford, to find and display the index.htm file (or default.html or index.html).

So your children could create their own web sites, put them into folders, and you can upload their folders inside of your own. If they want to upload more files or update existing ones, they can go to your folder, double-click their own folders, and drag files into it. Easier than you thought?

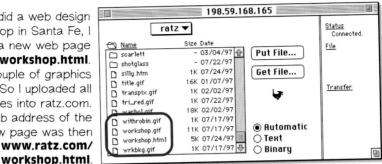

When I did a web design workshop in Santa Fe, I made a new web page called **workshop.html**. It had a couple of graphics on it. So I uploaded all those files into ratz.com. The web address of the new page was then **www.ratz.com/ workshop.html**.

I also changed the *home page* in ratz.com so it would have a link to the workshop page. That means, of course, that I had to upload the *changed home page* (default.html). I made the change, uploaded the file, and the new home page with the new link replaced the old home page.

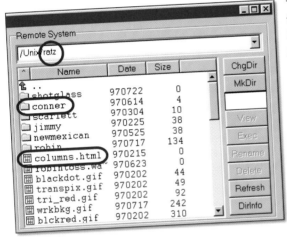

This ftp window also shows the files that are on the domain **ratz.com** (same as above, it's just from a different computer and a different ftp client).

On the web, you can get to ratz.com by entering **www.ratz.com**, right?

To get to each of the **files** within ratz.com, you can enter www.ratz.com, add a slash to tell the browser to look inside the ratz folder, then type the name of the file you want to view. Let's say you wanted to see columns.html. You would enter **www.ratz.com/columns.html**.

Each **folder** you see in the above window is another self-contained unit. My friend Julie Conner has her graphic design résumé on ratz.com, stored inside the folder called "conner." Thus the address to her site is **www.ratz.com/conner**.

The browser will go to ratz.com. The slash tells it to look down one more level, to a folder called "conner." If the browser is not told to find a specific HTML file (such as "columns.html"), it will look for and display the "index.html" or "default.html" that it finds within that folder.

So when you see a long web address divided by slashes, it's an indication of a large domain with lots of subfolders that contain subfolders, etc., until you get to the HTML file, which is the actual web page:

http://www.domain.com/folder1/folder2/folder3/folder4/folder5/webpage.htm

Oh boy, it's a Quiz!

Answer these questions to make sure you understand how to upload and update your files. Use the dialog box and folder window below to answer most of the questions.

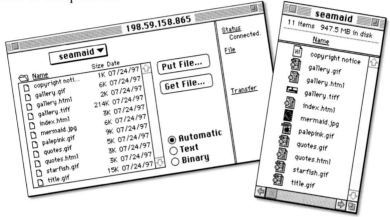

1. If you made and saved a change to the web page "quotes.html" in your web authoring software and posted it to this folder on the server, would it:

a. update an existing file

b. be added as a new page to the web site

2. If you made a brand new web page, saved it as "sea.html," and posted it to this folder on the server, would it:

a. update an existing file

b. be added as a new page to the web site

3. If you uploaded just the page in Question 2, above, would there be a link to get to this new page? If not, what should you do?

a. Don't worry—there would already be links to this page because they are created automatically when you make new pages.

b. No, there would not be a link; you need to make links on pages and upload every page with the new link.

5. How many of the files above should *not* have been uploaded? Which ones?

a. two . . . .

b. three . . . .

6. If you added a new photo to an existing page on your site, how many files would you have to upload?

a. one graphic file

b. one web page file

c. one graphic file and one web page

7. If you remove three pages from your site, what else would you have to do to the site?

a. Change your address

b. Remove the links from remaining pages and upload those changes

8. If you add a web site folder called "oceanmist," to the above window, what would the site's address be?

a. www.seamaid.com/oceanmist

b. www.oceanmist.com

4. What would the file structure look like for this web address (that is, name the folders inside of folders and any web pages that this address represents):

www.seamaid.com/oceanmist/foam/moonlady.htm

How and Why to Register Your Site

In Chapter 2 you read about how to use the various search tools. You know first-hand from using the Internet how important it is to be able to find the information you want. Yesterday, 500 web sites were added to the World Wide Web—how many of those do you know about today? None? Well, that's about how many people are going to know about yours tomorrow. If you have a business on the web, owning a web site should be just one part of a bigger picture and a bigger plan. If you simply post your site and wait for the crowds to appear, you're going to be disappointed and complain about how the hype doesn't match the results of "having a presence" on the web. But it will be your own dang fault.

Once your web site is up, your next job is to tell the world. We'll show you how to do that, in a variety of ways. If you are serious about marketing your web site, you need the book, *Getting Hits*, by Don Sellers, published by Peachpit Press. It is the best book, bar none, for learning how to really get in there and promote your site—using the Internet and many other means. Don tells you what each search tool is best at, how it puts you into its database, what you can do to increase your chances dramatically that your site will be found, and how to tell the rest of the world that it exists. Don's book is great, easy to read, and enormously useful. In fact, it's indispensable. You need it.

Search tools

First, a brief reminder. When you tell a search tool to find something, it doesn't go running all over the world looking for web pages with the information you request. *Each search tool merely looks in its own very particular database of information* to see if it has what you want. Every search tool builds its own database—that's why if you search two or three different ones you come up with two or three different collections of information.

There are **search engines** and there are **directories,** as discussed in Chapter 2. Search engines have "spiders" or "robots" that search the World Wide Web constantly and create the databases automatically. Directories are made by humans who look at the web sites and sort them into categories.

Each search tool has a little button somewhere on its main page that says something like "Add Your URL," "Submit your URL," or "Get Listed." Click each one and follow its directions. But don't be fooled into thinking you can then go to that search engine and look yourself up—even if you add yourself manually, it can take from several days to six weeks before you appear in the results (except maybe in the search engine InfoSeek Ultra).

Submission services that do it for you

If you don't want to or don't have the time to submit your URL to each individual search tool, there are lots of services on the web that will enter your web address in many search engines and directories at once. Drill down through the Computer and Internet category in Yahoo to World Wide Web:Announcement Services:How to Announce and Promote Your Site. There you will find a wealth of resources and information.

Below are two popular automatic submission services.

Submit It! www.submit-it.com
There is a free service that submits your site to about twenty search tools of your choice (chosen from their list). There is also a paid service that will submit your site to over 200 locations.

¡Register-It! www.register-it.com
Register-It will submit your address to 16 sites for free, plus it has several other great services, such as re-registering and updates. They also offer promotional services, such as submitting your site for awards, sending out press releases to reporters in your field, consulting, and more.

The best investment of your time and dollars is Don Sellers' book, *Getting Hits.* Don explains precisely how each search tool decides whether to add you to its list, and how to improve your chances of appearing at the top of the list of results.

Specialized search tools

There are many search tools that are very specialized. There are directories and engines that search only subject-specific sites, such as those that focus on travel, women, ancient history, orchids, dogs, humor, business listings, law enforcement, airports, etc., etc., etc.

There are several places on the web to find lists of directories. Try these:

Yahoo   Drill down through Yahoo to Computers and Internet:World Wide Web:How to Search the Web:Search Engines or Directories

Beaucoup!   www.beaucoup.com/engines.html

Search.Com   www.search.com Check their A–Z List of Specialty Searches, over 100 specialized search tools and lists.

Look through these lists carefully, and if one of the services supports your web site information, then of course register with them—it's your most direct route to being found by those looking for your specialty.

Link to me, I'll link to you

No matter what the topic, there is always someone determined to have a page with a link to every site on that topic. Chances are if you have some sort of special interest, you've found that lengthy link list (or collection of them) that pertains to your interest. If your web site should be on that list, e-mail them. They want you.

You probably know of other sites that have a similar interest as yours. If you would like them to link to you and you are willing to link to them in return, e-mail them and ask.

Popularity contest

In fact, one of the ways that some search engines determine if your site is valuable enough to be listed in their database is by how "popular" you are; that is, by how many other sites are linked to yours. So the more links to your site that you help generate, the more likely it is that people looking for you will find you.

To find out who is linked to your site:

- Go to AltaVista: www.altavista.digital.com
- In the Search edit box, enter: link:yourdomain.com
- You can enter a longer address, as well, such as: yourdomain.com/weber/family.html

You will get a list of the pages on the web that have links to the page whose URL you entered. You can click the links on the results to visit the pages of those who have honored you with a link to your site.

What search tools look for

These are things you can do to your site to make sure automatic search engines find you quickly. As we mentioned on the previous page, the popularity contest is important to some search tools. Here are other features of your web site that different tools take into consideration.

Title of your page

We talked about this before, but we want to emphasize the fact that many search engines use the title of your page to determine where to put you in their database, so be sure the title of each page is clear and succinct, yet tells the visitor (and the search engine) what to expect on that page.

First paragraph of your home page

When providing a list of results, some search tools display the first paragraph of your page. That's why you see descriptions of web sites like the one shown below, which don't give you much of a clue as to what the site is really about:

> 1. Tosselin Briards Page
>   TOSSELIN BRIARDS PAGE. ABOUT MY AIMS IN BREEDING BRIARDS. ABOUT BRIARDS (AND TRAINING) TOSSUMAISIA KUVIA - TOSSU'S PICTURE GALLERY. MUSTAT LAMPAANI -...
>   *http://www.uta.fi/~atnoko/tosselin.html* - size 4K - 23-Apr-97 - English

So one important feature of your web site should be a clear first paragraph that tells visitors what they can expect on the site.

> 2. Briards de la Petit Noblesse
>   Our Briard breeding is firmly based on the international cooperation with several well-known, reliable, and experienced breeders in Europe.
>   *http://www.dipoli.hut.fi/org/TechNet/org/briard/noblesse/noblesse.html* - size 2K - 27-Aug-96 - English

Stacking the deck

Some designers repeat keywords over and over and over again in various places in the code or even on the page (sometimes hidden) so search engines will display their site higher in the list of results. This works sometimes, but some search tools penalize sites that they think are stacking the deck in this way (which is also another form of *spamming,* or littering something—like your mailbox—with unwanted junk). We don't recommend you stack your keywords; if you do, be subtle about it.

Meta tags

One of the most useful little pieces of code you can enter on each page of your site is a **meta tag.** This is a really easy piece of code to write. There are several kinds of meta tags, but the most useful ones for you are the **Description** and **Keyword** tags—use both. Not all search engines take advantage of meta tags, but in the results of the ones that do you will see the description *you* write about your site instead of the first 250 characters that appear on the page. And you can make sure people find your site when they type in keywords related to your information, even if that word does not actually appear on the page.

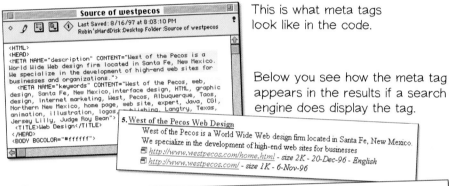

This is what meta tags look like in the code.

Below you see how the meta tag appears in the results if a search engine does display the tag.

This is the result of a search if a designer doesn't use the Description meta tag.

Description meta tag: Go into the code for your page and type this at the top, after the <HEAD> tag (it doesn't matter whether it's caps or lowercase):

```
<META NAME="description" CONTENT="
```

Then type a short description of your site. At the end of the list, don't type a space, but type: `">` So it might look something like this:

```
<META NAME="description" CONTENT="Mermaids, myths
of the sea, have haunted humans all over the world.
This site explores the myth, the magic, and the
truth of mermaids.">
```

Keyword meta tag: Go into the code for your web page and type this at the top, after the <HEAD> tag (as shown in the screen shot above):

```
<META NAME="keywords" CONTENT="
```

Then type a list of keywords the people might use to search for your site. Separate each word by a comma, then a space. At the end of the list, don't type a space, but type: `">` So it might look something like this:

```
<META NAME="keywords" CONTENT="mermaid, mermaids,
maids of the sea, ocean, underwater, jewels, sea,
foam, myth, fish, pirates, siren, sirens, treasure">
```

Getting your site noticed

Besides submitting your URL to every useful search tool, you need to also put that address out there in the rest of the world so people know to look for you on the World Wide Web.

Cross-marketing!

One problem with a printed piece is that, once printed, it still must be distributed to its market. On the World Wide Web, distribution is no longer a problem. Your family reunion web site is just as accessible as Disneyland's, Apple's, or Toyota's. The challenge is to make your web address known to the greatest number of people possible.

If your web site is personal, you may not care how widely publicized the web address is. But if you want to market your commercial site, you shouldn't rely entirely upon registering with web directories and search engines. Cross-market your site by using traditional media to greatly increase the chances of making your address known to your target audience. Print the address on your letterhead and in your brochures. Include it in print ads, radio, and TV commercials. Trade links with other sites that have some connection to you or that have an overlapping customer base.

Getting mentioned in magazines is always worthwhile. It involves sending press releases and clever notes to a number of different places, but the rewards of appearing in a magazine or a column can be great. Don't limit yourself to Internet magazines—if you sell a hog-farming specialty tool, send the hog-farming magazine a press release about your site.

You may decide that it's worth it to advertise your site on some other site, with your ad being a direct link back to your page. Much as we all complain about advertising, it works or it wouldn't be there. And many of us who hate it might be willing to accept several thousand dollars a month in exchange for putting a banner on our site.

Announce lists

Also check out the announce lists that give you lots of ideas for Internet resources for promoting your site. Here one to start with:

The Megalist   www.2020tech.com/submit.html
This place lists sites that distribute your URL
to other sites, reciprocal link services, regional
directories, sites that list your URL for free, and
"Other pages like this one."

Awards

There are hundreds of awards available on the web, many of them absolutely meaningless, some given out by people who should themselves be arrested for bad design. For those people, Url offers his own Chain-Yank Award.

Being listed on one of the more important awards sites, though, can do great things for you and your web site. Go to the sites that generate the awards and submit your pages. You can find a list in Yahoo—drill down to Computers and Internet:World Wide Web:Best of the Web.

Some of the higher quality web site awards come from c|net, Too Cool, Project Cool, and Cool Site of the Day. Several of the search engines, such as Lycos and Magellan, offer Top 5% of the Web awards. Go to their sites and submit your pages.

Just do us one favor. If you win an award, please don't litter your front page with icons of the awards. No matter how cool the prize, it's annoying to see little pictures of awards strewn all over the place. Have a link to another page where you can boast about the award, display its icon, and tell us why you won it and what it means to you. Giving the award a special place and telling us more about it will also give the award more credibility.

Resubmit regularly

If your address changes, of course you need to resubmit your site every-where. The most successful sites, though, resubmit regularly anyway, especially when there is new content. If you provide an online newsletter, resubmit every time you post a new newsletter with new content. If you add new products, resubmit. If you redesign with a new angle, resubmit.

Search for your own site

After you have registered your site everywhere possible, search for your own web site. If you plan to register other sites in the future, keep notes on which engines displayed your site first, how long it took, what worked and what didn't work, etc. If you hear or can garner any comments from visitors about how they found you, keep notes so you'll know what works and what doesn't. This is a cumulative experience.

Oh boy, it's a Quiz!

If you fill in all the blanks in this quiz, you will have what you need to start registering your site.

1. What is the best and most appropriate title for your home page? It's not too long, is it? It's not all caps, is it?

. . . .

2. What is the URL of your site? If it is not your own domain name, do you believe this URL is stable and will be up and available for a long time?

. . . .

3. What is your contact information, such as name, address, e-mail address, phone, and fax number?

. . . .

. . . .

4. Name at least ten keywords that you think someone might search by when looking for your web site.

. . . .

5. Write a 25-word description of your site.

. . . .

. . . .

6. Write a 50-word description of your site.

. . . .

. . . .

7. Develop a 500–1,000-word press release. Write it as you would like to see it printed in a newspaper or magazine.

. . . .

. . . .

. . . .

THE MACHINES ARE CONTROLLING THE WORLD, HE SAID.

HE SAID.

AND I SAID, WELL, SOMEBODY'S GOT TO.

Chapter One
The answers in the right-hand column fit into the blanks in order.

Chapter Two
1. Babe Ruth (InfoSeek needs only initial caps to connect the two words as one name)
2. mermaid -jewelry
3. "Vietnam war" Use quotes and capital V.
4. HotBot
5. Pollinia: Network Orchid Stuff
6. Hong Kong Search Engine (this list changes, so if this search engine isn't listed on this page anymore, I apologize!)
7. The full text can be found in several places. The Thomas directory is the best resource for government articles (thomas.loc.gov). The Declaration can be found at http://lcweb2.loc.gov/const/declar.html
8. Enter the company name in the browser's Location box. For example, enter ford, westinghouse, nfl, etc. In Internet Explorer on a PC, you'll have to enter the www and .com.

Chapter Three
1. a
2. c
3. c
4. c The difference is that the Heading 1 format would add space after the paragraph.
5. b
6. d
7. d
8. c

Chapter Four
1. c (cannot have a space in a name)
2. a,b,c,d
3. d
4. d
5. d
6. d
7. a
8. d

Chapter Five
1. Print, so you know the stockholders will receive it and look at it, whether or not they have computers.

2. Web, perhaps with a creative postcard that both shows off your talent and provides your web address.
3. Web, e-mail your customers.
4. Web, for those who can take advantage of it. Perhaps a quarterly supplement for others, depending on the product.
5. Web, perhaps Acrobat files (they can print the text fully formatted)
6. Print, high-quality, perhaps with a web site to publicize the book.

Chapter Seven
The first web page has some striking elements, but the general interface and navigation is not as clear, functional, and intuitive as the second web page.
A.
1. Buttons are too large, take up too much space—they're not THAT important.
2. The graphics (as indicated by the unloaded one) don't have alt labels.
3. Where is the rest of the navigation? I have to SCROLL to get to the rest of the navigation?
4. Black backgrounds are passé. Get some new colors.
5. I don't know where I'll go when I click that button.
B.
1. The entire visual impression is neatly contained within 640 x 460.
2. I can see the entire navigation system right here. Notice there are no scroll bars, an indication that there is nothing hiding.
3. Graphic buttons have matching text buttons.
4. I have a better idea of what to expect to see when I click a link.

Chapter Nine
1. CMYK
2. RGB
3. RGB
4. 256
5. The bit-depth
6. 256
7. 16.7 million
8. No, you will only see 256.

9. 65,536
10. Smaller, because more pixels have to fit into the same monitor.
11. With fewer pixels, it doesn't take so much memory to send bits of information to all the pixels.
12. So all the people with 8-bit monitors can see the graphics and background without dithering, and also so you can be assured that your graphics will look as good as possible on every sort of computer.
13, 14, 15. Check the chart on page 168 and make sure the values match across the columns.

Chapter Ten
1. JPEG, lots of colors, lots of blends, photographic quality.
2. GIF, flat color
3. GIF, graphic illustration
4. GIF, graphic illustration
5. a
6. b
7. b
8. d
9. So the visitor knows what to expect as the page loads, and in case a visitor is browsing without graphics (also, you can put secret messages in them).
10. 2

Chapter Twelve
1. Never. Very few people probably have that typeface installed on their computer, so it will change into their default font.
2. Never. Too hard to read and it is a sure sign of an amateur who doesn't know any better.
3. Never. Too hard to read.
4. Never. Too hard to read.
5. Sometimes. Sentences of large type are hard to read, and the large, childish size can make the text look dorky.
6. Never. See page 223
7. Sometimes (Rarely). If it's small, specify Arial or Geneva to make it as readable as possible. And make the lines shorter.
8. Never. duh.
9. Never. Italic is more difficult to read, especially on the screen. The more italic, the more difficult.

10. Never. Use this technique only if you truly don't care if people stick around your site or not.
11. Never. When you set type in all caps, it takes up 2 to 2.5 times as much space as lowercase. If you're going to take up that much space anyway, set the text in a point size the visitor can read.

Chapter Fourteen
1. The graphic is missing. Make sure it is in the correct folder, then either fix the code by hand (page 75) or delete and replace the graphic.
2. There is no space between the links. Use background-colored text or transparent GIFs instead of the Spacebar to separate the items.
3. The text is much closer to the edge of the table. Add more cell spacing or padding.
4. In the first cell, the space after the rule is bigger than it should be. Delete the space altogether until the text is next to the rule, then use a Break (Shift-Return/Enter) to bump the text down.
5. The line breaks are different in the browser because of the different font size. Let it go.
6. The rules above the text align differently—they align better in the browser. Let it go.
7. More of the page appears in the browser window. In this case it's because the graphic is missing. Fix the graphic, then let it go.

Chapter Fifteen
1. a
2. b
3. b
4. There is a folder named seamaid. Inside that is a folder named oceanmist; inside that is a folder named foam; and inside that is an html file (a web page) named moonlady.htm.
5. two: copyright notice and gallery.tiff
6. c
7. b
8. a

Robin's Obsessive Index

Colophon

I created the pages of this book entirely within PageMaker 6.5, which is the best tool for making books, on a Mac. I indexed it in PageMaker, as I always do. I used PageTools from Extensis, which saved me about a hundred hours. We made screen shots on the Mac with Captivate Select from Mainstay, and on the PC with ScreenThief from Nildram Software. We cleaned up all the screen shots in Photoshop on the Mac, where we also used PhotoTools from Extensis. John created the illustrations for the book in Adobe Illustrator and Photoshop, and wrote text in ClarisWorks. He also used Kai's Power Tools and PhotoTools. We used a PowerMac 8100, a PowerMac 7200, and a Hewlett-Packard PC running Windows 95.

We created real and dummy web pages in Adobe PageMill, Claris Home Page, NetObjects Fusion, GoLive CyberStudio, Symantec Visual Page, Microsoft FrontPage, and BBEdit.

The main fonts in this book are Nofret Regular for the body copy; Nofret Bold for the heads; Antique Olive for the bold callouts, heads, and chapter numbers; Gigi for the script in the chapter and quiz heads; and Langer for the captions. On the cover we used Tabitha for the title and Blur Medium for the rest of the copy.

The book was printed at GAC/Shepard Poorman in Indiana using computer-to-plate technology.

This is a chart of the 216 browser-safe colors. Each cell lists the hexadecimal code and RGB values (red:green:blue).

990033 153:0:51	FF3366 255:51:102	CC0033 204:0:51	FF0033 255:0:51	FF9999 255:153:153	CC3366 204:51:102	FFCCFF 255:204:255	CC6699 204:151:53	993366 153:51:102	660033 102:0:51	CC3399 204:151:53	FF99CC 255:153:153
FF66CC 255:102:204	FF99FF 255:153:255	FF6699 255:102:153	CC0066 204:0:102	FF0066 255:0:102	FF3399 255:51:153	FF0099 255:0:153	FF33CC 255:51:204	FF00CC 255:0:204	FF66FF 255:102:255	FF33FF 255:51:255	FF00FF 255:0:255
CC0099 204:0:153	990066 153:0:102	CC66CC 204:102:204	CC33CC 204:51:204	CC99FF 204:153:255	CC66FF 204:102:255	CC33FF 204:51:255	993399 153:51:153	CC00CC 204:0:204	CC00FF 204:0:255	9900CC 153:0:204	990099 153:0:153
CC99CC 204:153:204	996699 153:102:153	663366 102:51:102	660099 102:0:153	9933CC 153:51:204	660066 102:0:102	9900FF 153:0:255	9933FF 153:51:255	9966CC 153:102:204	330033 51:0:51	663399 102:51:153	6633CC 102:51:204
6600CC 102:0:204	330066 51:0:102	9966FF 153:102:255	6600FF 102:0:255	6633FF 102:51:255	CCCCFF 204:204:255	9999FF 153:153:255	9999CC 153:153:204	6666CC 102:102:204	6666FF 102:102:255	666699 102:102:153	333366 51:51:102
333399 51:51:153	330099 51:0:153	3300CC 51:0:204	3300FF 51:0:255	3333FF 51:51:255	3333CC 51:51:204	0066FF 0:102:255	0033FF 0:51:255	3366FF 51:102:255	3366CC 51:102:204	000066 0:0:102	000033 0:0:51
0000FF 0:0:255	000099 0:0:153	0033CC 0:51:204	0000CC 0:0:204	336699 51:102:153	0066CC 0:102:204	99CCFF 153:204:255	6699FF 102:153:255	003366 0:51:102	6699CC 102:153:204	006699 0:102:153	3399CC 51:153:204
0099CC 0:153:204	66CCFF 102:204:255	3399FF 51:153:255	003399 0:51:153	0099FF 0:153:255	33CCFF 51:204:255	00CCFF 0:204:255	99FFFF 153:255:255	66FFFF 102:255:255	33FFFF 51:255:255	00FFFF 0:255:255	00CCCC 0:204:204
009999 0:153:153	669999 102:153:153	99CCCC 153:204:204	CCFFFF 204:255:255	33CCCC 51:204:204	66CCCC 102:204:204	339999 51:153:153	336666 51:102:102	006666 0:102:102	003333 0:51:51	00FFCC 0:255:204	33FFCC 51:255:204
33CC99 51:204:153	00CC99 0:204:153	66FFCC 102:255:204	99FFCC 153:255:204	00FF99 0:255:153	339966 51:153:102	006633 0:102:51	669966 102:153:102	66CC66 102:204:102	99FF99 153:255:153	66FF66 102:255:102	99CC99 153:204:153
336633 51:102:51	66FF99 102:255:153	33FF99 51:255:153	33CC66 51:204:102	00CC66 0:204:102	66CC99 102:204:153	009966 0:153:102	339933 51:153:51	009933 0:153:51	33FF66 51:255:102	00FF66 0:255:102	CCFFCC 204:255:204
CCFF99 204:255:153	99FF66 153:255:102	99FF33 153:255:51	00FF33 0:255:51	33FF33 51:255:51	00CC33 0:204:51	33CC33 51:204:51	66FF33 102:255:51	00FF00 0:255:0	66CC33 102:204:51	006600 0:102:0	003300 0:51:0
009900 0:153:0	33FF00 51:255:0	66FF00 102:255:0	99FF00 153:255:0	66CC00 102:204:0	00CC00 0:204:0	33CC00 51:204:0	339900 51:153:0	99CC66 153:204:102	669933 102:153:51	99CC33 153:204:51	336600 51:102:0
669900 102:153:0	99CC00 153:204:0	CCFF66 204:255:102	CCFF33 204:255:51	CCFF00 204:255:0	999900 153:153:0	CCCC00 204:204:0	CCCC33 204:204:51	333300 51:51:0	666600 102:102:0	999933 153:153:51	CCCC66 204:204:102
666633 102:102:51	999966 153:153:102	CCCC99 204:204:153	FFFFCC 255:255:204	FFFF99 255:255:153	FFFF66 255:255:102	FFFF33 255:255:51	FFFF00 255:255:0	FFCC00 255:204:0	FFCC66 255:204:102	FFCC33 255:204:51	CC9933 102:153:51
996600 153:102:0	CC9900 204:153:0	FF9900 255:153:0	CC6600 204:102:0	993300 153:51:0	CC6633 204:102:51	663300 102:51:0	FF9966 255:153:102	FF6633 255:102:51	FF9933 255:153:51	FF6600 255:102:0	CC3300 204:51:0
996633 153:102:51	330000 51:0:0	663333 102:51:51	996666 153:102:102	CC9999 204:153:153	993333 153:51:51	CC6666 204:102:102	FFCCCC 255:204:204	FF3333 255:51:51	CC3333 204:51:51	FF6666 255:102:102	660000 102:0:0
990000 153:0:0	CC0000 204:0:0	FF0000 255:0:0	FF3300 255:51:0	CC9966 204:153:102	FFCC99 255:204:153	CCCCCC 204:204:204	999999 153:153:153	666666 102:102:102	333333 51:51:51	FFFFFF 255:255:255	000000 0:0:0

This is a chart of the 216 browser-safe colors. Both the hexadecimal code and the RGB values shown are in the order (as always) of red, green, then blue. That is, if the hex code is FFCC33, the value for red is FF, for green is CC, and for blue is 33. If the RGB values are 51:0:255, the value for red is 51, for green is 0, and for blue is 255. **Important note:** These RGB colors are printed on this page in CMYK! Many of these colors cannot be accurately duplicated in CMYK, so this chart serves only as a general guide.